CAESAR

CAESAR
A Life in Western Culture

MARIA WYKE

Granta Books
London

Granta Publications, 12–14 Addison Avenue, London W11 4QR

First published in Great Britain by Granta Books 2007

Maria Wyke's research on Julius Caesar is supported by

The Leverhulme Trust  Arts & Humanities
Research Council

A CIP catalogue record for this book is
available from the British Library.

1 3 5 7 9 10 8 6 4 2

ISBN 978–1–86207–662–4

Typeset by M Rules

Printed and bound in Great Britain by
William Clowes Ltd, Beccles, Suffolk

In memory of my father,
Barry Wyke

CONTENTS

ILLUSTRATIONS

ACKNOWLEDGEMENTS

I am extremely grateful for the generosity of the Leverhulme Trust, whose award of a Major Research Fellowship from 2000 to 2003 allowed me to initiate and develop my research into the reception of Julius Caesar, and for that of the Arts and Humanities Research Council (AHRC), whose award of Research Leave during 2006–7 gave me the opportunity to complete aspects of the research for my next monograph on *Caesar in the USA* (University of California Press) as well as to finalize this manuscript. The departments of Classics at the University of Reading and of Greek and Latin at University College London, in turn, kindly provided me with some undisturbed time to work on both these projects.

I am indebted to Christopher Pelling for his continued interest in and support for my work on the reception of Julius Caesar. In addition to lending me a draft copy of his commentary on Plutarch's *Life of Caesar*, he also provided comment on the papers I edited for the volume *Julius Caesar in Western Culture* (Blackwell, 2006). The contributors to that volume, and to the conference at the British School at Rome from which the volume arose, also provided me with invaluable ideas for this study.

I would also like to express my thanks to my publisher George Miller for his editorial skill and for his patience and consideration when domestic difficulties delayed the writing of this book, and to Mary Beard for recommending me as author to him. Bella Shand of Granta also provided invaluable help in resolving many of the problems in obtaining images and permissions.

Dominic Montserrat first introduced me to the value of metabiography, and David Oswell encouraged me to adopt it as an approach to the study of Julius Caesar's reception. I have also been lucky enough to receive help in many other forms. Bob Gurval drew my attention to a Fascist postcard of Julius Caesar in his collection and allowed me to use it as an illustration. Jane Dunnett passed on to me some relatively inaccessible source materials for the coupling of Mussolini with Caesar. In response to a paper I delivered at UCL in 2006 on Caesar's encounter with the pirates, Nick Lowe, Dorothea McEwan, Simon Hornblower and Mike Trapp all supplied useful comments or suggestions; and colleagues attending papers I gave elsewhere in London, Oxford, Exeter, Reading, Rome and Los Angeles contributed comments and criticisms which enabled me better to develop my discussion of Caesar's afterlife. As ever, Ned Comstock continued to send me relevant materials concerning film and television programmes about Julius Caesar and ancient Rome, and Amy Richlin gave me her warm and hugely enjoyable hospitality in the course of several stays in Los Angeles. Andrew Wallace-Hadrill kindly supplied the facilities of the British School at Rome for my study and for the conference on Caesar's reception which so advantaged my own work. Margaret Malamud introduced me to the delights of Caesars Palace and allowed me access to a number of her detailed studies on ancient Rome in modern American culture prior to their publication. I owe a big treat to Tilly Oswell Wheeler for playing over and over again, on my behalf, a single scenario from the strategy game *Rise of Rome* and for capturing various images from it for me.

Finally, I would like to express my constant gratitude to my husband David, and to my daughter and step-daughters Beattie, Tilly and Amelia, for making life with (and more often without) Caesar such fun. They are all more important to me than I could ever say.

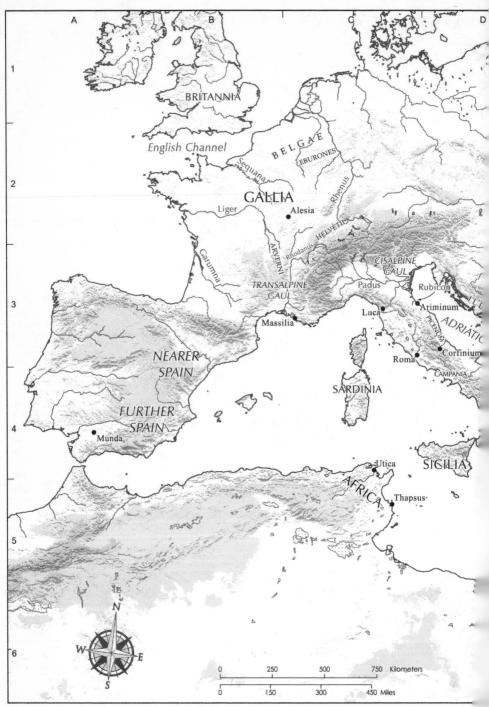

Campaigns of Caesar, Crassus and Pompey, 58–45 BC.

CRIMEA

BLACK SEA

PONTUS

• Nicopolis

• Zela

PARTHIA

Epidamnus/
Dyrrhachium

MACEDONIA

• Brundisium

• Pharsalús

ASIA

CARIA

• Carrhae

CILICIA

Amanus Mons

Euphrates

SYRIA

• Salamis

CYPRUS

JUDAEA

INTERNUM MARE

• Cyrene

Alexandria •

AEGYPTUS

Nile

Ancient World Mapping Center 2003

1

CAESAR'S CELEBRITY
From fame to fable

Julius Caesar hit the headlines in late summer 2003 when a perfectly preserved white marble head displaying his likeness was discovered on a small island in the southern Mediterranean. Although it was quickly identified as another posthumous Roman portrait, it was presented as more refined and pristine than the few other busts which have been most closely associated with the statesman's name. Italian archaeologists also claimed its physiognomy (the lines around the brows, the sad expression, the distant gaze) revealed both Caesar's authority and the strains under which it placed him, with perhaps even a suggestion of foresight into his impending demise and that of his whole epoch. Found on Pantelleria, a holiday hideaway for pop stars and Hollywood celebrities, the marble head was then shot by the fashion photographer Fabrizio Ferri to accompany newspaper and magazine reports. Julius Caesar's face had emerged elegantly from the warm waters of the Mediterranean into contemporary celebrity culture.

Why is Julius Caesar the most famous of all Romans? Why not the dictator Sulla, the military conqueror Pompey, or the emperor Augustus? Caesar's exceptional talents, his actions, and his murder, as they figure in many ancient narratives, all assist in the process of turning the Roman dictator into an embodiment of a profound transformation in the history of Western civilization from republic to empire. Caught on the threshold of epochal change, Julius Caesar is also deeply implicated in it. Consequently his biography has taken on monumental dimensions, and matured into a foundational and formative story. It has possessed extraordinary and lasting appeal because his image has not been fixed. Whether as founder or destroyer, Julius Caesar's life has become a point of reference from which to explore concerns about conquest and imperialism, revolution, dictatorship, liberty, tyranny and political assassination. Used as model or anti-model for warfare and statecraft, he has also been invoked to pose questions about more personal merits (such as audacity, risk-taking, courage and glory, leadership, good fortune and fame, even immortality) and about personal failings (such as arrogance, ambition, extravagance, lust and cruelty). Even from the time of his own writing about himself, Julius Caesar's life has been arranged, fictionalized, and sensationalized so as to become a set of canonic events and concepts whose telling reveals much more than just the minutiae of one individual's existence. Julius Caesar was a Roman leader of flesh and blood who existed in real time. He is also a quasi-mythic protagonist in the development of Western culture.

Fame

From the ancient sources (including Julius Caesar's own writing), there emerges the portrait of the most charismatic and talented Roman of his time. A spectacular and varied list of gifts, skills and capacities reveal a figure without precedent: a man of wide learning and sophisticated tastes, but also physical strength, endurance, courage, focus and energy; an eloquent and lively orator, a versatile and direct writer; a supremely shrewd general and magnetic leader, an astute and dynamic politician and statesman, an effective administrator, a clever self-publicist and showman, a successful lover, a favourite of fortune.

Blessed with such characteristics, and acting notionally in the name of the senate and the people of republican Rome, Julius Caesar conquered Gaul, vastly extended the boundaries of Roman rule, laid the foundations of France, and initiated the formation of what would become modern Europe. Then, in crisis-ridden Rome, he instigated a civil war against the republic's supporters and their leader Pompey, usurped power and established a permanent dictatorship. His populist, autocratic mode of government was cut short by his murder but eventually, after more than a decade of further civil war between his aspiring successors and his assassins, an enduring imperial monarchy was put in its place.

The Roman general and dictator constantly cultivated a public image for himself that was larger than life in order to arouse admiration and, therefore, increase his political authority, and also to achieve a lasting recognition (or *fama*) for those great deeds of state. Beyond the games and triumphs which he staged, and the honorific distinctions with which he adorned himself, his own commentaries on the war in Gaul and the subsequent civil war constitute a successful and enduring example of his self-promotion in pursuit of *fama*. In these works, the author refers to himself as 'Caesar' – a separable entity whose reputation can be favourably manipulated, polished and inflated. While the narratives affect third-person objectivity, a breathless haste and the limitations imposed by battlefield reporting, they tell tales of vast territories annexed and enemies utterly outwitted and overwhelmed.

Set alongside (and at times against) this self-presentation of 'Caesar' are the depictions which emerge from the works of contemporaries such as the poet Catullus, the orator and statesman Cicero, or the political historian Sallust. In his letters, speeches and philosophical essays, Cicero in particular offers no consistency: open hostility at times, at times expedient eulogy, frequently an oscillation between admiration and distaste. On at least one occasion, he expresses an apprehension that Julius Caesar will be granted the enduring fame he so desires, only for it to prove highly volatile:

> Posterity will be staggered to hear and read of the military commands you have held and the provinces you have ruled . . . battles without number, fabulous victories, monuments and shows and Triumphs. And yet unless you now restore this city of ours to stability by measures of reorganization and lawgiving, your renown, however far and wide it may roam, will never be able to find a settled dwelling-place or firm abode. For among men still unborn, as among ourselves, there will rage sharp disagreements. Some will glorify your exploits to the skies. But others, I suggest, may find something lacking, and something vital at that.
>
> (Cicero, *pro Marcello* 28–9. Trans. M. Grant, 1969)

Cicero found himself in a difficult political situation after he had been pardoned by Caesar for supporting Pompey in the civil war. For a while after Pompey's defeat, flight and death in Egypt, the orator stayed away from Rome and delivered no public speeches. Yet, breaking his silence at last in this speech of September 46 BC, he even manages to hint at a certain incredulity about the dictator's own reports on his glorious military activities, to the dictator's face.

After Julius Caesar was assassinated two years later, disagreements raged even more intensely and more urgently over how to evaluate his exploits abroad, his seizure of power, and his autocratic government at home. Cicero himself expressed astonishment, in a letter written soon after the dictator's death, that all his actions, writings, speeches, promises and plans now had more force than if he had still been alive (*Letters to Atticus*, 14.10.1). His murder conferred on Caesar both humanity and tragedy; the themes of betrayal by friends, brutal slaughter, and greatness suddenly brought low formed part of his biography forevermore. Only by recasting it as the noble killing of a usurper, tyrant and destroyer of the republic could the chief conspirators Brutus and Cassius bestow some nobility on the deed rather than the victim. Evaluation of Caesar's life thus became caught up in the dramatic horror of his death – was it a life that deserved to be taken away? – and constituted an integral part of the propaganda war waged between Caesar's assassins and his successors Mark Antony and Octavian, until finally, in 42 BC at Philippi in Macedonia, the two sides engaged in battle either to restore republican government or to inherit the dictator's power.

These bitter conflicts over the image of Caesar assumed striking visual form on the coinage issued by each side in the aftermath of his murder. A silver denarius issued in Rome around 43 BC by the official moneyer L. Flaminius Chilo (Figure 1.1) shows on the obverse a portrait of Julius Caesar, his head garlanded with laurel. The coinage minted shortly before the dictator's death had offered distinctively realistic representations of his face: the baldness, the deeply wrinkled brow, the large eyes with surrounding crow's feet, prominent nose, thin-lipped mouth, heavily creased cheeks, jutting cheekbones and chin, long, scraggy neck displaying sagging folds of skin, a pronounced Adam's apple. Now, after his death, the dictator's physical blemishes and peculiarities are partially obscured, though not yet wholly idealized as those of a god. His head is endowed with more hair, greater regularity of feature, smoother skin and a more monumental aspect. The reverse of the coin unites this fresh, physically forceful representation of Caesar with the

5

Fig. 1.1 Silver denarius, c.43 BC. Obv. portrait of Caesar. Rev. Peace.

goddess Peace, who leans on a long sceptre of power and holds a twisted staff of prosperity.

Conversely, a silver denarius issued by Brutus in 43 or 42 BC (Figure 1.2), from a travelling mint which moved with his encampment through Greece and Asia, displays a humbly bare-headed portrait of Brutus the general. With him is conjoined, on the reverse, a cap of liberty (or the *pilleus* customarily granted to slaves on the death of their master). The cap is inserted between two daggers below which sits the clear legend EID[ES] MAR[TIAE] – an archaic spelling of the Ides of March, the day in 44 BC on which the minter, along with some of his fellow senators, killed Julius Caesar. Here the promise of peace, prosperity and legitimate government which was being promoted for Caesar's successors in Rome is thoroughly rebuffed. Instead (and in order to stimulate military and civic support for the coming war), Brutus presents himself in the glorious republican tradition of tyrant-slaying: his heroic assassination of Caesar has freed the Roman state from servitude. This extreme polarity in the fame of Julius Caesar – between

Fig. 1.2 Silver denarius c.43–2 BC. Obv. portrait of Brutus. Rev. cap of liberty between two daggers.

superhuman provider for the Roman people and sordid master of slaves – has further ensured the enduring and diverse significance of the Roman statesman in Western culture.

This polarity is clear in later testimonies to the life of Julius Caesar which survive from antiquity – the biographies, histories and epic poems which have supplied a substantial part of the raw material from which the diverse Caesars of subsequent millennia have been moulded. Commemoration of Julius Caesar was an essential political strategy for his grand-nephew Octavian, who, by virtue of his adoption as Caesar's son and his inheritance of Caesar's name and estate, could now lay claim also to his soldiers, his civilian support and his disputed authority over the Roman state. Octavian named himself 'Caesar, son of Caesar' and officially recognized his father's divinity. Yet, once securely installed as emperor of Rome's vast dominions and now also entitled 'Augustus', his image was carefully constructed by his court biographer Nicolaus of Damascus as an heroic ruler to be distinguished from his politically inept predecessor. The tale of the father's assassination warns in the most graphic terms against the errors and dangers which the son must avoid in order to survive. Within the canon of virtues and vices collated by the imperial loyalist Valerius Maximus during the reign of Tiberius, it is possible to find Julius Caesar as a high celestial power, an ethical model of courage and clemency, whose death is parricide – the shocking murder of the father of the country. In contrast, under the emperor Nero, in the seemingly seditious epic on the civil war composed by the poet Lucan, the narrator makes of Caesar a demonic and destructive force of nature, an unscrupulous despot whose anticipated murder will be a fitting punishment and an example to all tyrants. During the reign of Trajan, when Julius Caesar appears to have taken on an exemplary function specifically as Rome's greatest general and conqueror, he was also instated as the 'first of the Caesars' and thus not just a crucial pivot between republican and monarchical systems of government, but also the divine founder of empire and of an imperial dynasty which bore his name. Yet, when the evaluation of Julius Caesar's life no longer needed to function as a vital signal of a Roman subject's patriotism or treachery, in later histories and biographies it became possible to acknowledge his elevated status as first Roman emperor while still detailing his excessive ambition and his abuses of power, and even endorsing his murder as a just punishment.

Fable

Julius Caesar's talents, actions and murder, their vivid and extensive representation in ancient sources, and the frequent, violent and sometimes fatal conflicts which took place over those representations have all contributed to his lasting fame – which, in turn, has developed into a way of addressing the concerns of the present and anxieties about the future. Yet the title of founder of monarchy and empire, which Caesar acquired in the second century AD, and his elevation to the position of first emperor provide further explanation. For 'Caesar' then became both the *name* of the Roman military leader and statesman and the *sign* of Rome and its imperial system of government. From the perspective of early Christianity and then the Middle Ages, Julius Caesar oversaw the profound transformation of the world from pagan to Christian and created an office which, under the Christian emperors, would become sanctified because it was divinely appointed.

While in some ecclesiastical literature Julius Caesar might represent the apogee of pagan pride before Christ advanced the teaching of humility, or was coloured more darkly still as an Antichrist, more often he personified supreme secular power on earth, and his monarchical mode of government a temporal counterpart to the spiritual government of God in heaven. Thus, in medieval literature, many features of Julius Caesar's ancient biography – which was dominated now by the authority of Lucan, whose civil war poem was read as a testimony to the benefits of monarchy – underwent epic and chivalric embellishment and invention. Already towards the end of the republican period (whose end is conventionally dated nowadays as 31 BC, when Octavian defeated Mark Antony in a sea battle and began to accrue far greater sovereign powers even than Caesar), and during the reigns of the first Roman emperors, Julius Caesar's life from birth to death had been fabricated by himself or others as unique and fated. In the Middle Ages, it was also deeply infused with an exemplary flavour – a celebration of ancient virtues (and, occasionally, a denigration of a few vices) delivered to aristocratic readers as a practical guide to their appropriate political role and moral behaviour at court. Sometimes miraculous tales were threaded into the surviving historical record to create a

Caesarian fable about a supreme courtly hero and champion, just conqueror and emperor, who was a form of pagan saint. In the hands of medieval clerics, court chroniclers and poets, the life of Julius Caesar was transformed into a kind of secular scripture.

Julius Caesar had himself already started the process of turning his biography into an heroic myth. Early in his life he had laid claim to both royal and divine ancestry, advancing himself and his family as descended from the first kings of Rome and the goddess Venus. Such ancestry rooted his biography within the narrative strategies fitting for an epic hero like Venus' son (and his supposed ancestor) Aeneas, and imply that a semi-divine mandate to greatness flowed through his veins.

Better to mark this extraordinary destiny, medieval literature and art elaborated a miraculous birth for the Roman statesman (although it is possible that comparable claims had been made for him in the earliest, lost sections of his ancient biographies). Authentication was supplied by retrieving its supposed historical record from ancient speculation about the origin of the family name 'Caesar': one of several classical explanations was that it came from the verb 'to cut' (*cadere*), and indicated that the first member of the Julian family who held it had been cut out (*caesus est*) of his mother's womb. Julius Caesar was not the first to bear this cognomen. Other etymologies for the name were also in circulation. Histories of ancient medicine made it clear that in republican Rome such an operation involved the death of the mother, yet Caesar's mother Aurelia did not die in childbirth. Nevertheless, medieval literature and iconography gave ample space to a birth which would be a suitably marvellous and auspicious beginning for such a great man. A lavish illustration for an extraordinarily popular medieval epic on Julius Caesar's deeds provides one such example (Figure 1.3). In conformity with medieval customs for lying in, the operation takes place exclusively among women. The

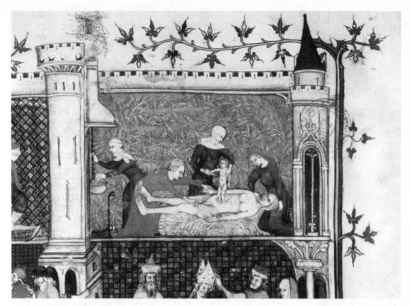

Fig. 1.3 Birth of Julius Caesar. Illustration from 14th-century French ms.

dead mother is laid out on a litter of straw to soak up her blood, while a servant prepares the boiled water with which to wash the newborn who has emerged from his mother's open abdomen. The entire event is literally framed within one chamber of the castle of Julius Caesar's great achievements.

The mature Caesar was also included in the medieval canon of the Western world's greatest military heroes. This collection of champions, or Nine Worthies ('*neuf preux*'), was first identified, cat- egorized, and made popular in the early fourteenth century in a poem composed by a French *jongleur* or itinerant ministrel. Joining a neatly composed arrangement of three Christians, three Hebrews and two other pagans (Hector and Alexander the Great), Julius Caesar along with the rest was made to embody chivalric goodness, wisdom, prowess and valour. Perfect warriors, the Nine Worthies conferred glory on their nations and provided patterns of both military virtue and moral conduct for imitation. They frequently appeared on frescoes, tapestries, enamelled cups and playing cards owned by medieval princes and noblemen. In a similar way to a collection of saints, their role was to exhort a supposedly degenerate present to live up to medieval ideals projected back into the past. In this line-up, Julius Caesar was conventionally distinguished by his imperial crown and the crest of a two-headed eagle emblazoned on his medieval armour. In a fourteenth-century tapestry of the Nine Worthies commissioned by the Duke of Berry (and now surviving only in parts), a majestic and heavily bearded Caesar sits enthroned within a fantastic Gothic niche. He grasps a broad, unsheathed sword and is surrounded by his courtiers (mainly musicians, but also a soldier and, directly above him, his lady). His heraldic symbol of the double-headed imperial eagle is woven in sable on gold (Figure 1.4).

Specific wars fought by the Roman general were widely narrated in the national chronicles and epic poems of the twelfth to fourteenth centuries, most notably in France, Germany and Britain. They were often invested with additional patriotic detail, whether to glorify the regions in which the works originated or their conqueror. A German epic, for example, commemorates how local barons, won over to Julius Caesar by his chivalric display of leniency, courtesy and generosity, came to his rescue when he would otherwise have been repulsed from the gates of his own city. Conversely, a chronicle of a city in the north-east of France recalls its strenuous defence against the Roman general, with the help of princes from other nearby areas, a number of kings from Africa and a few devils from hell. Completely fantastical victories might even stretch the Roman conqueror's military triumphs to regions such as India (in order to retrace the map of Alexander's conquests) and further on into the Biblical regions of Gog and

Fig. 1.4 Julius Caesar with courtiers. Nine Worthies tapestry, c.1400–10.

Magog. In areas which Julius Caesar conquered (and in some which he didn't), local chronicles claimed him for the founder of their cities or their peoples. Across Europe, he became a topographical trace, a local memory of a Roman presence which might invest a place with the importance attaching to his name.

Fabulous traits and deeds frequently migrated from one medieval worthy to another, moving in literature from Alexander to Charlemagne, Arthur and Caesar. Each becomes the conqueror of many countries; the perfect practitioner of prowess, leniency and wisdom; a hero in pursuit of a magic sword, tree or beast; born from or enjoying intercourse with fairies.

Every conqueror needs a distinguished horse which only he can ride. A number of classical sources note that Julius Caesar possessed such a horse, born on his own lands, whose front hooves resembled feet since they were divided in such a way that they looked like toes. This unusual condition was interpreted by a soothsayer as an omen that the master of such a horse would one day rule the world. Naturally, the horse would endure no other rider save Caesar. This observation in Caesar's ancient biography seems to recall the characteristics of Bucephalus, the wild horse tamed by Alexander, which provided that hero too with an oracle predicting world empire. In medieval romance, Alexander's horse becomes a horned creature so wild that it eats men. In a later medieval epic on Julius Caesar, in addition to unmistakable feet, his horse gains a fabulous horn on its head with which it can topple other riders and their mounts. A number of depictions survive in which this mythic horse (rather than its owner) is in sharp focus. A colourful earthenware dish of the early sixteenth century, which captures a moment in the triumph of Julius Caesar, appears to jettison the medieval horn in favour of a more rational spike attached to a harness, but all four of the horse's human feet remain clearly visible as it is ridden on parade by a youth, who carries a globe-tipped branch to signify that their master is ruler of the whole world (Figure 1.5).

The unique circumstances of Julius Caesar's death did not escape his medieval chroniclers and poets. They carefully reiterate the portents and disturbances of nature which classical authors describe

Fig. 1.5 Dish depicting Caesar's horse, *c.*1514

as having preceded the dictator's death, signifying its superhuman importance. According to ancient accounts, for example, some horses Caesar had dedicated to the gods would no longer graze but wept abundantly; a bull Caesar was sacrificing turned out to have no heart; a 'king' bird was torn to pieces by other birds in Rome's senate-hall; flames issued from men who were left unharmed by them; at night, lights were seen in the skies and crashing sounds were heard.

Medieval works also introduce new, even more elaborate omens. In a fifteenth-century poem memorializing history's most illustrious men, an Italian courtier amassed many of the miraculous events the medieval world believed to surround the murder of the Roman general: on that dark night, at the sixth hour, when the betrayal was arranged, terrible voices were heard clamouring in the sky, the earth quaked as if it were releasing a great sigh, fires with bloody tails circled through the air in battle, a lamb cried out 'Slaughter! Slaughter!', oxen pointed out to their ploughmen the pointlessness of carrying on . . . Some of these prodigies even echo those which, according to sacred scripture, marked the crucifixion of Christ and would herald the second coming. Generating a more explicit connection between Julius Caesar and Jesus Christ, the assassins Brutus and Cassius were generally damned in the Middle Ages for having betrayed the highest temporal authority and earthly counterpart of God. This type of execration finds most vivid expression in Dante's poetic depiction of a spiritual journey in which he came across the Roman senators in the nethermost pit of Hell. There they are perpetually mangled in the three mouths of Lucifer alongside the betrayer of God, Judas Iscariot.

Finally, attending to the close of Caesar's life, his relics became an object of veneration. Medieval guidebooks to Rome frequently drew the attention of pilgrims to a red granite obelisk which stood close by the Church of St Peter. This they identified as both a memorial in honour of Caesar and his tomb for, they asserted, the bronze sphere which sat high at the top contained his cremated remains. Thus Julius Caesar found a place on the sacred map of Rome.

Caesar in Western culture

If Julius Caesar acquired in antiquity the highly volatile fame which Cicero had foretold. During the course of the Middle Ages, however, he became far more than a famed (or infamous) historical figure. Now he was a fable, almost a myth, more than human and almost holy. Consequently, the ways in which Caesar has been received into Western culture have been extraordinarily diverse, and on numerous occasions profound. He has been constantly reshaped and adapted to new contexts and for fresh purposes. Whether perceived as conqueror or civilizer, founder or destroyer, democrat or autocrat, murderer or victim, he has appeared and reappeared for the purposes of imitation, education or entertainment, from the poetry of Dante to the casino at Caesars Palace in Las Vegas.

Caesar has been deployed to legitimate or undermine the authority of kings, to justify or denounce the coups of generals, to launch or obstruct revolutions, to demonstrate incisive literary style and perfect grammar, to teach military strategy and tactics or the workings of fortune and destiny, to display luxury, to play out sexual excess, to stimulate expenditure and consumption. Moreover, the history of Caesar's reception is not only a matter of re-presenting him in ways that speak to the present (in paintings, plays, novels, operas, films and computer games, as well as in political speeches and historical treatises); it is also often a matter of adopting aspects of his life in someone else's, or replicating his murder for political reasons – a matter of becoming or removing a new Caesar.

How then might we investigate a reception history so vast and so diverse? Already towards the end of the Middle Ages, the reception of Julius Caesar – the use of his biography – began to fragment further. The emerging humanist interest in scholarly investigation, in antiquarianism and philology, entailed close scrutiny of Caesar's own commentaries and comparison of them with other classical sources. This, along with the pursuit of historical analysis, led to a dilution of the Roman dictator's fabulous and sacred aura. He now became a man of letters (as well as the general and statesman), perhaps rather more admirable for his writing style than his actions. If we consider Julius Caesar's reception exclusively at the level of state and of politics, it is possible to piece together some broad trends. Critics, for example, have observed various fluctuations in the fortunes of the political Caesar from the fifteenth to the twentieth centuries. With the initiation of violent debates about republicanism and citizenship in the Renaissance, and the re-establishment of republics, some humanists drew on Cato, Cicero and Brutus as symbolic champions of their civic liberty, while casting Caesar as the enemy for being a usurper and tyrant. In the counter-moves of the hereditary princes and monarchs of Europe, and the intellectuals who staked out the ground for them, the founder of European monarchy received swift rehabilitation or even greater admiration.

In the era of revolutions in late eighteenth-century America and France, Brutus became yet more noble, Caesar ever more villainous. The conspirator was widely and practically deployed in the French Revolution as historical and secular support for the armed struggle for liberty. On the other hand, at the beginning of the nineteenth century, Napoleon Bonaparte ensured that Caesar replaced Brutus, and imperial replaced republican Rome, as admirable and reproducible models for leadership and government. So closely did Caesar seem bound to the French emperors and their expanding empires that 'Caesarism' was developed as a political theory in the latter half of the century better to understand the novelty of Napoleon III's regime, blending as it did authoritarianism with populism. By the start of the twentieth century, Julius Caesar had once again reached the elevated standing of a great man of world history, only to fall drastically into disrepute again after the death of the Italian dictator Benito Mussolini, who had so closely and so spectacularly shaped himself in Caesar's image.

From the fifteenth to the twentieth centuries, Julius Caesar may have careered between political model and anti-model, but he never disappeared from sight. In recent decades, his apparently diminished importance has been linked to the equally diminished standing of classics in Western educational systems, and the disappearance of pragmatics as an integral aspect of historical study. The Roman republic seems far too distant and too different from the present to offer any guidelines for political or moral life in a global economy, although the Roman empire is often used still to supply general parallels for the rise – and warnings of the inevitable fall – of that modern superpower, the United States of America.

Yet politics is not the only cultural terrain on which Julius Caesar reappears. Other routes to investigate Caesar's reception entail scrutiny of different aspects of his biography (such as military expertise or even prose style), or a close engagement with a particular location of reception, a period, a person, a mode, an author. Here, instead, I propose to take the biography of Julius Caesar itself as my starting point and as the structuring device for this book. The next eight chapters will investigate the first surviving accounts and the reception of a whole range of canonic events in the dictator's biography (such as capture by pirates, war in Gaul, the encounter with Cleopatra, dictatorship and assassination). They also follow his life chronologically from youth to death and deification. Each begins with an examination of how that event was first articulated, whether by Caesar himself or by other classical writers. Then I explore selected receptions in some detail, ones which in my view best illustrate Julius Caesar's key appropriations for Western culture (military, political, erotic, commercial, recreational, ethical, theological) and demonstrate the diversity of his use across cultures, periods and media (from medieval French chronicles to American newspapers and Internet discussion boards). In that sense, this book constitutes a metabiography – that is, not an exploration of a life at its time of living but of key resonances of that life in subsequent periods.

Metabiography provides me with scope for an investigation which moves beyond the more thoroughly explored areas of

Caesar's political career and assassination and into, for example, the impact of his youthful capture by pirates (Chapter 2) or his deification around the time of his death (Chapter 9). Conversely, those events whose reception history has already attracted considerable critical attention I reconsider here by submitting them to a sharper focus – so Chapter 3 is concerned not with all the years of war in Gaul but mostly with the surrender of the Gallic chieftain Vercingetorix. The civil war is largely represented by the crossing of the Rubicon with which it began (Chapter 4), and the triumphs which followed it (Chapter 6), while I explore Caesar's assassination through its reconstruction in the text of Shakespeare's play and its performance on the American stage (Chapter 8). Metabiography also allows me to expose unexpected links or ruptures in the history of Julius Caesar's reception, such as those in the representation and re-enactment of Caesar's encounter with Cleopatra, from Lucan to Las Vegas via Handel and Hollywood (Chapter 5), and to give space to a very diverse range of media such as computer games (Chapter 2) and political cartoons (Chapter 7). Nevertheless, in this metabiography I can still only offer a selection and not a survey. Parts of Caesar's life, for example, are wholly omitted, so that here he never visits Britain and scarcely engages in civil war. Caesar's life and the reception of it are together far too full and long to be treated comprehensively.

Julius Caesar himself lived and wrote his life with a view to its future reception. He sought out fame; contemporaries such as Cicero acknowledged that he would attain it. Ancient narratives which reconstruct his life at times manifest an awareness of its original self-conscious construction ('Caesar writes that he', they sometimes add to their accounts). At other times, they highlight its present reconsideration or its future significance. In that sense, metabiography is not discontinuous with the actions originally ascribed to the Roman dictator, and can serve to shed yet further light on the ancient public entity 'Caesar', if not on the private person who remains forever hidden (what, for example, did the tale of capture by pirates do to enhance the young Caesar's political appeal?).

The metabiography of Caesar, as with other types of study of the reception of classical antiquity, can also serve to shed light on the present. By isolating in each chapter an individual event in the life of Caesar and then examining that event's appropriation at different times and places, across diverse media, by numerous individuals, I hope to expose shifts in the reconstruction, value and use of Julius Caesar and, therefore, to understand the kind of present or future he is asked to encourage or warn against.

2

AUDACITY AND ADVENTURISM
Capture by pirates, c.74 BC

Julius Caesar's childhood and youth are scarcely documented in the ancient sources. Almost always in classical and later texts (except for literature designed for children or students of Latin), he is presented as a mature figure, powerful or on the road to power. Perhaps, some conjecture, before he accumulated a fortune, a following, senatorial stature, military command and political authority, contemporary witnesses did not notice anything extraordinary about him. (The dictator Sulla, though, is reported to have remarked percipiently of Caesar as a young man that he would one day deal the death blow to the cause of the aristocracy: Suetonius, *Deified Julius* 1.3). Furthermore, ancient political biography such as that by Plutarch or Suetonius displays little concern for the individuation of character or the development of a psychological profile. Generally, their narratives do not seek to explain their subject's personality as highly distinctive or as shaped by experiences early in life. Instead, their concern is to illustrate a permutation of recognizable characteristics embodied by their subject, general traits which belong to preset categories and whose assembly encourages readers actively to assess their ethical value. Thus, when the ancient biographers record the fabulous tale that some time around 74 BC Caesar travelled to Rhodes and on route was captured by pirates, the future dictator may still be young but he is already fully formed.

Julius Caesar had begun his public life in confrontation with the aristocratic party and its leader, Sulla. Caesar was linked to the party's opponents by both blood and marriage; he was nephew to Marius, son-in-law of Cinna. After they had both died and Sulla had established a temporary dictatorship at Rome, the young man was rendered vulnerable. In 81 BC, nonetheless, and aged only nineteen, Caesar refused the dictator's order to divorce Cinna's daughter Cornelia, and fled the city until his relatives pleaded successfully for his life. Then, until Sulla's own death in 78 BC, Caesar stayed away from Rome. He undertook military service in Asia and Cilicia, winning a civic crown in recognition of his bravery during an attack on the Greek state of Mytilene. On his return to the capital, he engaged in the various traditional activities which launched Romans on a political career, such as a foray into forensic prosecution, until in 74 BC he sailed to Rhodes to round off his oratorical training.

Plutarch offers the most elaborate version of the ensuing events in his *Life of Caesar*. Cilician pirates – the most bloodthirsty variety – took the young man captive off the coast of Pharmacusa (an island south of Miletus). They originally demanded twenty talents for Caesar's ransom, but he laughed at such ignorance of their captive's worth and promised them fifty. While his companions procured the money from various cities, he remained almost completely alone with the murderous crew. But he held them in such contempt that

> whenever he lay down to sleep he would send and order
> them to stop talking. For eight and thirty days, as if the men
> were not his watchers, but his royal body-guard, he shared in

their sports and exercises with great unconcern. He also wrote poems and sundry speeches which he read aloud to them, and those who did not admire these he would call to their faces illiterate barbarians, and often laughingly threatened to hang them all.

(Plutarch, Life of Caesar 2.1–2. Trans. B. Perrin, 1919)

The pirates were amused by this behaviour and put his boldness down to boyish simplicity. Once the ransom was paid and Caesar set free, however, he instantly manned some ships at Miletus, pursued his kidnappers and captured most of them. He kept their money, lodged the men in prison, and then sought their punishment from the Roman magistrate responsible for safety on those waters, namely the governor of Asia. When the governor delayed (with an eye on the money to be made), Caesar bypassed him, extracted the pirates from prison and crucified them – just as he had jokingly promised them on the island where they had held him. Although it is here transposed to shipboard, an etching by the nineteenth-century Italian artist Bartolomeo Pinelli pictures dramatically a moment from the adventure as Plutarch had narrated it: when Caesar declaims to the brigands (Figure 2.1).

The episode probably contains a kernel of truth, since piracy and kidnapping had been a constant obstacle to maritime traffic in the eastern Mediterranean, against which Roman countermeasures were frequently required. Yet, given that Julius Caesar was the only recorded survivor of this sojourn with pirates, it is hard to imagine that anyone other than Caesar originated their details, especially given their potential to serve his own interests. Caesar's authored adventure, put into circulation to enhance his public image, would then have invited even greater elaboration as pirates became favoured actors in the complex plot twists of the novel or prose romance (a genre which took shape only from the mid-first century

Fig. 2.1 Caesar, prisoner of pirates, B. Pinelli, *L'istoria Romana* (1818–19).

AD) and regularly featured as a topic of Roman exercises in decla-
mation: for example, a child refuses to support his father because
the father had refused to ransom him from pirates as punishment for
having previously killed his own brother for adultery. Is the son
acting against the law on the support of parents? (Seneca,
Controversiae 1.7.1–18).

In the tale of Julius Caesar's capture by pirates, then, we find
entangled the threads of his own self-serving narrative, literary
embroidery and historiographic illustration (rather than explanation) of the famous statesman to come. More than doubling the
ransom displays Caesar's early confidence in his own value, as well
as his intelligence in declaring that value in order to protect himself
from harm. Paying the ransom demonstrates his ability both to
convince the local populations of the coastal cities of Asia to collect
such a large sum, and to command the allegiance of the agents who

collect it and bring it back to him. His comportment with the pirates confirms that, though a boy (actually some twenty-six years old now), he is neither playing games nor is he afraid in the face of death.

Velleius Paterculus, an historian of Rome who lived during the reigns of both Augustus and Tiberius and wrote in adulatory terms of the imperial house, brings out further the story's evident contrast between the bold and decisive actions of the young Caesar and the timidity and inactivity of the Roman governor (*Roman Histories* 2.41.3–42.3). As a youth and a private citizen, Caesar has no public office, and operates without authority against a superior's orders. Whilst a senior magistrate of the Roman state does not act to restore law and order on the high seas, Caesar has the organizational skills to collect money like a public tax gatherer, swiftly assume direct command of an armed fleet, win victory in a naval battle and punish the pirates with absolute finality. No wonder the governor is filled with jealousy. Even death by crucifixion does not receive any overtly hostile treatment in the ancient sources, since it was a common means of punishing criminals in ancient Rome. Suetonius elsewhere lists among the signs of Caesar's clemency that he first arranged for his kidnappers' throats to be cut (Suetonius, *Deified Julius* 74.1), since crucifixion was known to be a particularly slow and agonizing way to die.

At its most eulogistic, the episode appears in *Memorable Words and Deeds*, dedicated by its author Valerius Maximus to the emperor Tiberius. The writer uses historical events and biographical incidents as ethical models for current actions. Set out as an account of the conduct of great men in Roman life's various aspects, the work narrates the past didactically as a guide to the present conduct of its aristocratic readers. An education in ethics through the narration of words and deeds which are to be emulated or scorned, the sixth book contains a section illustrating how famous men have emerged from youthful episodes of humiliation inflicted on them by fortune to become brilliant men of state. Valerius Maximus portrays the young Julius Caesar as already a god incarnate, with the result that his reversal of fortune is dramatically expanded to leap the divide between divinity and captivity. Thus, Caesar's swift revenge for the insult to his dignity – his ascension from abject prisoner in a pirate galley to brightest star of the universe – becomes a climactic example. By means of Caesar's response to capture by pirates, as from other historical examples, Rome's aristocrats can be educated in virtue and dissuaded from vice.

Through the course of the Middle Ages and the Renaissance, Valerius Maximus' volume of aristocratic culture became a form of secular bible, a source of reference for anyone who could read Latin and faced a moral decision. But the early nineteenth-century etching by Bartolomeo Pinelli brings to the surface the ethical and political ambiguities already underlying the ancient accounts of Caesar's adventure with the pirates: is it an example of virtue or of vice? From one perspective, it prefigures the dictator's commendable traits of self-assurance, strategic thinking, charisma, audacity and decisiveness; from another, it exposes his key vices, such as arrogant self-sufficiency, reckless bravado, bloodthirsty cruelty and, crucially for Pinelli, imperiousness.

Pinelli's depiction of Caesar's adventure appears in a volume of one hundred plates illustrating the history of Rome, *Istoria Romana* (1818–19). In contrast to the elaborateness and exclusiveness of history paintings, the artist's sequence of prints depicts a simple and populist narrative of the city's past from its foundation. His political sympathies (during a period of nascent nationalism in Italy) are apparent. For, within Pinelli's graphic history of the Roman republic, the Caesar cycle begins with a representation of the general 'contravening the laws by crossing the Rubicon'. After the representation of Caesar declaiming on board the pirate ship, there follow such evidently tragic episodes as the death of the 'unfortunate' Pompey, the presentation of his dismembered head to Caesar, and Pompey's funeral. Julius Caesar's assassination follows swiftly on his emergence from the waters of the harbour of Alexandria (where he had nearly drowned) and the suicide of Cato, who did not wish to survive 'the slavery of his own country'. The pirate etching itself is captioned 'Julius Caesar, prisoner of pirates, imperiously commands them, as if he were their master'.

Within his visual history of Rome, Pinelli presents the youthful adventure on the galley as a prefiguration of how Caesar will handle the ship of state. Already a widely used metaphor in classical literature, the ship of state appears prominently in the political biography of Julius Caesar. According to Plutarch, at the outbreak of civil war between the ambitious rivals Caesar and Pompey, the city had been left to anarchy 'like a ship drifting without a helmsman' (*Caesar* 28.5). Pinelli uses the Plutarchan details of Caesar's adventure with the pirates to depict in extravagant terms the future statesman's power. But his will be no steady hand on the political rudder: though prisoner, he acts like an imperious captain; though citizen, he will come to act like a disdainful tyrant.

While before the twentieth century, there occur only incidental engagements with the story of Caesar's capture by pirates, curiously a whole cluster of relatively detailed versions of the episode emerge in the popular culture of the tail end of the twentieth and the beginning of the twenty-first centuries. In detective fiction, historical novels, television adventure series and digital gameplay, Caesar encounters the pirates over and over again.

In 1999, 'Little Caesar and the Pirates' appeared in a collection of short mystery tales, *The House of the Vestals*, by Steven Saylor. These tales are related to an ongoing series of historical novels collectively entitled *Roma sub rosa* (explained as meaning both the secret history of Rome and the history of Rome's secrets), whose investigative

hero and first-person narrator, Gordianus the Finder, begins his fictional career around 80 BC, during Sulla's dictatorship, and, with
each novel in the series, finds himself progressively more entangled
in the momentous events of Julius Caesar's career. The novels have
met with considerable commercial success and the author, a history
and classics graduate from the University of Texas at Austin, has
been praised for his vivid and meticulous recreations of republican
Rome and the skill with which his narratives interweave history and
suspense. The novels lay partial claim to the authority of scholarship
through the use of a strong sense of historical chronology, a close
dependency on ancient sources (most notably Cicero's speeches and
letters), and the regular attachment of 'historical notes' which disclose the author's research strategy and purpose.

Within Saylor's associated collection of short stories, 'Little Caesar
and the Pirates' opens at the baths in Rome, where Gordianus is
regaled with a story of 'pirates, ransom, revenge – *crucifixions!*' by his
good friend Lucius Claudius. While following Plutarch's account
closely, the bravado of young Caesar is presented as a choice piece of
recent Forum gossip and its telling is met with both distaste and
scepticism by this tale's own hero, Gordianus:

> [Lucius] 'Many times while he was their captive he
>   boasted that he would see them crucified, and they
>   had laughed, thinking the threat was mere boyish
>   bravado – but in the end it was Caesar who laughed,
>   when he saw them nailed naked upon crosses. "Let
>   men learn to take me at my word," he said.'
> [Gordianus] I shivered, despite the heat of the bath. 'You
>   heard this in the Forum, Lucius?'
> [Lucius] 'Yes, it's on everyone's lips. Caesar is on his way
>   back to Rome, and the story of his exploits precedes
>   him.'

[Gordianus] 'Just the sort of moral tale that Romans love
to hear!' I grunted. 'No doubt the ambitious young
patrician plans a career in politics. This is the very
thing to build up his reputation with the voters.'

(Saylor, *The House of the Vestals* 1999: 142)

Soon after this exchange, Gordianus is asked to deliver a ransom to
pirates who have kidnapped another young patrician named Spurius
(for whom, we learn, Caesar has been a great idol). Spurius, however, turns out to be the antithesis, the diminutive, of great Caesar –
the 'little Caesar' of the story's title, with all its modern associations
with petty gangsterism. This latter 'kidnap' is indeed spurious, as the
clever investigator soon comes to realize. Caesar's capture is now
replayed as farce. The 'victim' has set up his own kidnapping in
order to defraud his stepfather of much-needed money. The 'kid-
napper' is no bloodthirsty Cilician pirate but a poor Neapolitan
fisherman in the pay of, and in love with, the boy. The relay boat
sinks under its weight of gold, and Gordianus tries to protect its hap-
less crew from the angry stepfather who has lost both his gold and
his dignity and has sent a warship to exact a Caesarian vengeance:

[Gordianus] I clutched my arm and staggered to my feet.
'You can't kill them. The kidnapping was a hoax!'
[Captain of warship] 'A hoax, was it? And the lost gold –
I suppose that was only an illusion?'
[Gordianus] 'But those men aren't pirates. They're simple
fishermen. Spurius put them up to the whole thing.
They acted on his orders.'

(Saylor, *The House of the Vestals* 1999: 180)

The opening of 'Little Caesar' acknowledges that, even in youth,
Caesar has already become a set of fictions, fictions which need the

proper evaluation of an expert like the first-person narrator. The use to which the tale of 'Caesar and the pirates' is then put in the mystery plot also acknowledges the dubious ethical function of the episode (as the model on which Spurius has drawn for his own appalling conduct). The final horror of the slaughter of innocent fishermen helps recast Caesar as *anti*-model.

The collapse of the tale of a young patrician's bravery at sea fits particularly well into Saylor's broad project of demonstrating, through retrojection into a familiar but even more sordid past, the corruption of contemporary political life and its loss of moral principle – historical fiction as the present's 'distant mirror'. For it smacks of disclosures, in the years which immediately preceded the first publication of Saylor's mystery tale, about the youthful exploits of another charismatic and patrician leader who was also destined for assassination, John F. Kennedy. Political biographies were drawing attention to the disastrous military operation which underlay the highly celebrated account of JFK's wartime heroism (when, in 1943, he had rescued the men of his rammed torpedo boat PT-109 by swimming with them to remote shores and sustaining them until help could arrive), and to the extensive exploitation of the incident to characterize Kennedy as warrior and hero in his later political career.

Fictionality lies both at the core of 'Little Caesar' and on its surface. It is a central theme of the story but is also brought to the attention of readers in the framing circumstances of the story's publication. The piece was composed some years after the novel series *Roma sub rosa* was launched and, alongside the others in *House of the Vestals*, it was explicitly offered to fill in for readers the missing years the fictional hero Gordianus had passed between the publication of the first novel (*Roman Blood*, set in 80 BC) and the second (*Arms of Nemesis*, set in 72 BC). Critics have long argued that the strategies of detective fiction focus readers' attention on the processes of narration: the detective hero pieces together clues to criminality in a manner akin to an author's plotting of their literary work. Heroes of detective fiction are perhaps most like authors of histories in the manner in which they thread together separate strands of the past in order to produce a credible story. And the overlap of detective fiction and historical narration is most noticeable in the narrative structures of historical mysteries like 'Little Caesar', where both author and detective are simultaneously piecing the past together. In his tale, Saylor takes advantage of this overlap to dramatize through Gordianus his own authorial stratagems. Both, we are invited to understand, are evaluating and exposing from below the 'secret truth' behind the stories out of which elites have composed the history of republican Rome. Part of the reader's pleasure in this particular Saylor tale lies in recognizing that such detective fiction can plausibly challenge history as a mechanism for revealing the dirty truths about Julius Caesar.

Whilst Caesar is already a distant and dubious ethical model in Saylor's short mystery tale, he is very much a direct physical presence in Vincent Panella's novella *Cutter's Island: Caesar in Captivity* (2000). Composed in the first-person voice of a young Julius Caesar, divided into segments which correspond to the days of captivity and their immediate aftermath, the novella's point of view and structure (as private diary written in the present tense) deliberately work against the external perspective of the ancient biographical tradition and even the writings of Julius Caesar himself, in which his military campaigns are catalogued in an ostensibly objective, distanced third person. The enforced idleness of captivity and bouts of fever become literary devices to justify an interior narrative: Caesar's intimate ruminations on his life to date, presented as vivid visual and emotional flashbacks to his sexual and political awakening. Captivity now becomes a formative experience, close contact with the pirates' leader – here fleshed out as an individual with the fictional name Cutter – a dance of deception in which, as Caesar tells us in his prologue, he came to know himself. Eventually Caesar finds the strength to shake off his self-doubt and, as his story draws to a close, he is at last entirely confident of his own destiny:

> The air rings with the sound of hammers and the agonies of the guilty. I canter my horse along the tide line. Above the groans and cries my name flies in the air, as though the gods are speaking it. *Caesar! Caesar!* On the lips of men, in the lapping tide, my name bubbles up in the salty foam, the chant of two syllables. *CAE-SAR! CAE-SAR!* The tidal flow sings my destiny, rising, rising, foaming, yet steady and white like the swan. My name sails above the cries of the doomed. There's no way to tell them that I am doomed to this as they to death.
>
> (Panella, *Cutter's Island* 2000: 189)

The author's role becomes akin to that of a probing psychoanalyst who brings into words the formative confrontation that turned Caesar from an indulgent and indecisive young poet and politician into a cunning dictator in a brutal world.

Both a crucial formative experience and destiny are also the concern of an episode in the television fantasy-action series *Xena: Warrior Princess*. It is not Julius Caesar, however, who matters here but the pirates. Filmed in New Zealand, the series was widely syndicated in the USA during the six seasons it ran from 1995 to 2001. It was broadcast on approximately two hundred stations across the States and also shown in many other countries worldwide. It starred Lucy Lawless as a mythic warrior princess who constantly struggles to renounce her past life as a ruthless warlord. In 'Destiny', while lying fatally wounded and delirious, Xena relives in flashback the encounter ten years earlier that had caused her original transformation into warlord: the capture by her pirate crew of an audacious young Roman soldier who then reveals himself – accompanied by stirring music to underscore the revelation's significance – to be 'Caesar, Julius Caesar'.

The narrative style in *Xena* has been categorized as pastiche, or post-modern camp. The liberties it takes with both chronology and geography are notorious: Xena is Greek, yet in her heroic adventures she meets characters ranging from Caesar to Santa Claus. The visual carries greater significance than the verbal, suggestive double meanings and intertextual references are legion (such as that here to James Bond, the hero of fictional espionage). The series also acknowledges this rejection of realism in its regular use of self-reference and irony. For audiences familiar with the pirate adventure of the historical Julius Caesar, irony is pleasingly put into play in 'Destiny' at what would otherwise be an unusually romantic moment. When Caesar (Karl Urban) has been ransomed and it is Xena who is about to sail away, the Roman declares, 'A moment won't pass when I'm not thinking about you.' They kiss on the seashore. He adds, 'Now go. I'll find you, I promise.' Sure enough, Xena has been duped. Revenge quickly follows on reunion, as Caesar's soldiers return to take over her ship and seize its crew. Her legs violently and loudly broken, Xena is crucified along with the others, to be rescued only much later by a girl who had been hiding on board.

As the memory of all this fades towards the end of the episode, viewers understand that the encounter with Caesar is absolutely central to the character of their hero. Julius Caesar holds a special place in Xena's heroic quest (and he will reappear across seasons and episodes): it was from this first meeting with him that she had understood her destiny to be cold self-advancement and ruthless conquest and, by the end of the episode, that recollection restores her to life and her proper destiny – the fight against evil and the protection of the innocent.

Xena: Warrior Princess has excited substantial interest from critics, particularly from the perspective of feminist or queer analysis of popular culture. It is one of the first television series to feature a woman within an epic plot of warfare and heroic quests and achieve wide popular appeal. The close friendship between Xena and her fellow-warrior Gabrielle has been construed as one of many indicators of a rich lesbian subtext. It generated hot debate as to whether, or to what degree, it challenges modern conventions of gender and sexuality or makes available queer readings and subversive pleasures. It also spawned a large fan base (the *Xenites*) who communicated with each other via the Internet, and inspired comic books, action figures, novels and magazines, even Xena club nights and cruises.

This, at first, may seem a rather unexpected context in which to find Julius Caesar playing a significant role. Yet throughout the whole series, Xena and her partner Gabrielle frequently alter the founding myths and legends of Western culture. Along with geographic and temporal boundaries, they attack the Western canon and replace it with a revisionist myth of women. This challenge to traditional history becomes especially pronounced when they meet such significant historical figures as Julius Caesar. The utility of the pirate adventure lies in its possibilities for presenting the perspective of the subaltern – of a woman, of the pirates, of the crucified victims of the Roman empire. In a narrative where it is the Roman and the male who is doubly Other, we are reminded that the hero's name is a permanent indication of her status as both female and foreigner. Julius Caesar's adventure with the pirates is retold as a story about a female pirate's formative experience, about her destiny. And, at the most dramatic moment of crucifixion, the camera temporarily gives viewers the elevated perspective of Rome's victims.

The pirate adventure enables *Xena: Warrior Princess* to challenge traditional conceptions of heroism, as well as history. Heroism is everywhere redefined to encompass women who are independent agents, and as the heroes' quest the pursuit of imperial expansion is replaced by the protection of women, the family and the home. Yet Caesar is presented not just as Xena's antithesis, but also as her disturbing reflection. By means of its depiction of the present-day warrior princess as constantly haunted by her warlord past, the overarching narrative of the series works to challenge any obvious distinction between hero and villain. Retelling the pirate adventure makes this possible because its ethical ambiguity has long been recognized: the murderous pirates are matched by their murderous captive.

Finally, this version of Caesar's capture by pirates plays out traditional gender relations in the most dramatic – and tragic – terms. Caesar stands for a hard, military masculinity, and a conventional heterosexuality of hero and his temporary helpmeet, in response to which Xena sheds her armour for the soft, silky attire of an old-fashioned alluring femininity and invites him into her shipboard boudoir (Figure 2.2). Submission to such traditional gender roles leads directly to the radical reversal of Xena's position of power: from captor, she becomes captive. Captivity thus reveals in exaggerated terms the consequences of woman's sexual subordination to man. Presented in the episode 'Destiny' as a recollection of a terrible mistake, Xena's seduction by a domineering male provides a pointed contrast to the gender role and ambiguous sexuality ascribed to Xena elsewhere in the series: Julius Caesar has taught her to scorn the treachery of men.

In contrast, however, there are no women in the scenario 'Caesar Vs. Pirates' which is part of the digital strategy game *The Rise of Rome* (released by Microsoft in October 1998). Economically, such games now comprise a key sector of computer technology. Their consumption matches or even outranks cinema attendance in terms

Fig. 2.2 Xena tries to seduce Caesar. Scene from the 'Destiny' episode of
Xena: Warrior Princess (1997).

of both market size and cultural impact, and is sustained by a global entertainment industry. *The Rise of Rome* forms an expansion to *Age of Empires*, and invites players to build the Roman empire against strong and constant opposition by expanding a small village community into a thriving civilization that can vie for world dominance (that is, game win). Digital game play involves scaling a ladder of technology: creating, controlling and upgrading people, military units and transportation; collecting and managing resources (from food to gold); building and repairing structures (from storage pits to sentry towers); exploring terrain; trading or creating alliances; and, most importantly, combat (using a wide variety of units from axemen to centurions, armoured elephants to catapult triremes) and finally – if successful – conquest. Destiny here belongs to no individual but to the nation, and the game world works on the assumption that global competition equals extreme physical violence (categorized as killings and razings) and all-out militarism.

In the Rome expansion, as well as multiplayer games, there are twenty single-player scenarios divided into four separate sections, each of which links its groups of scenarios in a predefined order, notionally following the evolution of the Roman empire. Julius Caesar's encounter with the pirates constitutes the first scenario of the campaign 'Ave Caesar' after 'Rise of Rome' (first scenario: battle against the Samnites) and before 'Pax Romana' (first scenario: battle of Actium). In this new gaming context, Julius Caesar's pirate adventure has no ethical or emotional dimension. Gamers are not offered the opportunity to simulate kidnap, ransom, and release (those events are already in the past when the game begins) but only to immerse themselves in a vengeful attack on the pirates of the Mediterranean. Thus, the mission is transposed to Julius Caesar that, historically, was assigned to his rival Pompey (the year is even given as 67 BC, when Pompey had received an unprecedented command against the pirates and succeeded in almost obliterating their presence in Mediterranean waters). The scenario instructions read:

> Pirates in the Mediterranean have been a plague on trade for decades. Now that we control most of the Mediterranean coastline, it is within our power to wipe out the pirate nests and make the Mediterranean trade routes safe from predators. You have been given responsibility for these areas and the mandate to wipe out the pirates. *Objective:* Destroy all enemy docks. If Caesar dies, the mission will be lost.

The narrative of such digital games breaks with the linear plot or rounded characters of conventional plays, novels and films. Rather, it is geography which marks out narrative development – what changes and develops over time is not the psychology of a character but a map of territory and waters won or lost. Closure is rare; the actual play is more important than its outcome. The player (not their digital avatar) is the source of action; the simulations on screen (of different islands, woods and settlements, barracks and docks, fishing boats and warships, blue-coded Romans and red-, yellow- or brown-coded pirates) not static objects to be read but options to select. Gamers affect the activity on their screens within predefined rules for engagement: enlarging their community, managing its economy, organizing material and social structures, controlling the military (including the Roman general himself). Direct hands-on control and the requirement to take swift decisions intensify the players' sense of their own power to shape events and create the illusion that they are winning (or losing) the battle against the pirates, that they are building (or destroying) the Roman empire, that they are making history. The perspective of players (their god's eye) over the audio-visual map they are creating, and on Caesar always astride his horse, constructs them as external directors who engage with their Roman avatar only by moving him around the map (Figure 2.3). They do not stand in for him.

However, in terms of the back-story and the narrative momentum through the 'Ave Caesar' campaign, the player is also directly addressed as Caesar. Game players are informed at the outset that they are seeking revenge for their earlier kidnap by pirates. If they succeed in their mission to destroy the three colour-coded sets of pirate docks then at the end of the game, on the screen entitled *Achievements*, the sub-heading 'Aftermath' leads to the information that they are now in line for promotion and new responsibilities, namely a move up to the second scenario (the invasion of Britain), followed by the third (besieging Alesia) and so on. At this juncture, the interactive strategy software for *Rise of Rome* positions game players as a cyber-Caesar. But if players fail to complete the mission, they are humorously mocked for failing to live up to the game's

Fig. 2.3 Scene from Caesar vs. Pirates, in *Age of Empires: The Rise of Rome* (1998).

version of masculinity, of Roman history, and of Julius Caesar's youthful escapade. If Caesar is out-manoeuvred, the screen reads as follows:

> The pirates have made a mockery of your boast to return and eradicate them. Rome is disappointed, but because you paid for the expedition personally there will be no recriminations. The job of eliminating the pirates has been given to a real man, Pompey. You can go along to keep his armour oiled.

3

COURAGE, CRUELTY AND MILITARY ACUMEN

War in Gaul, 58–51 BC

When Julius Caesar left Rome in March 58 BC for an extraordinary provincial command, his political conduct had already been the subject of intense criticism. During the eight years that he would campaign in Gaul, his military conduct would also meet with increasing disapproval from sectors of the Roman senate. And when he next entered Rome, just over nine years later, it was as an aggressor, at the head of an army, in an act of civil war. Caesar had become an outstanding politician and a decisive military commander over the course of the 60s. But, especially as praetor (a judicial magistrate) in 62 and as consul (one of the two supreme magistrates of the Roman republic) in 59, his populist actions had involved considerable violence and illegality and had been vehemently opposed by conservatives in the senate. Attempts had been made to prevent his election as consul and to commit him in advance to a paltry administrative command over Italy's woods and footpaths when his term of office was complete. When he finally did win authority over his three provinces of Cisalpine Gaul, Transalpine Gaul and Illyricum, however, Caesar was overjoyed (the sources say) and boasted that he had got exactly what he had wanted in the face of his adversaries (Suetonius, *Deified Julius* 22.2).

Even in antiquity, it was clear that warfare in Gaul represented a fresh chapter in Julius Caesar's political biography. He passionately desired a great command, an army, and an unprecedented war in which to give his ability *(virtus* or 'virtue', 'manliness', 'courage') the opportunity to shine (Sallust, *War of Catiline* 54.4). This is because the Roman who displayed great military ability was usually rewarded with the highest honours. Pompey had entered into temporary alliance with Caesar two years before Caesar's departure for Gaul, after the experienced general had failed to capitalize politically on his successful eradication of pirates from the Mediterranean, his crushing defeat of Rome's long-standing enemy Mithridates (King of Pontus), his great victories across Asia, Bithynia, Pontus, Syria and Cilicia, and his foundation throughout the east of Roman colonies. In 58 BC Julius Caesar, from his base in the Roman province of Gallia Narbonensis (Provence), might have an opportunity to expand Roman dominion west and north across the vast territories of what are now modern France and Belgium as far as the northern seas, the river Rhine and Germany, perhaps even beyond the ocean to Britain, which stood at the very end of the earth. War in Gaul would be a new kind of activity for Caesar, a new aspect to his life which also gave him the chance gradually to build fresh and substantial political support within a devoted army while continuing, through his agents, to sustain his plebeian support at Rome. War in Gaul could also consolidate his reputation not as the leader of a faction at Rome, but as the commander of Rome's troops abroad – not least because Caesar became the author of his own history, principal eye-witness to his own military success.

Julius Caesar's seven books of commentary on the Gallic war *(Commentarii de bello Gallico)* are unique – the only surviving narrative by a participant in a large-scale Roman war abroad and, furthermore, one written by the commander-in-chief. An innovative literary genre, the books are composed in the third person as a general's campaign reports dispatched year by year in haste to Rome from winter headquarters at the frontline, and famously open: 'Gaul as a whole is divided into three parts.' We now possess no comparable sources by which to evaluate their accuracy. If they were first published annually in draft and then re-edited as a unit in 51 BC (as modem scholars generally conclude), their author would scarcely have had pause to compose wholesale falsifications, but by deliberate neglect, selection, and emphasis, the image of 'Caesar' the courageous general and skilful strategist could be consciously shaped.

Without orders from Rome, and exceeding the limits of his proconsular authority, Julius Caesar proceeded to subject all of Gaul to Roman rule, levying legions for himself additional to those which had been allocated by the senate and people, and ultimately conquering a territory larger than any ever acquired by a previous Roman general (even Pompey). Despite operating over a vast area beyond the borders of his province, the general is first presented to his readers undertaking a series of small-scale, local campaigns in conscientious performance of his duty, as a Roman governor, to protect Rome's allies against marauding Helvetians and Germans, and it is by these campaigns that he represents himself as gradually drawn into a full-scale, just war. Always at the service of the senate and people of Rome (never with an eye to his own personal interest), he comes to the rescue of Rome's allies, avenges Rome's defeats, and guards its empire.

As book follows book there accumulates a relentlessly self-aggrandizing account of incredible marches, frightful battles, skilful sieges, and a whole continent explored, penetrated and subjugated. The most important attributes expected of an outstanding general are all here on permanent and clear display: courage, military acumen, authority, good fortune, fortitude. From such material develops the fame of soldier Caesar – who, despite his sophisticated manners and patrician background, can immerse himself fully into the everyday dangers and privations of military life (eating little, sleeping less, dictating multiple letters on the move: Plutarch, *Life of Caesar* 17) – and strategist Caesar, who blends in happy synthesis prudence and audacity (scouting terrain to avoid ambush, disguising himself as a Gallic guerrilla to cross through German lines: Suetonius, *Deified Julius* 58). While, in his own account, Caesar becomes a military genius by demonstration rather than description, his enemy – the Gauls – are typified by their baseness and incompetence, their barbarity and treachery. The direct style in which all this is packaged (no preface, no dedication, no justification for writing, simple Latin, limited vocabulary, little embellishment) is designed to embody the directness and transparency of its author. And, whilst the first person plural 'our' (used for example of soldiers, provinces, customs, authority) draws readers into Caesar's self-advertisement, the third person singular 'he' cultivates a tone of distanced objectivity and a role for Caesar as the selfless instrument of the will of the Roman senate and people.

Not all Julius Caesar's critics were so persuaded. In 56 BC, we find Cicero (recently returned from exile for executing Roman citizens without appeal during the conspiracy of Catiline, and now enlisted into Caesar's service) compelled to argue in the senate in the most extravagant terms against those members who would dismiss the general from his provinces and break off his prolonged command: there is nothing now beyond the peaks of the Alps as far as Ocean for Italy to dread, because Caesar has either crushed, or terrified, checked and subdued, the tribes in that region; the senate should not recall a commander so distinguished by Fortune's fullest favours or so fired with devotion to the high service of the state *(de provinciis consularibus* 33–5). While in 55 BC, although Caesar had now gained a five-year extension to his command and won from the senate public rituals of thanksgiving lasting twenty days for his military achievements of that year, his constant opponent Cato countered that the Roman general should instead be handed over to two Germanic tribes – the Usipetes and the Tencteri – as an act of atonement for the treachery he had demonstrated in breaking truce with them and slaughtering their women and children.

Renewed rebellion in Gaul in 54 BC required Julius Caesar to spend the next few years regaining lost territory. By the beginning of 51, his opponents (including Pompey, who had broken away from Caesar some three years earlier) were again attempting prematurely to recall the proconsul to Rome from his provinces so that, reduced to the vulnerable status of a private citizen, they might indict, condemn and ruin him. Caesar's seven books of commentary on the Gallic war were now published as a unit to counter such opposition, culminating in the seventh with a dramatic description of the great crisis of 52 when the Celtic tribes, led by the brutal and ambitious Avernian prince Vercingetorix, were crushed, and finally abandoned all hope of common liberty. Although such an account of Caesar's Gallic war may have had some success in improving his popularity in Italy in the short term, later judgement on his military conduct was often far more critical. Body counts are catalogued in Caesar's own writings as tallies of his great victories. In the biography by Plutarch, they prove that Caesar fought more battles and killed more enemies than any other Roman general: 800 towns taken by storm, 300 tribes subdued, three million armed men defeated, of whom a million were killed and a million taken prisoner (Plutarch, *Life of Caesar* 15.5). But in the estimation of Pliny the Elder, such numbers do not speak of the glory achieved by an individual but of the great injury inflicted on the human race (*Natural History* 7.92).

Later centuries have continued to split judgement between the courage and the cruelty of Julius Caesar, between the value of Romanizing Gaul and the cost incurred to accomplish it. Manifestly, Caesar's conquest of Gaul had epochal consequences which extended far beyond the end of his command there. After conquest, colonization was a gradual process spread over centuries. Roman dominion was no longer to be confined to limited regions around the Mediterranean, for the area the general had subjugated was double that of Italy alone, and pushed the boundaries of empire right out to the Atlantic, the North Sea and the river Rhine. Caesar's conquest, some historians argue, concluded the prehistory of Western Europe by the imposition there of efficient Roman administration, the beneficial provision of Latin rights or Roman citizenship, and the deep infusion of Roman culture. Unification and Romanization then laid the groundwork for the later emergence of France and, through the embrace of the West into the empire, initiated the development of first medieval, and then modern, Europe. Yet it is possible to overvalue the long-term benefits of the Roman conquest (as Luciano Canfora has noted), to become blinkered by a vision of an historic destiny that is teleological and imperialist.

Caesar's war began as an act of unprovoked aggression. It resulted in devastating genocide and the slow destruction of a sophisticated Celtic civilization. And all this for Caesar's own cynical political ends: to match and exceed the military glory of Pompey, to win honour, fame and authority at Rome, to provide a foundation for civil war, a rung on the ladder to kingship, another step towards the destruction of the republic. It is hardly surprising that such reassessments of the Gallic war have been most frequent and most pronounced in modem France, and that they focus most often on Caesar's concluding account of the pan-Gallic rebellion of 52 BC and the surrender of the chieftain Vercingetorix.

From the outset of the seventh book of Caesar's commentaries on the Gallic war, Vercingetorix is presented as the leading chieftain responsible for inciting revolt against Roman rule. Caesar distinguishes the rebel youth from the other chieftains because he leads a civil state (not just an army or a tribe), and supplies him with personal details of family, direct speech, drives and aspirations. His conduct is characterized by brutal military discipline, while his talk of common liberty is mere rhetoric designed to mask his real desire for kingship over all Gaul (7.4).

The final decisive confrontation between Roman general and Gallic chieftain takes place after Vercingetorix has withdrawn into the town of Alesia, a natural citadel, standing on a high plateau and bounded by rivers and other hills. Impossible to take by storm, the site invited the most methodical and (in due course) the most celebrated of siege tactics. Caesar encloses the fortress with a double concentric ring of fortifications: in the terminology of the Napoleonic excavations, first an inner 'contravallation' some nine miles long to block the Alesians in, and later an outer 'circumvallation' some thirteen miles long to keep the relief army out. To these are added parapets, towers, camps, and a system of ditches and spiked booby traps. Following several tense weeks, hemmed in by enemies on either side, outnumbered five to one, Caesar's legions repel the combined forces in a series of battles lasting four days and win an exceptional victory, assisted by a cavalry attack which surprises the enemy in the rear (Caesar, *Gallic War* 7.68–88). On the fifth day, the victorious general 'orders the weapons to be delivered up, the chieftains to be brought out. He himself takes his seat on a rampart in front of the camp. The leaders are brought out to him there. Vercingetorix is handed over, arms are thrown down' (7.89).

In sharp contrast to later narratives, paintings, performances and other reconstructions of the same events, the Roman general's account of the ritual of surrender is clipped and concise in the extreme. The passive voice is frequently employed in order to underline the rebel leaders' loss of power; as physical index of their loss of political liberty, and their submission to Rome, they have lost control over their own actions and are forced to obey the commands of Caesar seated on high.

Already within antiquity, historians restored agency to Vercingetorix as well as conferring on him dignity, drama, a little heroism and much pathos. In Plutarch's version, the Gallic chieftain, once leader of the whole war, dons his most beautiful armour and decorates his horse before riding out through the gates of the citadel. He first circles around the seated Caesar, then leaps off his horse and strips off his armour before he abases himself at Caesar's feet *(Life of Caesar, 27.8–10)*.

Cassius Dio concurs that Vercingetorix himself chose surrender and his own humiliation. He also adds a dash of psychological invention when he describes the Gaul's hopes that he might be able to obtain pardon from Caesar because of their earlier friendliness:

> So [Vercingetorix] came to him without any announcement by herald, but appeared before him suddenly, as Caesar was seated on a tribunal, and threw some who were present into alarm; for he was very tall to begin with, and in his armour he made an extremely imposing figure. When quiet had been restored, he uttered not a word, but fell upon his knees, with hands clasped in an attitude of supplication. This inspired many with pity at remembrance of his former fortune and at the distressing state in which he now appeared.
>
> (Cassius Dio, *Roman History* 40.41. Trans. E. Cary, 1941)

In these later accounts, Caesar always remains seated on high and unmoved. Yet not only is he without pity, he is also cruel: he commands that Vercingetorix be put in chains and transported to prison in Rome, where he remains for a further six years, only to be brought out for display in Caesar's Gallic triumph and, finally, executed.

From the nineteenth century, Vercingetorix becomes a central character in the formation of a French national mythology, the foremost hero of the nation, the instigator of unified France. Often exploited as a goad to political action, the Gallic chieftain is presented in opposition to any present-day enemy transposed back into the body of Julius Caesar. Through works of historiography, public statuary, theatrical performances, historical novels and especially school curricula, his legend and that of a villainous Caesar become firmly embedded in the national culture of modern France. Yet already in the medieval period, when Vercingetorix has not yet been singled out for 'nationalization', we can find subtle critiques of Caesar's actions in Gaul and small-scale improvements to the characterization of the rebels rising to the surface of vernacular translations of Caesar's commentaries on the war.

Li Fet des Romains (*The Deeds of the Romans*) is – despite its sweeping title – a biography of Julius Caesar in French prose, compiled by an anonymous cleric around 1213–14 from a selection of Latin texts. Taking for its narrative structure Suetonius' life of *The Deified Julius,* it inserts sequentially translations of Sallust's *War of Catiline,* Caesar's seven books on the Gallic war (despite conforming to the conventional medieval identification of that work's author as one 'Julius Celsus'), the concluding eighth book by Aulus Hirtius, and Lucan's *Civil War,* while drawing on various medieval works for some elaboration. It also demonstrates the influence of medieval epic and romance in its narration of Roman history as a collection of heroic deeds. This is Caesar's first sustained appearance in French narrative, and his life is portrayed comprehensively from birth to death. The Roman general's own account of his conquest of Gaul translates easily into the vocabulary of a medieval tale of consummate battles and valiant single combat fought between chivalrous warriors. His qualities can be readily honed to match those of the ideal medieval knight: qualities such as intelligence, bravery, technical skill in warfare, courtesy and largesse. Thus *Fet* legitimates, by historicizing, chivalric ideology.

Yet the chronicle also exhibits some ambivalence towards its hero. The latter half of the work, where it depends rather more on Lucan than on Caesar, narrates the Roman hero's decline towards his own destruction as he develops idiosyncratic vices (the sins of pride and lust, and excessive ambition) and fights in a civil war for his own advancement and not for the greater good. The narrative possesses a double didactic purpose, its compiler affecting through his anonymity the status of an inheritor and transmitter of lessons to be learned from the actions of Julius Caesar, lessons he has humbly received through the writings of the classical historians and poets. Politically, *Fet des Romains* is designed to educate its beleaguered aristocratic audience about their present-day struggle with the French king Philippe Auguste through the representation of an historic conflict between aristocratic rule and Caesarian authority. Ethically, it is designed to demonstrate from history that even the greatest of heroes can be lured away from chivalry by his own ambition. Moreover, even the first half of *Fet* (where Caesar's heroic reputation is more secure) displays concern over the Roman general's occupation of Gaul. For Gaul, not Italy, is now the homeland of both the translator and the reader of this medieval Caesar.

Fet des Romains lets slip its patriotic stance through the methods by which it translates the Latin commentaries of Julius Caesar. In some sections, it abbreviates or omits the original wording. In others, it fabricates. At times, it even explicitly contradicts the Roman general's narrative. The chronicle systematically reworks the Roman perspective on Gaul and Vercingetorix. It removes or diminishes the barbarism which Caesar had ascribed to Gaul: the geographic perspective is resituated, so that 'beyond the Alps' now marks out Italy. It creates for readers in its place a genealogical connection to the terrain of their prehistory: Gaul is named France, the tribal barbarians are 'François', Vercingetorix is from Clermont. It rejects the attribution of inferiority and fickleness to the Gauls that is a constant feature of Caesar's text. Instead, they are rendered more courageous and less debased. The Latin original is revised to recreate the war as a chivalrous joust between two nations on an equal footing in a civilized Europe. The uprising of 52 BC is undertaken for the sake of liberty and the security of all France. The Gallic chieftains are driven by their noble ancestry and the obligations of national honour, and Vercingetorix is matched against Caesar in an epic contest. He may still suffer from the self-interested ambition with which Caesar first furnished him, but he is Caesar's match in military acumen and prowess.

The Vercingetorix of this medieval tradition is an elected leader who comes to decisions collectively. And in the climactic moment of surrender he achieves complete autonomy: he chooses to hand himself over, he is not given up. Surrender is an act of voluntary submission, undertaken ceremonially sovereign to sovereign, to which Caesar responds, not with further campaigns of attrition, but by holding most courteous council with the other French princes. He then bestows such generous gifts on them that he conveniently emerges as a courtly ruler whom it can be no dishonour to serve.

Despite the ambivalences and contradictions generated by these various revisions of Caesar's account of war in Gaul, *Li Fet des Romains* provides a first taste of the kind of nationalistic prehistory of France which was to come – one where rebellion against Caesar was not a crime but, rather, a noble struggle for liberty against tyranny. The vernacular chronicle was remarkably popular throughout the Middle Ages both in France and in Italy (where it was retranslated into Italian). For close on three hundred years it had greater success than works in Latin on the Roman conqueror of Gaul, and circulated widely as a secular manual for princes and clerics on the life of Caesar, on military, political and moral conduct, and on the early history of France.

Julius Caesar's *Gallic War* became the object of close scrutiny in the Renaissance. It achieved wide circulation in numerous editions: admired for the purity and simplicity of its Latin, it was regularly prescribed for students as an introduction to the language. In translations, commentaries and military treatises, however, Caesar's political ambition was often deplored at the same time as his battlefield strategy and tactics were admired and even held up as a model for imitation. In *L'arte della guerra* (*The Art of War,* 1521), for example, while demonstrating a republican hostility to the political Caesar, Niccolò Machiavelli celebrates the Roman general's great strategic choices (exploiting victory to the full, valuing infantry), his great tactical choices (concentrating forces on a single point, selecting an opportune moment to attack), his anticipation of the reactions of the enemy, his adaptation to circumstance. Now that contemporary warfare was once again a match for ancient warfare in scale and level of complexity, ancient military practice appeared applicable – both theoretically and directly – to the modern conduct of war.

This intimate relationship is graphically displayed in Melchior Feselen's depiction of *Die Stadt Alesia von Julius Cäsar belagert (The city of Alesia besieged by Julius Caesar,* 1533). Viewers are informed by the garlanded inscription which sits high in the sky, without any apparent trace of irony, that 'this painted tablet depicts with what great slaughter of men Alesia yielded to the exalted Caesarian eagles' (Figure 3.1). Caesar's infantry and cavalry are attired in current military fashion and carry on their flag the double-headed eagle of the Hapsburgs. And the spectacular celebration of Caesar's siege tactics and the scale of his victory is conducted in terms of

Fig. 3.1 *Siege of the City of Alesia by Julius Caesar* (1533), Melchior Feselen.

contemporary German military formations and equipment, most notably the rings of cannon primed to bombard the Gallic city.

The ever more acute and explicit split in the French perspective between Julius Caesar's courage and his cruelty, between his military acumen and his ruthless ambition, is tangibly demonstrated by a pair of works published in 1559 by the Renaissance humanist and professor of philosophy and eloquence at the Collège Royal, Petrus Ramus. One is a work of military science, *liber de Caesaris militia (Treatise on Caesar's Military Command),* in which reflections made by Julius Caesar in his commentaries on the Gallic and civil wars are extracted and reassembled to build up a methodical set of rules for action on the modern battlefield. The other, *liber de moribus veterum Gallorum (Treatise on the Customs of the Ancient Gauls),* is expressly described in the introductory chapter as written from personal love of country. Although Vercingetorix is not yet singled out as a national hero, Ramus presents a radical counter to the perspective of his Roman model. The Gauls are 'our ancestors', their land a form of Arcadia, their deeds most worthy of celebration.

It was not until the nineteenth century that Vercingetorix was singled out from among the Gauls and furnished with the characteristics that would make him the primary national hero of France. National sentiment had emerged during the Revolution and been fed by Napoleon's victories across Western Europe at the beginning of the century, but defeat in 1813 and the subsequent occupation of Paris had called for a redefinition of the nation. And the history of the Gauls provided one opportune route to a new legitimacy – a genealogy for noble resistance against foreign invasion. Amédée Thierry's *Histoire des Gaulois,* published in 1828, is generally regarded as an innovation, a work of historical scholarship that spoke to contemporary patriotic needs by fully fleshing out Vercingetorix as tragic martyr and heroic match for Caesar.

Although Thierry's account of the Gallic uprising was based upon Julius Caesar's version of events, it thwarts Caesar's purpose in the execution of its narrative. Composed not just as a history, but also as a dramatic tale of adventure and romance, the *Histoire des Gaulois* reshapes the young Gallic chieftain as a genuine and ardent patriot, blessed with all the right virtues, a match for Caesar in all

military qualities, driven to regain the Gallic freedom of his ancestors. The night before his surrender, Vercingetorix is alone. Calm
and resigned, he ponders within the walls of Alesia whether his
death might be sufficient revenge for Caesar, whether to sacrifice
his life might at least obtain the conqueror's mercy for his unfortunate companions. At dawn he summons his troops, and reminds
them for the last time that what has been driving them has not been
his personal cause but all of theirs – the glory and the freedom of
Gaul. Then he mounts his horse and heads for the Roman camp.
There follows (as in Dio's account) the shudder of the Roman
spectators, the silence, Caesar alone, inflexible, unshakeable.

This form of romantic historiography went through many editions and reprints in the course of the nineteenth century, and had
an extraordinary impact on later historians, as well as political
polemicists, novelists, dramatists and artists, who between them
developed for the young Gallic chieftain engaging features not
available from the commentaries of Caesar – a face, gestures and a
voice. From these small origins grew a cult of Vercingetorix as
national martyr, noble defender of the independence of Gaul, hero
of modern France. With the right kind of amplification, Caesar
could be shaped to embody cruel assaults on the integrity of the
nation, his noble opponent resistance against those assaults. It
became the responsibility of Vercingetorix to give individual, heroic
form to all the values to which the French nation aspired, and to act
as heroic model for the continuous struggle of the mother country
against foreign invasion.

In a work of melodramatic fiction, the sentimental novel *Les
Mystères du peuple* (*The Mysteries of the People*) serialized in the
Parisian press from 1849, the socialist journalist Eugène Sue explicitly compared the Prussian and Cossack invasion of France in 1814
with Rome's conquest of Gaul. Vercingetorix only has a small role
to play in this otherwise brutal family chronicle, but his heroization

(champion of democracy, four years of constant struggle, defeated only by betrayal) is matched by a corresponding blackening of the character of Caesar:

> And so the next day, at dawn, the sun rises over the ramparts of Alesia. – What is that tribunal, covered in cloth of crimson, which rises between the entrenchments of the Roman camp and the high walls of the besieged Gallic city? – Who is that man, pale, bald of brow, eyes sunken and blazing, cruelly smiling, who sits above the tribunal? – Yes . . . who sits above the tribunal, in his ivory seat, he alone seated in the middle of his generals standing about him? – That man, bald and pale, is Caesar . . .
>
> (Sue, *Les Mystères du peuple* 1977 I: 336)

Cynical and sadistic, Julius Caesar is here a trader in slaves and the craven killer of a Gallic martyr. His subsequent assassination becomes appropriate punishment for having rebuffed the heroic supplication by Vercingetorix.

State intervention in the 1860s brought a new scientific dimension and civic recognition to the Gallic war and the actions of Vercingetorix. Napoleon, in his own analysis of Julius Caesar's text dictated in exile (*Précis des guerres de César*, or *Notes on the Wars of Caesar*, 1836), had expressed enormous admiration for the Roman as statesman, but as general he found him to be unnecessarily cruel, prone to errors of both strategy and tactics, and unsuitable for modern imitation. His nephew Louis, however, saw his own resuscitation of French empire as gloriously prefigured in the imperialism of Caesar, and the subjugation of Gaul as Western civilization's manifest destiny, so that in the second volume of his own monumental but unfinished history of Julius Caesar (*Histoire de Jules César*, 1865–6) he lauded the great advantages of Roman colonization.

To provide supporting evidence for the second volume's study of Caesar's campaigns in Gaul, Louis Napoleon Bonaparte – Napoleon III – sought out the collaboration of a whole array of scholars. The emperor instituted a national commission responsible for the topographic, historical and archaeological study of ancient Gaul, and visited the sites which were duly excavated in meticulous detail under his sponsorship. These included, from 1861, the terrain of Alise-Sainte-Reine where, it was thought, Vercingetorix had taken his last stand. At the time, political opponents of the emperor queried the identification of the site as Alesia, but that identification was subsequently confirmed, after more than a century, by further government-sponsored excavation.

Thanks to the initiative of Napoleon III, it became possible systematically to trace on the ground the outline of the vast and sophisticated siege-works which Julius Caesar had catalogued in the seventh book of his commentaries. Over the course of some five years, the complete topography of the blockade of Alesia was explored, from the famous double concentric ring of fortifications (the contra- and circum-vallations) to the Roman camps in the plain below and up on the surrounding hills. The excavators also found the grim remains of battle (the bones of men and horses) as well as weapons, ceramics, and coins which had been minted by at least twenty different Gallic tribes. Now permanently on display in a museum of national antiquities at Saint-Germain-en-Laye, these materials became public mementoes of both the enormity of Gallic losses and the splendour of Celtic civilization.

Although the emperor Louis Napoleon imagined himself a modern disciple of Julius Caesar, after the success of the archaeological work he had commissioned he personally financed a colossal bronze statue of Vercingetorix to be raised in Alise-Sainte-Reine in 1865. Designed by Aimé Millet, its features were modelled on those of the emperor, and on its base was engraved an inscription that adapted a quotation which Caesar had rendered rather more obliquely: 'Gaul united / forming a single nation / animated by the one same spirit / can defy the world. / Vercingetorix to the assembled Gauls / (Caesar, De Bello Gallico, VII, 29) / Napoleon, Emperor of the French / To the memory of Vercingetorix.' Both physical features and inscription allow the emperor to take a share of the glory that was owed the Gallic hero, but the statue's posture (a warrior and his weaponry in repose, a resigned expression) evokes Vercingetorix's unfortunate fate, and indicates the dangers that might attend too direct and personal a comparison in the political or military domain. Nonetheless, the sponsorship of Napoleon III, and the labours of the various academic institutions and experts he initiated, provided corroboration for the legend of the Gallic chieftain who was not yet a very widely known figure. The site at Alise-Sainte-Reine would eventually become embedded in the national memory and launch the siege of Alesia and the surrender of Vercingetorix as the first chapter in most school textbooks on the history of France.

Within two months of declaring war on Prussia in July 1870, the emperor and many of his troops were captured on French soil. Paris was besieged; capitulation, loss of territory and compulsory indemnity on a vast scale followed. This national crisis considerably enhanced the political utility of the ancient encounter between the Roman general and the chief of the Avernians. Thereafter, in popular political discourse, the disastrous events of 1870–1 were regularly assimilated to those of 52 BC with consolatory outcome: the occupation of French territory by German troops was comparable to the invasion of Gaul by Julius Caesar's legions, the gruelling blockade of Paris with that of Alesia, the gallant resistance of the republican leader Léon Gambetta with that of Vercingetorix, the imperial aggression of the German chancellor Otto von Bismarck with that of the Roman proconsul. But the lesson of ancient history, so went the consolatory argument, would teach the people of France that they would have their revenge. Just as France had been born from Gaul and the Roman empire had eventually fallen, so now a second France would arise, stronger and more vengeful still, and the German empire would be crushed.

This was the history lesson that the children of France should be taught, claimed the polemicists. Félix Mahon, for example, wrote a story for schoolchildren about the adventures of a young Gaul who became a companion of Vercingetorix at the time when he was campaigning against Caesar (*Les Aventures d'un jeune Gaulois au temps de César*, 1882). In the preface, the author made explicit the historical analogy he saw between the ancient Roman invaders (accompanied by their German auxiliaries) and the more immediate enemy from across the river Rhine, and claimed *Les Aventures* was a patriotic fiction designed to put the young on guard against identical dangers with which the future was sure to menace them.

During the period of the Third Republic (1870–1914), therefore, Vercingetorix first entered and then stayed in the French education system, now fully formed as a national myth of resistance and retribution, as a lesson about the foundation of France. In the history and Latin classes of secondary schools, Julius Caesar and ancient Rome still held centre stage. In this context, the siege of Alesia marks the bridge from Gallic savagery to Gallo-Roman civilization. The leader of the Avernians is stripped of moral virtue; the Roman governor is the bringer of order, rationality, nationhood. But in primary education, and its history textbooks, the pride of Vercingetorix overshadows the victory of Caesar. Illustrations based on or reproducing well-known history paintings often reinforced the education in civics and ethics which the school texts were proposing. The grand tableau *Vercingétorix jette ses armes aux pieds de César* (*Vercingetorix throws his weapons at the feet of Caesar*), for example, painted by Lionel Royer in 1899 and acquired a few years later for public display in the museum of Puy, also provided the source for the illustration of the surrender which appeared in a school history of France by Ernest Lavisse (first published in 1913 and frequently republished). It has been used regularly ever since, appearing in another such history published by Larousse in 1976 (Figure 3.2).

The painting captures and freezes the surrender at the moment of its greatest defiance (the second part of the surrender, Vercingetorix's recorded prostration, has been reproduced far more rarely). The ramparts of Alesia burn in the top left corner. The victorious Romans are scattered in some disorder. Julius Caesar is denied an imposing tribunal. He does not sit alone on high, but is instead surrounded by a thuggish pack of protective legates, before a forest of standards. The Roman is distinguished by his wreath and blood-red cloak, and his expression of intense viciousness. His Gallic enemy, in contrast, is adorned with a white cloak and shining breastplate, astride the elaborately ornamented white horse mentioned in

Fig. 3.2 *Vercingétorix jette ses armes aux pieds de César* (1899), L. Royer.

Plutarch's account of the events. The theme of degradation and slavery is given concrete form by the half-naked Gallic warriors who flank this historic encounter cruelly gripped by their Roman captors, and by the bowed head of the Gallic horse. But Vercingetorix sits tall and virile, with flowing hair and long moustache, pointing with his open hand – in a gesture of peaceful conciliation – to the weapons he has just thrown at Caesar's feet. He gazes down at Caesar. The conquered here dominates his conqueror.

Vercingetorix endured well into the twentieth century as national hero, not least because the vulnerability of France in two world wars kept giving historical analogy fresh relevance. If, in the latter part of that century, scholarship became more concerned with the economy and society of ancient Gaul than with the virtues of its leaders, the national myth continued to circulate in schools and in at least one hugely successful strand of popular culture. Set in 50 BC, shortly after Vercingetorix has surrendered and (most of) Gaul has been conquered by Julius Caesar and his legions, *Astérix* replaces one mode of heroic Gallic resistance against the might of Rome with another. The character Asterix first appeared in 1959 within a magazine cartoon strip by René Goscinny and Albert Uderzo. He was launched in the form of self-contained albums in 1961 and has continued to appear regularly ever since in cartoon albums, animated feature films, live-action star-studded epics (such as *Astérix and Obélix contre César*, 1999, and *Astérix & Obélix: Mission Cléopâtre*, 2002), on merchandising, in digital games, an amusement park and an official website (including blog). In most of the Asterix narratives, Julius Caesar is a major protagonist. The phenomenal commercial success of this brand of French graphic literature has given its cartoon-strip Caesar a global reach. Outside France, he has been read, seen or experienced by millions of children, teenagers and adults across the globe.

The cartoon strip offers two distinct versions of the surrender of

Vercingetorix: the 'fiction' stored in Julius Caesar's memory and the comic 'real' version (Figures 3.3 and 3.4). The album *Le Domaine des Dieux* (*The Mansions of the Gods*, 1971) opens with Caesar's recollection of what happened back in 52 BC. Out of breath, his breastplate and clothing torn, his shield, helmet and spear on the ground beside him, Vercingetorix knelt in humiliated supplication at Caesar's feet. The Roman (at least in his own memory of the encounter) was sternly resplendent, washed in the golden glow of dawn. In *Le Bouclier Arverne* (*Asterix and the Chieftain's Shield*, 1968), however, the first panel offers a flashback to the 'real' event. Vercingetorix here stands impressively erect, tall and muscular. In an arrangement reminiscent of Royer's historical painting, he takes up the entire front plane of the cartoon image, dominating the scene. And, in a gesture of proud contempt, he throws his weapons *on* the

Fig. 3.3 Caesar recalls the surrender of Vercingetorix, *Mansions of the Gods* (1971).

Fig. 3.4 Vercingetorix throws his weapons at the feet of Caesar,
Asterix and the Chieftain's Shield (1968).

feet of Alesia's conqueror, who shouts in pain and, in subsequent
panels, jumps off his seat and hops off in search of easier conquests.
This humorously literal rendition of the traditional throwing down
of weapons is a formative scene. The same event appeared on the
first page of the first album, *Astérix le Gaulois* (1961), where the surrender of Vercingetorix is offset by the terror of the Roman soldiers
who flee before the onslaught of his comic-strip replacement in a
fantastical genealogy of Gallic resistance – little Asterix from the
north-western region of Armorica, whose small village of
indomitable Gauls still holds out against the invaders. From album
to album, and from films to theme park, the comic's fictional Gallic
hero repeatedly wins out over his Roman conqueror.

The defining representation of the surrender of Vercingetorix in
Astérix does not draw on Julius Caesar's account in the seventh
book of his *Gallic War*, but on the grand nationalistic vision prof-
fered in the historiography, novels, paintings, drama and
schoolbooks of France. The pleasurably subversive originality of the
strip for French readers lies in its replacement of the tradition's

magnificently defiant national hero with a whole village of prepos-
terous avengers, and in its caricature of the otherwise villainous
Roman conqueror as a whimpering and wretched clown, supercil-
ious, hot-tempered and irritable. The comic epic of Gallic
resistance to Roman conquest replays the national mythology of
France in irreverent, parodic key, and takes apart the sacred images
of French cultural heritage, the now dusty clichés initiated during
the Third Republic. Yet it also directly explores in comic mode
problems which were associated with the Fifth Republic from the
1960s onwards.

Read from the perspective of the internal politics of post-war
France, the conflict between a small village of Gauls and the mighty
Roman army evokes that between the French provinces and centralized government. Asterix is the little man of France embroiled
in a nostalgic struggle against modernity. The obedient Roman
legionnaires, indistinguishable and often nameless, literally uniform, stand in for contemporary bureaucracy, regimentation and
conformism. Read from the perspective of post-war foreign relations, the Roman enemy is suggestive of the United States of
America and the great growth of its economic, cultural and military
power in the latter half of the twentieth century. The endless struggles of Asterix against Caesar then constitute a protest projected
back into the past against the 'new Romans', whose heartless effi-
ciency, mass production and cultural homogeneity appear to
threaten Europeans with the loss of their individuality and
distinctiveness. Thus, self-referentially, Asterix is so named because
he is a small star who was originally designed to counter the larger-
than-life supermen of the American comics.

But all these perceived oppositions are only ever playfully put
(through sight gags, puns, anachronisms and parodic discrepancies).
There also remains a deliberate imprecision in the supposed rivalry
between Asterix and Caesar. In the very first album, they are

initially opposed as symbols of independence and imperialism, bravery and brutality. 'Gallicity', however, is subsequently punctured. Reduced to a profound desire for celebrations, the village aptitude is more gastronomic than patriotic. Romanness is associated with greed and aggression, but also grandeur and sophistication. Julius Caesar and his Roman soldiers are not even especially concerned with the tiny village as a territory to acquire. It is small and insignificant, and you need a magnifying glass to find it on the map. Genuine danger comes from the Germans, the common enemy of Gaul and Rome. Asterix proceeds in the first album to disclose to Caesar a conspiracy against him and benefits accordingly from the general's clemency. More and more frequently across the albums they are allies. And in the final obligatory banquet scene in *Le fils d'Astérix* (*Son of Asterix*, 1983), the Gallic hero and his village chieftain even attend a dinner presided over by Caesar and Cleopatra. In this comic utopia, everyone (except the Germans) can party.

4

REVOLUTION AND RISK-TAKING

Crossing the Rubicon, 49 BC

Caesar presented the decisive capitulation of Vercingetorix at Alesia and the preceding stages of the war in Gaul to Roman readers as a complete narrative towards the end of 51 BC. The publication of the seven books of military commentary laid stress on the enormous scale of the Roman general's achievement and, at a time when his opponents were stepping up their attempts to block Caesar's future political progress at Rome, spoke to the massive power-base he had acquired thanks to his dedicated soldiers. A smooth transition from one inviolable magistracy to another, from his proconsulship in Gaul to a second consulship at Rome, would leave Julius Caesar completely immune to prosecution. So his enemies in the senate were working to block Caesar from any special entitlement to stand for another consulship while still absent in his provinces. They wished instead to deprive him as soon as possible of his command, and to return him to the city as a vulnerable private citizen. Reduced to that status, they would be able to put Caesar on trial and ruin him.

The war was clearly over, they argued, and Gaul therefore had no further need of its general and his army. When, in March 50 BC, official discussion began in the senate on a replacement for Caesar in Gaul, his supporters made various conciliatory gestures on his behalf: Caesar would give up his command if Pompey gave up his armies and his long-running absentee governorship of Spain; or Caesar would reduce his command to fewer provinces and fewer legions. But always he would be sure to keep some small level of protecting *imperium*.

A sweeping senatorial vote in early December in favour of the first proposition was immediately superseded by the arbitrary action of one consul who, the following day, accompanied by the consuls already designated for the next year, approached Pompey with a request to intervene in defence of the city now under threat from Caesar's legions. When the new consuls took office on 1 January 49, a despatch from Caesar was read out to the senate in which he threatened to come down from Gaul to avenge the country and himself, if Pompey were not required to resign his command at the same time. In response, the senate voted that Caesar should dismiss his army by an appointed date or be declared a public enemy. Even though the vote was vetoed there and then by two tribunes who were supporters of Caesar, an emergency decree was passed within the week granting dictatorial powers to the senate's appointees to protect the state against the wayward proconsul. New governors were appointed to his provinces, and the rebuffed tribunes fled to Caesar, who was already stationed with one legion at Ravenna, the city of Cisalpine Gaul closest to the borders of Italy. Without waiting for reinforcements (as his opponents had both expected and hoped), Caesar immediately launched his small force into northern Italy. In so doing, he and they crossed the Rubicon, the frontier river of his province.

At the start of his own account of subsequent events in his commentaries on the ensuing civil war, Julius Caesar conceals the significance of his crossing the Rubicon in January 49 BC. He says of himself only that 'once he has ascertained the inclination of the soldiers, he sets out for Ariminum with the legion' (*Bellum civile* 1.8). But a Roman general should not enter Italy while still in command of his troops; constitutionally it was an act of sedition against the senate and the people of Rome. Immediately thereafter, Pompey (taking a lead in defence of senatorial government and the military protection of the republic) called for the evacuation of the capital, which he abandoned in the company of the consuls and a majority of the senate. 'Crossing the Rubicon' was thus a crucial decision: it established Julius Caesar as a revolutionary, willing to take extraordinary risks, to challenge the established order, to instigate civil war. Only Caesar narrates this momentous event with such concision. He does not mention the river at all.

The account in Suetonius' biography of the deified Julius, thought by modern scholars to draw on the lost record of eyewitness and participant Asinius Pollio, is much more detailed and dramatic. As soon as Caesar heard that the veto of the tribunes had been overridden and they had abandoned the city, he sent on a few cohorts in secret to the banks of the river and then, not to arouse suspicion, concealed his purpose by doing all the usual things: attending a public show, inspecting the plans for a new gladiatorial school, dining in sizeable company. Finally, after the sun had set, Caesar set out in the utmost secrecy, with only modest numbers, in a carriage drawn by mules which he had borrowed from a baker's nearby. When his torches gave out, he lost his way. But at daybreak he found a guide to lead him on foot along the narrowest of paths, until he overtook his cohorts at the river Rubicon (*Deified Julius* 31). The biographical narrative suggests that the waiting soldiers would already have been alert to the significant step they might be about to take, that Caesar was even more sharply alert to its importance and its extreme consequences, and that he suspected his enemies had infiltrated even his closest entourage. For these reasons, he had to avoid drawing attention to his seditious movements: he did not ride his celebrated horse, chose an innocous-looking and humble mode of transport, took the back roads and, in the end – most surreally of all – got lost.

There follows a supernatural event which was surely needed to raise the morale of the troops, who had been waiting all night for their missing leader. Suetonius now narrates that, having reached the extreme limit of his province, Caesar paused for a little while in order to consult with his intimates, remarking that it was still possible to turn back but that, once across, the sword would decide everything. But, while he was hesitating, he received a sign: a tall and beautiful figure appeared suddenly nearby, seated and playing a reed pipe. When shepherds and soldiers gathered to hear the sound, it snatched a trumpet from one of them, leapt to the river and, sounding the war-note with a forceful blast, strode across to the opposite bank. Caesar – thanks to this miracle, able to break the moment of collective hesitation – cries out, 'Let's go to where the signs of the gods and the injustice of the enemy summon us. The die is cast.' (*iacta alea est*: Suetonius, *Deified Julius* 32). If the Latin text is correct here, the shift from the imperative 'let's go' to the indicative 'the die is cast' marks the speed of the final decision. Caesar is already hot on the phantom's heels.

Although they both dispense with the supernatural sign (perhaps, critics think, a trick organized by Caesar himself), the Greek historians Plutarch and Appian appear to supply pieces of the same account drawn from the single eye-witness testimony of Asinius Pollio. Plutarch even observes explicitly that the future author was one of those few with whom the Roman general consulted when he paused at the riverbank. Yet Plutarch in particular gives the same material a somewhat different spin, weakening the traces of Pollio's pro-Caesarian perspective. He starts with the smallness of Caesar's force, the boldness, speed and secrecy, the gladiators and the dinner, sunset, carts, the circuitous route. But then, when he came to the river which separates Cisalpine Gaul from the rest of Italy (it is called the Rubicon), and began to reflect, now that he drew nearer to the fearful step and was agitated by the magnitude of his ventures, he checked his speed. Then, halting in his course, he communed with himself a long time in silence as his resolution wavered back and forth, and his purpose then suffered change after change.

(Plutarch, Life of Caesar 32.4–5. Trans. B. Perrin, 1919)

With his friends, Pollio among them, the paralysed general weighs in the balance the consequences of crossing: the fame which would be left to posterity, the evil to all mankind. Fame wins. Swapping calculation for passion, and declaring 'let the dice fly high' (the proverbial idiom of the gambler which, Plutarch notes, men usually utter as prelude to a plunge into desperate and daring fortunes), he rushes to cross the river. Cast as tragic actor, Plutarch's Caesar is caught in a moral quandary. Protagonist of this drama, he is flawed by a craving for glory, and it is this flaw which precipitates his tragic downfall.

In an addendum, Plutarch also notes that the night before the crossing Caesar had an unnatural dream in which he had incestuous intercourse with his own mother. The dream appears deliberately displaced here from the earlier context in which it occurs when told in other ancient sources for Caesar's life. Here it is labelled 'unnatural' and therefore unambiguously monstrous, indicative of Caesar's desire to penetrate territory which is forbidden to him. This terrible dream and Caesar's prolonged agonizing (not a characteristic he possesses elsewhere in Plutarch's account) occur almost halfway through the Roman statesman's biography. Together all these narrative devices mark the crossing of the Rubicon as an extraordinary turning point for Caesar, for Rome, for history.

Even before this, writing in the reign of emperor Nero, the poet

Lucan had turned the event into a horror tale of epic proportions, set in the dead of night. In the opening book of the historical epic *Bellum civile* (*Civil War*), having already conceived in his heart immense upheavals and coming war, the Roman general arrives at the Rubicon's little stream where he comes face to face with his distressed country:

> clearly to the leader through the murky night appeared
> a mighty image of his country in distress, grief in her face,
> her white hair streaming from her tower-crowned head;
> with tresses torn and shoulders bare she stood before him
> and sighing said: 'Where further do you march?
> Where do you take my standards, warriors? If lawfully you
>   come,
> if as citizens, this far only is allowed.' Then trembling
>   struck
> the leader's limbs, his hair grew stiff, and weakness checked
> his progress, holding his feet at the river's edge.
>
> (Lucan, *Civil War* 1.186–94. Trans. S. H. Braund, 1999:8)

In her sorrowful appeal to him, Caesar's mourning *patria* accentuates the Rubicon as a sacred boundary across which her warriors, if they are law-abiding citizens, should not march. Lucan's narrator of the incident which launched the civil war between Caesar and Pompey of 49–48 BC is positioned as a survivor who possesses only limited knowledge about the imperial future in store for Rome. Full of a fascinated contempt that borders on admiration, the narrator constructs Caesar as a demonic force of nature and as epic myth. He provides a poetic counterbalance to Caesar's own evasive commentary, and to his claimed descent from the mythic hero Aeneas who, in a variety of encounters with apparitions and deities in the course of Virgil's earlier epic, had been invested with responsibility to found Rome as a resurrected Troy – and was not, as here, accused of planning impiously to attack her.

The physicality of the leader's terrified response – the effect on his limbs, hair, and feet – puts on vivid display the doubts and hesitations which later would be expressed as interior musings ('he communed with himself') in Julius Caesar's Greek biography. Readers are invited to see Caesar's fear as he stops at the riverbank. Lucan's poetic 'image' works literally in the opposite direction to the 'sign' of Roman historiography (and its pro-Caesarian vestiges), commanding that the general step back and not advance across the river Rubicon. Lucan's Caesar, however, does not stop for long. Soon, having recovered his composure, he audaciously casts aside the questions and pleas of his *patria* and prays instead to Jupiter, the gods brought over from Troy by the Julian clan, the tutelary divinity Quirinus, the fires of Vesta, the city of Rome itself. Claiming to be their soldier, passing any blame over to those who would make him their enemy, he asks that they favour his (conspicuously unspecified) plans. The Roman general immediately breaks the bonds of war and carries his standards over the stream now swollen up to oppose him.

At this climactic point, Julius Caesar is at his most poetic, shaped in the highest heroic mode. An extended simile compares him to a Libyan lion: concentrating his anger against the hunters who pursue and wound him, the lion whips himself into such frenzy that he impales himself on their spears. The epic narrative device suggests that the general, whose dignity has been wounded by Pompey and his opponents in the Roman senate and whose anger has been roused, in crossing the Rubicon heads only towards self-destruction. Over now on the other bank, Caesar substitutes war for peace, and his Fortune for law. Agreements are done with, now the only judge must be combat (1.224–7).

In his own commentaries Julius Caesar omitted to mention both the act and the significance of crossing the Rubicon. That omission was rectified in subsequent classical literature by two apparitions who took on human form either to invite the general over or to bring him to a halt at the riverbank. The beautiful sign in Suetonius' account sounds the call for crossing, Lucan's weeping image begs for a standstill. And it is between these two choices that Plutarch's Caesar spends a great deal of time wavering. The Roman epic places emphasis on the audacity and anger of the statesman who can confront and overcome so challenging an obstacle to his self-regarding plans as his own sobbing country; Roman historiography highlights the ability of the first of twelve Caesars to respond rapidly to an indicator of his own destiny. Curiously, as critics have noted, the 'for' and the 'against' of Caesar's choices meet in the same narrative some thousand years later.

Li Fet des Romains (The Deeds of the Romans) was encountered in the preceding chapter as an early thirteenth-century, secular manual written to educate the medieval aristocracy of France in ethical and political conduct, and as a French translation of Latin texts that realigns Julius Caesar's life to accommodate a more favourable stance towards Gaul and its chieftains. The passage of its protagonist across the Rubicon takes up several pages at the start of its second half. The narrative at this turning point shifts focus from the Roman general's conquest of 'France' to his instigation of civil war back home, yet both are presented as the imposition of tyranny over liberty. Although Suetonius provides the framework for this medieval life of Caesar, Lucan takes on prominence as we find the hero's chivalric values spoiled by his political ambition, his military prowess punctured by its exercise in a civil war. First, then, by the riverbank comes a dishevelled female apparition, hair disordered, arms bare, issuing her complaint. Caesar's limbs tremble, his feet delay. The apparition – subsequently identified more specifically as Rome – rehearses her general's transgression of the law, he in reply his private grievances. But next, after the Roman general has addressed his soldiers and cautioned them that they can still turn back, while still he doubts, there comes another apparition of a giant trumpeter in supernatural support. As swiftly as a pouncing lion, the commander and his troops cross. Poetry and history thus intertwine in an equivocal narration of medieval Caesar at the Rubicon.

The ancient externalization of Caesar's choices on which *Fet* drew made this scene especially suited to illustration. Among the many spectacular renditions of Caesar at the Rubicon produced to accompany fourteenth- and fifteenth-century editions of the medieval life, a more clear-cut meaning is often attempted in order to close down the text's contradictions. A French miniature of around 1475, painted by Jean Fouquet to illustrate a manuscript which appears to have contained two medieval works – one of world history up to Caesar's first campaigns in Gaul and the other the life of Caesar (*Histoire Ancienne jusqu'à César et Faits des Romains*) – depicts both apparitions at the banks of the Rubicon but in different planes (Figure 4.1). Three trees of diminishing size lead the viewer's eye into the deepening perspective; the winding river and the distant mountains further develop a sense of spatial depth. Julius Caesar is marked as military leader by his location at the head of his troops, in gold armour, mounted on a white horse (itself caparisoned with a black double-headed eagle crest on cloth of gold), poised at the edge of the Rubicon.

Directly opposite the general, but stationed on the other bank of the river, stands Rome. No longer as pathetic as Lucan's *patria*, her hair is down but not disordered; her shoulders and arms are covered, not bare, and they rest alongside her body so that her gesture is scarcely readable as an attempt to push Caesar back. In the foreground at the bottom right, however, stands a veritable giant already immersed in the stream. Composition sets the tiny, limp, downward-pointing arm of Rome against the giant's long, firm, upward trumpet in an arrangement which suggests that instead it is he who

Fig. 4.1 'The crossing of the Rubicon' (c.1475), J. Fouquet. Detail of French miniature.

is pushing her back. The semi-nudity of the musician and the glaring whiteness of his turban and loincloth evoke an innocent quality for his summons, while their flowing folds mimic the gratifying sound of his war cry. This is no horrifying encounter in the dark, no furtive crossing. The ambiguities of the text (where the Rubicon was a narrative bridge over to the deterioration of chivalric Caesar) are glossed over. Crossing the Rubicon is here depicted as a Roman general's triumphant destiny, an audacious step that invites imitation.

For Renaissance tyrants, eighteenth- and nineteenth-century generals and twentieth-century dictators, Julius Caesar's action in crossing the Rubicon came to represent a willingness to take an audacious political gamble and conveniently provided classical legitimacy – sometimes a national genealogy – for violent challenges to established government. It was even taken as an advocacy of the splendour of usurpation. And just as men of state have desired to replicate Caesar's military acumen, his acquisition of vast territories, his accession to supreme power and his triumphant displays of his achievements, so they have desired to follow in his footsteps and cross their own Rubicons.

Cesare Borgia regarded his naming as an omen. 'Caesar' was the title of the great Roman general and conqueror who, in his view, had raised it to the level of a timeless symbol of military glory and supreme power. Spanish rather than Italian by birth, the young cardinal considered himself to be born from ruling stock, and felt his Christian name to be a sustenance for his ambitions and a prediction of their future success. Around 1497 he arranged for a silver ceremonial sword to be forged for him that testifies materially to the devotion he bore to his namesake and, specifically, to his aspiration to imitate the crossing of the Rubicon. The sword still survives in the Fondazione Caetani in Rome, its scabbard in the Victoria and Albert Museum in London. It was most probably consecrated for use by Cesare Borgia when, in his capacity as papal legate, he crowned Federigo as King of Naples, because the ceremony of coronation required a weapon which displayed symbolically the supreme jurisdiction of the Church, even in matters temporal. Delicately engraved with Latin inscriptions and classical emblems mainly of a bellicose nature, the blade looks like the weapon of a Roman general rather more than the symbolic instrument of a Renaissance cardinal (Figure 4.2).

An inscription engraved by the handle, at the base of the blade's face, indicates that Cesare Borgia's sword evokes Julius Caesar as a kind of protecting deity or guardian spirit: *cum numine Caesaris*

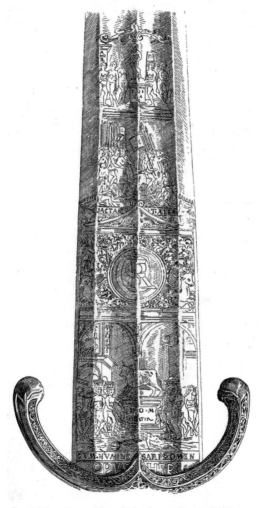

Fig. 4.2 Parade sword made for Cesare Borgia (1498).

omen ('with Caesar's divine will, good omen'). The invocation governs the general composition of the blade's various sections on both face and reverse. On the face, above a scene of ritual sacrifice (the Borgias' symbolic bull waits on a pagan altar ready for slaughter), below a tiny statue of Cupid surrounded by nude worshippers, and adjacent to the initials 'CB' incised within a circular frame, a scene is engraved that shows a squadron of cavalry. They wave banners on which the letter 'C' stands out and are in the process of fording a stream. Immediately beneath this scene, leaving no room for doubt as to its point of reference, is a quotation from Suetonius: *jacta est alea* ('the die is cast'). Incised on the reverse of the blade by its handle is an elaborate procession, including a Roman cart led by four horses on which sits the triumphant Caesar clutching a laurel branch in his hand. Above it appear classical scenes of the peace and cultural life which the Roman general's victories have permitted. With Caesar's Rubicon engraved on one side of the blade and his triumph on the other, the silver sword tangibly displays Cesare Borgia's intimate relationship with Julius Caesar as his future's protection and prediction.

Soon after the coronation ceremony, in August 1498, Cesare Borgia officially cast off his cardinal's purple to take up the role of a general leading the papal armies to war. With the consent of his father Pope Alexander VI, Cesare Borgia now began a military career as Duc de Valentinois (or 'il Valentino'), crossing over from the relative safety of a cardinalate to the dangerous uncertainty of military command and combat. His understanding of the importance of this step and its perils is represented in the composition of the silver sword. The cardinal places himself under the protection of Julius Caesar, even holds his namesake's audacious political gamble in his hand, just as he is about to undertake his own personal Rubicon – the risky renunciation of his spiritual authority in order to become a conqueror of earthly kingdoms. Within two years,

Cesare Borgia would view himself as having fulfilled the dual pro-gramme, the grand prediction, sketched out on his silver sword – from Rubicon to Rome, from risk to victory and a triumphal parade.

In February 1500, the duke processed through Rome in tri-umph and, in continuing homage to Julius Caesar, included among the second day's parades a spectacular allegorical representation of the Roman general himself, both crossing the Rubicon and tri-umphing in ancient Rome. Soon confirmed as captain-general of the papal armies, the duke proceeded to further military cam-paigning and conquest on Italian soil. In his military career, Cesare Borgia even recoined Julius Caesar's celebrated declaration 'the die is cast' into the personal motto of a gambler ready for complete suc-cess or complete degradation: *aut Caesar aut nihil* ('either Caesar or nothing'). But in death, when little of political substance had been gained for the papacy from his campaigning against the states or kingdoms of Milan, Romagna and Naples, his opponents mocked his ambitions and his Caesarian motto: 'You conquered all, you hoped for all, Caesar. But all is lost, and you begin to be nothing.'

Whilst Cesare Borgia took hold of the crossing of the Rubicon as inspiration and omen for the crucial decision to change his public standing, it could also be used – in a more closely fitting historical precedent – to sanction a change of state. Thus the *coup d'état* instigated by Napoleon III on 2 December 1851 was code-named 'opération Rubicon'. The myth of ancient Rome's civic virtue and republican liberty had been put to substantial use in French political discourse in the period of the Revolution: its heroes included the first Brutus (Lucius Junius), who led an upris-ing against the early kings of Rome and originated the Roman republic, and his descendant the second Brutus (Marcus Junius), who assassinated Caesar, the would-be king of Rome, in order to preserve that same republic. Both Napoleon Bonaparte and his

79

nephew Louis worked to replace that political genealogy for France, substituting republican with imperial Rome, the first and second Brutus with Caesar.

Many stages in Napoleon Bonaparte's career were compared with the successes and failures of Julius Caesar, by Napoleon in his lifetime and by his admirers and critics then and in the following centuries. As general, he won striking victories in northern Italy and Egypt. As revolutionary, he overthrew parliamentary democracy in the *coup d'état* of 18 Brumaire 1799. As consul between 1799 and 1804, he obtained virtually supreme, dictatorial powers. And as emperor of the French from 1804 until his abdication in 1814, he conquered in rapid succession Austria, Belgium, Holland, Italy, Prussia and Russia. Critical comparison rendered Napoleon a usurper and military dictator who had replaced the republicanism of France with a disguised despotism.

Napoleon himself did not take ancient Rome for his only historical model, his greatest Roman precedent for the transition from consulate to empire was Augustus not Julius Caesar, and his own careful reading and analysis of Julius Caesar's commentaries on the Gallic and civil wars were charged with criticisms of the Roman's military and political failings. Nonetheless, in the epilogue to his *Précis des guerres de César* (*Notes on the Wars of Caesar*, 1836), in an implicit statement of self-justification when now in exile, Napoleon wrote in the most eulogistic terms of Julius Caesar's usurpation of power: it was a legitimate act, undertaken when the deliberative assemblies were no longer able to function, for the necessary protection of all the citizens of Rome, of whatever party.

Julius Caesar thus had an intimate role to play in the gradual formation of Napoleon's legend as an extraordinary, populist soldier-statesman and world conqueror – the modern French Caesar. For this reason, and because of Louis Napoleon Bonaparte's own direct fascination with the Roman general and dictator, 'opération Rubicon' became the title of the dossier on which he drew, for the details of plans, proclamations and arrest warrants to discuss with his fellow plotters, on the eve of his *coup d'état* of 2 December 1851. And although he was no professional soldier, Louis Napoleon ceremoniously rode in the next day on horseback in a general's uniform, as the army filled the city streets and martial law was declared. The double parallel which he was attempting to establish, between himself and both the Roman and the French Caesar, was not lost on Karl Marx, who published a scathing attack on the coup, 'The Eighteenth Brumaire of Louis Bonaparte', in a New York journal only a few months later. The work was subsequently revised and republished in the 1860s and entered the canon of Marx's works on the nature of the class struggle.

Famously, Marx noted that history constantly repeats itself, but first as tragedy then as farce. Revolutions in France from 1789 to 1814 had dressed themselves in the costumes and the language of the Roman republic or the Roman empire to glorify their new struggles, but now a grotesque mediocrity – Napoleon III – plays the Roman hero by hiding under the mask of his uncle. For Marx, such historical analogy was unpersuasive: the coup was inspired by a desire to protect the middle class against the new urban proletariat. Ancient and modern class struggle had nothing in common, so one could hardly elucidate (let alone glorify) the other.

Napoleon III's devotion to Julius Caesar was far greater than his uncle's. His *Histoire de Jules César* (1865–6) is the longest work on the Roman statesman written by a sovereign. Its bulky two volumes stretch from birth to the Rubicon (authorship of the third volume was transferred elsewhere when the emperor was detained by political complications), and throughout Julius Caesar is shaped as an early-day Bonapartist, so that his actions in this retelling provide seemingly perfect historical authority and vindication for the present ruler, his *coup d'état*, and his revival of empire and the preceding emperor.

Bringing the narrative to a halt at the Rubicon meant the emperor could fashion a Caesar fixed in the ascendant, never in the midst of civil war or suffering the stab-wounds delivered by his friends. As we reach the conclusion of the second volume, as the narrative edges towards the moment of Caesar's decision to march on Rome, as Roman society calls for a master to bring it back to order, the leader of the popular party is deeply troubled. He recalls that in a dream on the previous night he had violated his mother. Was not the country in effect his mother and, despite the justice of his cause and the grandeur of his designs, his enterprise an attack on her? But then he witnesses an apparition, tall of stature, playing martial airs upon a trumpet and summoning him to the other bank. Hesitation ceases: he hurries onward and crosses the Rubicon.

In an article published in *La Cloche* in September 1872, Emile Zola declared the *Histoire* a farcical enterprise in which the emperor had wished to justify 2 December 1851 by rewriting the Rubicon. Critics quickly recognized that, through Julius Caesar and his supernatural summons, Louis Napoleon was replaying his own momentous political step in heroic mode. The emperor produced no direct, personal record of the *coup d'état*, and its importance as the founding event of his empire was never acknowledged in the various ceremonies instituted during the course of the regime to celebrate his rule. Hounded by polemics against his initial actions, he provides only anxious self-justification rather than celebration, and that only indirectly as he retells Caesar's crossing of the Rubicon rather than lauding his own.

Mussolini, however, had no compunction about celebrating his 'March on Rome', or comparing his action in the most explicit terms to that of Julius Caesar. For the Fascist dictator represented himself, both in the very moment of taking power and for many years into his regime, as following literally in the Roman general's footsteps, crossing the same Italian terrain, heading towards Rome, for the same glorious political purpose. The March on Rome of 29 October 1922 – gradually mythologized as a revolutionary march on the capital by armed squads of Black Shirts, Mussolini riding horseback at their head, bent on taking power by force – was a complete charade. The Fascist units did not seize power militarily; they were invited to do so by the king, who had sent a telegram to their leader in Milan asking him to form the next government. Mussolini did not arrive at Rome on horseback but paid for a ticket on a night-sleeper, and was legitimately sworn in as prime minister the next day. The Black Shirts arrived in Rome twenty-four hours after their general, but were permitted to pass through the blockades of a substantial garrison of government troops in order to parade before the royal palace. At this point, the myth of the March on Rome was launched and, in later commemoration of the event, there was fabricated a close historical parallel (virtually an identity) with Julius Caesar's crossing of the Rubicon, on his famed horse, at the head of his brave Roman legion, to appropriate the supreme powers of the state.

Regular commemorations of the March as a founding event of the Fascist regime, and one tightly bound to the memory of Julius Caesar, began with the first anniversary on 29 October 1923. Ceremonies were held in a sequence of five cities, moving down the peninsula of Italy to end at the capital, where 'il Duce' suppos-edly repeated his triumphal entry, processing down the city streets, until he reached the remains of the Roman forum. There, as the concluding ceremony, before the ruins of the temple which had been erected in Julius Caesar's honour after his death, Mussolini placed a laurel wreath on the altar. The Fascist leader thus estab-lished a public ritual of veneration which would be repeated annually until the regime's collapse in 1943.

In addition to any general association between Mussolini and Julius Caesar, specific and sustained comparison of the March on

Rome and the crossing of the Rubicon was promoted by numerous popular works. Among a series of booklets which began to appear almost immediately under the title *Mussolinia* and were designed to build up a home library of Fascist propaganda, one early number by Tito Vezio was entitled 'Le due marce su Roma: Giulio Cesare e Benito Mussolini' (*Mussolinia* 1, 1923). It opens:

> Two profound crises of social putrefaction, alike in some respects, overcame Italy in the course of centuries.
>
> The first occurred in the last century before Christ and, with the downfall of the old aristocratic factions, marked the triumph of democratic monarchy and of Julius Caesar.
>
> The second, almost two thousand years later, that is in 1922, was characterized by the collapse of revolutionary socialism, and by the victory of Fascism and of Benito Mussolini.
>
> In both cases, two men, endowed with great strength of mind, superior intellect, and exceptional energy, and favoured by events, succeeded in rescuing Italy from ruin.

Vezio then summarizes Caesar's 'march on Rome' before he details the modern sequence of events, and ends by coupling Julius Caesar and Benito Mussolini once again at the end as 'the two restorers'. Here and elsewhere in other Fascist historical narratives (both popular and scholarly), 49 BC is depicted as the year in which Caesar initiated a political revolution, marched on Rome, violently uprooted a rotten republic, repressed the corrupted privileged classes and established a new dictatorial order, all for the benefit of the people. Caesar and the Rubicon are here reshaped better to match Mussolini and his March; both are impulsive and virile generals, both are saviours of Italy and its people.

Thus one of a series of twelve Fascist postcards depicting heroes

of Roman history presents Julius Caesar as the final hero and cul-
mination (Figure 4.3). And of all the moments which could have
been selected from his career, it is the crossing of the Rubicon that
is depicted. No apparitions are needed here either to invite or to
deter. Caesar the *imperator* takes up most of the visual frame,

Fig. 4.3 Fascist postcard commemorating the Rubicon crossing.

supremely confident, riding robustly at the front of his troops, gripping his muscular white horse, manfully pointing the way with his wide, unsheathed sword, already immersed in the river. This was the hyperbolic iconographic style associated with Fascist *romanità* (or the quasi-mystical quality of modern Romanness) that, on posters, in school textbooks, cartoon strips, stamps and public art and statuary, reshaped events and figures from ancient Rome to fit the contours of Fascism in order to display a glorious genealogy for the regime, even a unity between past and present. And there is, here, a hint of Mussolini's physiognomy in Caesar's stern countenance.

Mussolini himself drew out the Fascist side of the parallel in an article he published in the official Fascist daily newspaper *Il popolo d'Italia* in the year of the tenth anniversary: 'This, this too, is an epoch that can call itself Caesarian, dominated as it is by exceptional personalities who reassume in themselves the powers of the State, for the well-being of the people, against the parliamentarians, just as Caesar marched against the senatorial oligarchy of Rome.' The main topic of the article concerned the decision of 'il Duce' to have two bronze copies made from an imperial statue of Julius Caesar housed in Rome's Palazzo Senatorio (where the Roman had been portrayed as a breast-plated *imperator* or general). One copy was erected in Rome before Caesar's forum – where it still stands – and the other in Rimini's central square where, Mussolini confirmed, Julius Caesar had once stood on a plinth to address the soldiers of the thirteenth legion after he had already crossed the Rubicon, and from there had launched his march on Rome.

As the site of ancient Ariminum (to which Caesar had mentioned advancing in his own commentaries), and the modern town closest to the river Rubicon, Rimini became a crucial locus for the celebration of the perceived connection between Fascism's initiatory March and Caesar's crossing. The Fascist leader instructed its citizens that every year, on the Ides of March, they were to venerate 'the founder of Roman empire' by adorning his statue with spring flowers. The instruction was published in *Il populo* and the ceremony inaugurating the statue (which was attended by huge crowds) received full coverage in the national newspapers and on radio. Given the Fascist focus on marching to Rome, Rimini effectively took over from the Rubicon as a more convenient topographic memorial to Caesar. Here also Fascist ritual could constitute itself as almost a re-enactment of the events of 49; the official orator at the inaugural ceremony, for example, was a general who had participated in Mussolini's March.

Thus annual rituals of veneration and commemoration, topography, sculpture, rhetoric, newspaper articles and radio broadcasts, postcards, popular pamphlets and historical scholarship, all of these and more worked to create a positive identification between Benito Mussolini and Julius Caesar as exceptional leaders, between the March on Rome and the Rubicon crossing as forceful revolutionary acts, and between the Italian masses and Caesar's soldiers as loyal and obedient followers. None of the Napoleonic indirectness here. Such identification across the centuries, if consumed appropriately by the masses at whom it was directed, could provide historical legitimation for the regime's beginnings, coat Fascism in a veneer of tradition, locate it in a national history, unify those who witnessed or participated in its ceremonies, and point to its imperial future. Yet those rituals of identification were not always so piously perceived or performed, at least according to the reflections of the film director Federico Fellini, who, in his semi-autobiographical film *Roma* (1971), recalls a childhood spent in Rimini in the 1930s. In one short sequence we see a small army of uniformed children from the town on a school trip to the Rubicon, where they are pestered by their pompous old schoolmaster to re-enact the glorious crossing. This poor substitute (both for Caesar and for Mussolini) triumphantly leads his giggling charges across a tiny trickle, on foot, with rolled-up trouser legs and a handkerchief for a helmet.

'The die is cast' (or 'let the dice fly high', as we have it from Plutarch) was originally a Greek proverb which became embedded in the narrative of a Roman action which, in turn, became proverbial. Julius Caesar's crossing of the Rubicon has been imbued with such celebrity in Western culture that the phrase 'crossing the Rubicon' now possesses its own proverbial meaning – taking a decisive step from which there is no return. It has thus been used regularly of momentous and irrevocable political decisions which involve some permutation on heads of state, troop movements, passage across a geographic boundary, the outbreak of war or an assault on legitimate government. For example, 'crossing the Rubicon' was used in all (or most of) these respects in a British newspaper with regard to President George Bush in the lead-up to the invasion of Iraq early in 2003:

> Just after 5 p.m. yesterday, when the United Nations Security Council voted 15–0 to disarm Iraq, the US President George Bush crossed the Rubicon. 'The world must insist that judgment must be enforced', he told us.
>
> The Rubicon is a wide river. It was deep for Caesar's legions. The Tigris river will be more shallow – my guess is that the first American tanks will be across it within one week of war – but what lies beyond?
>
> For Rome, civil war followed. And, be assured, civil war will follow any American invasion of Iraq.
>
> (Robert Fisk, *Independent*, 11 November 2002)

But so diffuse has the phrase become that the irreversible step need not be in the domain of politics, or be taken by a head of state, or concern a geographic boundary or the onset of war (civil or otherwise). *Rubicon*, for example, is the name of an American insurance and risk management company whose website explains that the company takes its name from Caesar's need to weigh up the risks of a fateful decision. It goes on: 'No less critical for you, is your "decision" on whose shoulders should rest the protection of your personal and business assets.' Even the purchasers of insurance policies now have to weigh up critical risks and cross their own Rubicons. Nor is the expansion in application of 'crossing the Rubicon' merely a recent phenomenon. In 1690, the phrase was pressed into sexual service by a character in John Crowne's Restoration play *The English Friar*, who lamented 'Some Caesar pass'd my mother's Rubicon; wou'd I had his commentaries.' The legend of Julius Caesar's sexual prowess would only have added extra force to this particular example.

5

LUST, LUXURY AND LOVE
Cleopatra and Egypt, 48–47 BC

Not just a celebrated soldier and statesman, Julius Caesar is also a notorious lover and debauchee. Suetonius catalogues his costly tastes and wild extravagance: the passionate collection of gems, statues, paintings, attractive slaves; the gift to his mistress Servilia of an outrageously expensive pearl; the construction and immediate demolition of a lake-side country house because it failed to satisfy his exacting standards. The Roman historian also details Caesar's sexual conquests (from Roman matrons to foreign queens), as well as the rumour that he once played queen himself to the King of Bithynia – a rumour with which he was teased by his own soldiers and taunted throughout his career by his political opponents. In sum, quotes Suetonius, Julius Caesar was branded 'every woman's man and every man's woman' (*Deified Julius*, 49–52).

But it is for his encounter with Cleopatra VII, Queen of Egypt, that Caesar has achieved erotic celebrity. The ancient sources, between them, sketch the outline of a thrilling affair (even if it was soon to be outdone by the more substantial account of the tragic coupling of Cleopatra and Mark Antony). Set against the backdrop of war in Egypt, a captivating, brilliant, sophisticated and seductive aspirant to great power, only twenty-two years old at most, meets a jaded, powerful Lothario, now a mature fifty-two-year-old general. Recently ousted from Alexandria in a power-struggle with her joint ruler and brother-husband Ptolemy XIII, the queen contrives that she be returned secretly to the capital of her kingdom by a loyal servant on a tiny skiff at dead of night. Gaining entry into the royal palace concealed inside a bedding bag which the servant carries, she is carefully composed and adorned to look majestic yet pitiful. She is then unravelled before the Roman statesman at this their first, extraordinary meeting. There follows, for Caesar, love at first sight, luxurious banquets lasting until dawn, a tourist trip up the Nile towards the southernmost boundary of the Egyptian kingdom floating ostentatiously on Cleopatra's state barge accompanied by a convoy of four hundred ships, and finally departure. Later, for Cleopatra, the birth of 'little Caesar' (Caesarion), residency in her lover's villa across the Tiber at Rome, high honours and rich gifts, but then flight back to Egypt immediately after the assassination.

The Roman Lothario, however, is utterly circumspect about his meeting with Cleopatra. In his own commentaries on the civil war (*Bellum civile*), Julius Caesar first recounts the justice of his reasons for crossing the Rubicon in January 49 BC. Then through the course of his work's three books, the general catalogues his achievements in war against fellow Romans. From the Rubicon, he marches swiftly to Rome and on south down the Italian peninsula in hot pursuit of Pompey, who just manages to escape with the senatorial opposition across the sea to Greece. Then the author crosses west to Spain, where he manoeuvres cleverly against the subordinates of Pompey and – despite flood and famine – forces their armies to surrender. By the beginning of the third book, and the winter of 49, Caesar is back in Rome delivering well-considered edicts. But he soon sails stealthily across the Adriatic to the east, where he creates vast entrenchments and bold blockades against Pompey outside Dyrrachium, a port on the north-west coast of

Greece. There his enemy's successful sorties lead to chance setbacks which are soon surmounted. Caesar makes constant offers to the Pompeians of peace, displays repeated acts of clemency towards his Roman enemies and frequently attempts to achieve reconciliation. He is blessed by good fortune, and by the courage and devotion of his soldiers, in contrast to the greedy squabbles which surface among his republican opponents. At last in the autumn of 48, and more than halfway through the final book, he meets Pompey's vastly superior forces on the plain of Pharsalus in Thessaly, where he achieves a decisive victory in a set battle, overruns his rival's camp and suffers few losses.

Only towards the very end of these commentaries, determined to pursue Pompey now in flight, and so prevent the renewal of hostilities, does the author state (in the third person) that Caesar arrived in Egypt, to find Pompey dead and Alexandria also in a state of civil war. There, nonetheless, he was forced to stay because of contrary winds:

> Meanwhile, thinking that the dispute between the rulers was a matter of concern to the Roman people and to himself, because he was consul, and that it had an even greater claim on his attention because it was in his previous consulship that an alliance had been made by law and by decree of the senate with Ptolemy (the father), he made it known that it was his decision that King Ptolemy and his sister Cleopatra should disband their armies and conduct their argument by judicial process before himself rather than by armed struggle between themselves.
>
> (Caesar, *Civil War* 3.107. Trans. J. Carter, 1997: 135)

The general presents himself as summoning the royal brother and sister into his presence, in his capacity as Rome's consul, in order for him to arbitrate over their petty rivalries for sole occupancy of their father's throne. It is as if, with Pompey now dead, the conflict between Romans is also over and the winning disputant has become impartial judge over the armed struggles of others. Yet Caesar does not go on to mention his decision to give the kingdom to Cleopatra, and thus avoids any reference to his intimacy with the queen.

Some historians have speculated (following classical sources) that the subsequent war of succession fought on Egyptian soil was unnecessary and driven by love of Cleopatra, for Caesar became seemingly detached from Roman politics and the progress of the Roman civil war, besieged in the royal palace at Alexandria and embroiled in a local conflict so dangerous that it almost cost him his life. Others, such as Luciano Canfora, counter that it was not a pointless erotic interlude, but a politically motivated struggle to extract much-needed funds with which to fight on against Pompey's successors, and to secure an important client-kingdom for Caesar which had been previously aligned with Pompey (by placing on the throne a ruler who would not foment nationalistic uprisings nor present themselves as a fresh rival to Caesar in the Roman political arena). But, whatever Caesar's motives for spending nine months in Egypt, Cleopatra has almost no role to play in Julius Caesar's own representation of his stay. In the official Caesarian tradition (including the continuation of Caesar's commentaries in an anonymous book dedicated to the war he fought at Alexandria), Cleopatra is scarcely present – once mentioned as a loyal member of Caesar's camp, never as his lover.

Almost one hundred years later, Lucan turned history into hexameter verse. Fictionalizing the Roman dictator, he conferred huge thematic importance on his stay in Egypt towards the end of an epic narrative on the Roman civil war. Julius Caesar arrives in Alexandria at the beginning of book 10 of Lucan's *Bellum civile*. The whole episode borrows from and binds itself to Virgil's *Aeneid* in a correlation that exposes Caesar's visit as an utterly shameful waste of time. Like mythic Aeneas, the dictator dallies at the North African court of an enemy of Rome, acquiring a taste for oriental luxury. But, unlike Virgil's Dido (noble and tragic Queen of Carthage), Lucan's Cleopatra is a sordid, painted whore who sags under the weight of her jewels. The Queen of Egypt is here depicted poetically as a feminine mirror held up to an equally sordid Caesar. And each uses the other, like prostitute and client.

First Cleopatra is openly denounced by the epic narrator as the 'disgrace of Egypt', 'promiscuous to the harm of Rome' (10.59 and 60). Then, on her first night with the Roman general, she conceives an ambition even to assault the city itself and lead Caesar as a captive in her triumph. Accordingly, that first night elicits a sustained polemic against the behaviour of her Roman lover which makes even Antony's subsequent crazy love (10.70) seem forgivable:

> Even in the midst of madness, in the midst of frenzy
> and in the court inhabited by Pompey's shade,
> while drenched with blood of the Thessalian slaughter,
>> adulterously
> he shared his anxieties with Venus and combined with
>> war
> illicit union and progeny not born from wife.
> O the shame! Forgetting Magnus, he gave you brothers,
> Julia, from a loathsome mother, and he let
> the routed party gather strength in Libya's furthest realms
> while he spends time disgustingly on love beside the Nile,
> since he prefers to make a gift of Pharos, not to conquer
>> for himself.
>
> (Lucan, *Civil War* 10.72–81. Trans. S. H. Braund, 1999: 208–9)

The narrator borrows from the rich stock of abuse that, outside the time frame of the poem, would be deployed in the lead-up to the battle of Actium to win support for Augustus as he fights against the Egyptian whore and her besotted, adulterous lover Antony for republicanism, liberty, masculinity and the Roman West against tyranny, slavery, femininity and the barbarous East. The epic narrator here twists the propaganda round in order to transpose it ingeniously back in time onto Augustus' adoptive father and his coupling with Cleopatra. He thus denounces Caesar for having abused his Roman family (forgetting the murder of his son-in-law 'great' Pompey; contaminating his stock with Egyptian brothers for daughter Julia), and for having created spurious offspring on ille- gitimate beds out of a loathsome mother (v.78). In the middle of the madness of war, the already married Roman thought to give time over to adulterous, disgusting love (v.80). And, finally, forget- ting himself as general, he let his opponents regroup while giving conquered territories away as a lover's gift to his mistress. Following this vile night of passion, Lucan's Cleopatra then delivers a speech of seduction by which she corrupts Caesar's judgement. Thus the epic narrative of the civil war gives the lie to Julius Caesar's official version of his stay in Alexandria (according to which he com- ported himself impartially between the two Egyptian siblings) by cleverly exploiting the official version of a later Roman encounter with Cleopatra – an encounter which was publicized and denounced by Caesar's own adopted son.

Egypt and Cleopatra, in Lucan's poetic account, are a physical antithesis of Rome and its traditional moral and political values. Both land and queen begin to separate the Roman from his *roman- itas* and stimulate his desire to replace republican liberty with oriental tyranny. In the course of his Egyptian sojourn, the similes used of the epic protagonist change disturbingly from the ferocious propul- sion of a caged lion and pent-up volcano as Caesar is cornered

(10.445–8), to the helpless domestic withdrawal of an unwarlike child and a woman within a captured city's walls as he wanders from room to room of the palace hiding behind closed doors (10. 458–60), until he achieves the desperate barbarity of the oriental Medea thinking to toss the head of his companion King Ptolemy in the way of his pursuers (10.464–7). Alexandria and its queen weaken, effeminize and orientalize the Roman general (just as, according to Augustan propaganda, they would Mark Antony).

Julius Caesar's commentaries on the civil war end abruptly with his placement of a garrison on the island of Pharos (on which a tall lighthouse guided entrance into the harbour of Alexandria), thus making possible the shipment of food and reinforcements. On shore, he had increased his defences around the palace and, while squabbles were breaking out among the enemy on the outside, he had slain the young king's guardian (and controller of the kingdom) who had remained in his company inside. Thus, according to his own account, the Alexandrian war was now about to commence from a position of relative strength for Caesar (*Civil War* 3. 112). Radically rewriting Caesar's ending, Lucan's poem – at least in the form in which we have it – closes equally abruptly with Caesar at his most vulnerable. He has seized Pharos, but is encircled by all the fearfulness of war. With no hope of escape or even of an honourable death, he stands perplexed (10.542). And it is Cleopatra who has reduced Caesar to this perplexity.

Consumed as history rather than poetic fiction, Lucan's Cleopatra and her Roman lover achieved wide circulation in the Middle Ages, translated, adapted and expanded to suit medieval tastes and purposes. *Li Fet des Romains* (*The Deeds of the Romans*) has already been encountered in the two preceding chapters as a hugely influential example of the medieval conversion of classical culture into contemporary languages and literary genres which, through the instrument of ancient history, explored the political and ethical concerns of aristocratic society. This early thirteenth-century chronicle historicizes and interrogates chivalry's principles of martial valour and Christian manners through its translation of the life of Julius Caesar into French prose.

Caesar was a particularly fine exemplar for this mode of didactic historiography. As the quintessence of both sovereignty and military power, he could display in action, on a suitably heroic scale, the ideal knight's virtues of prowess and fame. But medieval Caesar could also play out the subversion of chivalric values (such as honour, loyalty, generosity and courtesy) when they are transferred from the context of conquest to that of civil war – now they become instruments of personal ambition rather than the greater good, and their presentation is based on the words of Lucan rather than Caesar himself. So Caesar's encounter with Cleopatra in Egypt appears in the second half of *Fet* embedded in a narrative of the Roman general's fearsome military exploits as he attempts to replace liberty with tyranny. Heavily expanded from Lucan's account, the affair becomes a kind of black romance, because cast in such negative terms – a cautionary tale for the French chronicle's aristocratic readership about the dangers of luxury and of lust.

The most extensive alteration of Lucan's account occurs in the descriptions of the Egyptian queen's royal palace and her person, both put on display in their extraordinary magnificence to celebrate, and further secure, Caesar's favour after that first night of infamy (according to Lucan, *Civil War* 10.104–35). The palace is here identified as a setting so beautiful and so rich, so great a delight to see, that it is most suited to its purpose of moving Caesar to lust. It is furnished excessively with a medieval decor made out of, for example, sard, almandine, marble, porphyry and chalcedony. Borrowed from other medieval romances, there are statues of white ivory, fine gold or silver, decorated with emeralds and topazes, their eyes sparkling with sapphires – a sculpted inkling of the

bejewelled woman who is to come. The space in which the
Egyptian queen will further work her charms is refurbished
anachronistically to give the narrative greater persuasive force. The
ancient world of Ptolemaic Alexandria is rendered more familiar,
converted into a material copy of the medieval present, better to
draw thirteenth-century readers into its admonitory romance; and
located here is an equally remodelled Cleopatra, already marked as
immoral by her immoral habitat.

The compiler of *Fet des Romains* lingers far longer than Lucan
over the beauty of the queen, a beauty which conforms to the
ideals of medieval poetry: tall, long blonde hair, wide forehead, fine
eyebrows, straight nose, full lips, round chin, and so on down the
body of the beloved. However, the medieval Cleopatra is distinguished from the heroines of contemporary romance (whom she
otherwise resembles physically) by the cosmetic artificiality of her
beauty and the perversity of its purpose. The queen displays her
body dishonestly, as if it were a sumptuous piece of merchandise. A
dazzling gold necklace illumines her throat; a wide scarf of gold
thread which crosses over her dress brings a golden glow to her
breasts. She has already removed the fastenings of her cloak better
to expose the contours of her shoulders. Hers is not the intrinsic
beauty that accompanies moral goodness. The chronicle's Cleopatra
is a decorated, painted surface designed to ensnare Caesar, and thus
to damage Rome.

This medieval love affair is a dreadful seduction, and the weight
of blame is placed squarely on the woman. Cleopatra cannot move
Caesar to favour her greed for power by the merit of her words; she
must instead contrive the decorative display of herself and her
palace as objects of luxury to incite him to lust, and in this way
obtain favour. The Roman is indeed so successfully corrupted that
he wants to hold her in his arms and have done whatever she
chooses. He immediately falls in love; she does not. He submits to

base corporeal desires, abandoning his Roman self. She is driven to an act of prostitution by her sordid need for political survival. All this is a deformation of chivalric, Christian love, not least because it involves a union outside marriage, the celebration of an adulterous life which, in this prose account, has now been stretched even more shamefully to a period of two years. Finally, it is not Julius Caesar but Caesar's knights who understand the moral damage being done both to Rome and to chivalry when their leader submits to a woman like this. As the adulterers sail down the Nile, the knights ride after them and directly reproach their lord:

> 'Caesar, you abase the honor of Rome when you make us follow after you and after a woman who is not your spouse. In this manner you do not conduct yourself like a leader of Rome, you who still have much to accomplish. This is the life of the libertine. All chivalry is dishonored by the fact that we thus follow you.'
>
> (*Li Fet des Romains*, Flutre and de Vogel 1937: 657, ll.10–14. Trans. G. M. Spiegel, 1993: 174)

The history lessons for the aristocratic readers of *Fet des Romains* are clear: as in war, so in love, Julius Caesar fails to meet the standards of medieval chivalry; adultery is an obstacle to martial valour; chivalric failure is certain to lead to ruin.

This medieval morality tale of the conqueror conquered by the folly of love became so well known that it came to take up a vital place in the representation of Love triumphant. In *I Trionfi*, a poem in the vernacular composed gradually over the years from 1338 to 1374, the Italian humanist Petrarch presented a novel form of dream-vision in which there appeared to him, first as spectator and then as participant, a series of six triumphs. In turn, he narrates, there came Love, Chastity, Death, Fame, Time and Eternity, each in triumphal procession in the Roman manner, and each parading captive the figure who had triumphed just before them.

Opening both poem and dream is a parade of famous individuals who have been conquered by Love (Love is later paraded by Chastity, the exercise of which leads to victory over Love's debased power). The poet and his readers learn how long a catalogue of heroes and heroines, gods and goddesses, kings and queens have succumbed to amatory passion, and even Petrarch himself is pulled into Love's victory parade from his initial position as bystander. But pride of place at the front of Love's triumphal procession goes to the canonic *triumphator*, Julius Caesar, from whose world the Roman triumph has been appropriated as the poem's structuring allegorical device:

> He who so lordly and so proud appears,
> First of us all, is Caesar, whom in Egypt
> Cleopatra bound, amid the flowers and grass.
>   Now over him there is triumph; and 'tis well,
> Since he, though conqueror of the world, was vanquished,
> That Love, who vanquished him, should have the glory.
>
> (Petrarch, *Triumphus Cupidinis* 1.88–93.
> Trans. E. H. Wilkins, 1962: 8–9)

An extraordinarily popular poem in the early Renaissance, *I Trionfi* gained an immense literary circulation in the fifteenth and early sixteenth centuries (in a wide variety of editions, translations, commentaries and imitations), as well as a very rich visual afterlife in court pageantry and spectacle, in paintings, tapestries, frescoes, woodcuts and stained glass, on wedding chests, armour and medals, in illuminations and miniatures.

One such influential commentary, composed by Bernardo Ilicino around 1475, secured an allegorical and processional reading for the poem as a call to virtue: the soul may grow from youthful engagement in carnal desire to the mature pursuit of salvation and heavenly bliss, if it undertakes the appropriate inner journey. Julius Caesar then becomes the first example of an outstanding individual who yielded to one of the providential forces in life, but might have overcome it had he proceeded unswervingly along virtue's path. A nude Venus, hair flowing down her back, burning torch clutched in her hand, stands on a pedestal at the top of a miniature designed by Jean Bourdichon to illustrate an especially decorative edition of Ilicino's commentary on *I Trionfi*, a translation into French of 1503 intended for the library of king Louis XII (Figure 5.1). Directly below Venus, we see a blindfolded Cupid adorned with multi-coloured wings, flaunting in each hand his regular props of arrow and bow. He stands victorious on top of a burning wagon drawn by four white, winged horses, named for the four fundamental characteristics of amatory passion: Bold Folly, Injustice, Intemperance and Imprudence. And directly beneath Cupid, in the centre foreground, stands Julius Caesar, the foolish lover. He gazes back in distraction at Cleopatra. She holds him by the shoulder, the beloved who has led him astray.

If, however, we retrace our steps for a moment back to the second half of the thirteenth century, we find a split in the reception of Caesar's affair with Cleopatra, and another – altogether more romantic – route for it to take. Only a few decades after *Li Fet des Romains* had narrated the Roman general's amatory folly in Egypt, the *Hystore de Jules César* attempted drastically to revise Lucan's authoritative account in order to produce a medieval Caesar who would be doubly ideal – a knight of exemplary achievement on the battlefield and of social refinement in personal affairs (including those of the heart).

Written in the mid-century in vernacular prose by the French cleric Jean de Thuin, the *Hystore* declares its didactic purpose and reveals the high class of its anticipated audience at the outset: 'it is

Fig. 5.1 'The triumph of love' (1503) by J. Bourdichon, illustrating a
commentary on Petrarch's *Trionfi*.

proper that [Caesar's] deeds be recounted in such a way that all the
high men who have lands to protect and to govern, because they are
accustomed to maintain themselves in gentility and in all good things,
can find in it examples and lessons' (Settegast 1881: 2; trans. Spiegel
1993: 187). Unlike the earlier French chronicle *Fet*, however, here the

examples and lessons Caesar's life offers to its audience of landown-
ers and lords are meant to be all to the good. For in the *Hystore*, the
Roman is an embodiment of earthly sovereignty, the founder of
empire and first emperor, as the conclusion indicates: 'Thus Caesar
was emperor of Rome and the most powerful prince in the world,
for he had subjected to himself its three parts, all of which he had
conquered; never was there king nor emperor who conquered as
much in his lifetime as Caesar did' (Settegast: 1881: 245; trans. Spiegel
1993: 210). This is a history of the glorious rescue of Rome from self-
destruction and the subjugation of the world by a generous and
merciful conqueror driven only by a proper desire for glory.

Within this narrative casing, where the author claims to be trans-
lating the ten books of Lucan's civil war poem into French prose,
the *Hystore de Jules César* instead is compelled radically to rewrite
the Latin epic. Lucan's poetic account is abbreviated, his narrator's
diatribes against the Roman general systematically cut out, his first-
century vision feudalized, his battles transformed into tournaments
of heroic single combat. Clearly too a new perspective is required
for Lucan's tenth book, where epic emphasis on virtues such as
prowess, fortitude and loyalty is now integrated with a courtly
romance demonstrating courtesy and refinement.

The description of Cleopatra which opens the tenth book of the
Hystore portrays the queen as a genuine beauty rather than a painted
whore, and thus begins the process of transforming the whole
encounter with Julius Caesar into a great love affair. This Cleopatra
does not entice the Roman general for a cunning political purpose,
instead she appeals to his sense of chivalry – asking, as a defenceless
lady, that he should come to her rescue against her brother and his
wicked advisers. As ideal knight, Caesar is moved both by her
beauty and by the imperatives of the chivalric code to place his
martial valour at her service: 'Certainly, my lady, greatly should one
give assistance, with all willingness, to a woman who requests aid as

sweetly as you do, and it is a great honor and great courtesy and great nobility to help a woman who is deprived of protection' (Settegast 1881: 164; trans. Spiegel 1993: 204). And for this, Cleopatra's knight is rewarded with a kiss.

Just at the point of sexual consummation, the narrative of Caesar and his beloved Cleopatra is abruptly halted to allow for the intrusion of a prolonged treatise on courtly love. Love is first defined, then its causes, processes and nature are explored. Finally, true love is distinguished from false. This 'love casuistry', sandwiched between the details of the developing affair between Caesar and Cleopatra, works to shape the affair's ethical value. For Caesar's love for the queen demonstrates in performance the codes for courtly love that interrupt it. His conduct conforms – as much as Roman history will allow – to the stated ideals of reason and moderation. The beloved is virtuous and hesitant (her lover is even constrained to bribe a chamberlain in order to enter her bedchamber). Her love is fair recompense for his heroic feats of arms on her behalf.

History, however, requires that this love proceed beyond a courtly kiss to consummation:

> and Caesar acted with such ardor that the lady granted all his wishes. Thus they went to sleep together in one bed, lying arm in arm, kissing and embracing and experiencing such delight as lovers do, when they are joined together by love and the desire for one another.
>
> (Jean de Thuin, *Hystore de Jules César*.
> Settegast 1881:190; trans. Spiegel 1993: 209)

Despite the romantic tone of the *Hystore de Jules César* at this point, the romance also must come to an end. Caesar fights for Cleopatra in the Alexandrian war, but then he must go on to further martial feats and the conquest of Rome itself if he is to play both the ideal courtly hero and the conquering monarch. This medieval chronicle extends far beyond the parameters of Lucan's civil-war poem to reach its climax in the general's triumphal entry into Rome and his coronation as absolute sovereign. Even in romantic historiography, Caesar's encounter with Cleopatra is only an interlude.

Romantic versions of the affair between Julius Caesar and Queen Cleopatra have proliferated in Western culture, in paintings, plays, operas, historical novels, in films and television docudramas. Over the course of the seventeenth and eighteenth centuries, for example, some fifty different operas were performed on the stages of Europe (in French, Italian, German or English) in which the events of the Roman civil war often became just a backcloth to the grand Egyptian love affair which was made to occur during its progress. The most famous of these, George Frideric Handel's *Giulio Cesare in Egitto* was first presented on the London stage in 1724.

The opera was composed when Handel was director at the Royal Academy of Music, which had been recently established under the patronage of George I to put on in London recurrent seasons of Italian opera. Opera seria, of which *Giulio Cesare* is an example, originated in the Italian royal courts, and its libretti – full of mythic heroes and noble rulers performing with dignity both their statecraft and their affairs of the heart – were written for the benefit of their elite audiences as a celebration of monarchy and an exhibition of ideal conduct. Now on the London stage, as much earlier in the French *Hystore*, the presentation of Julius Caesar's stay in Egypt would carry this sort of positive, exemplary force. Having inherited from medieval romance the tradition of Caesar as chivalric warrior and lover, both the Italian libretto by Nicola Haym and Handel's score endeavoured to characterize Caesar and Cleopatra as passionate young lovers, and to fix them forever in the moment of their blissful love.

Opening Act 1, Handel's Caesar makes a grand ceremonial

entrance 'on a plain near Alexandria' as clement victor over Pompey. A choral ensemble of Egyptians acclaims his arrival accompanied by the triumphant tones of four horns ('May the Nile rejoice on this day! / Every land smiles for him, / Every anguish disappears'). But, although he is characterized throughout the opera as manly conqueror, Caesar's part was originally scored for the high voice of an alto castrato, and was sung at first performance by the celebrated Senesino. High registers dominated the vocal arrangement and musical instrumentation of opera seria, and were closely associated with the genre's lover-hero who was therefore regularly characterized as especially youthful. Thus this operatic Caesar is played as a much younger man than his historical counterpart, as passionate young lover as well as noble statesman. And, since only a few members of the London audience would understand the Italian libretto (even though full text and English translation were usually supplied), plot and characterization were elaborated by means of the vocal registers, the strong and distinctive emotional tones of the arias, the semantic role of each instrument, the elaborate stage spectacle.

Before the second act opens, an ambitious Cleopatra has already seduced the honourable Caesar by pleading for his help against the tyrant Ptolemy while persuasively disguised as a defenceless serving-maid. Lucan's Cleopatra had secured the seduction of the Roman general with a lavish banquet in her luxurious palace (*Civil War* 10.104–71); Handel's Cleopatra, in the second act, stages another, appropriately musical, seduction by displaying a spectacular entertainment of Virtue, seated on a throne, in a palace on Mount Parnassus. Once revealed, this 'Virtue' ironically sings an aria that celebrates erotic passion ('I adore you, O eyes, / Love's darts') accompanied by nine 'Muses' who all play stage instruments. The spectator Caesar (along with the opera's audience) is again captivated. But already by the end of Act 2, the queen has cast aside all such frivolity, and fearing now for Caesar's life, she reveals her true identity and her reciprocal love.

In the final third act, after Caesar has heroically rescued his beloved from imprisonment by her cruel brother and placed her on the throne of Egypt, the two ardent young lovers sing a final (and rare) duet which anticipates their lasting love. The intensity of their accord is demonstrated musically by the merger of their voices. The opera ends in a lavish pageant, with the return of the stately horns, and the populace looking forward to peace and liberty under the protection of their Roman lord:

CLEOPATRA AND CAESAR
A great joy will fill my breast,
if you will always be faithful;
thus bitter grief will leave my heart;
there will remain only love,
constancy and faith.
POPULACE
Let there return to our hearts
fairest joy and pleasure;
with our hearts free from all sorrow,
let each one again rejoice.
(*Giulio Cesare in Egitto* Act 4.4.
Trans. Dale McAdoo, 1967)

The happy ending is so strong a convention of opera seria that even Julius Caesar and Cleopatra are permitted one, and throughout the opera (as with the medieval *Hystore de Jules César*) little trace of the Lucanian diatribe against Caesar's Alexandrian dalliance remains. So there is no bloodying of Julius Caesar's erotic bliss with the suggestion that he was responsible for the death of his fellow-Roman Pompey or that he was forgetful of that savage deed.

Instead, in Act 1, Scene 3, Caesar responds to the sight of Pompey's funeral urn by weeping and singing a tragic accompanied recitative on the frailty of human achievement ('Soul of great Pompey, / Your trophies were but a shadow'). Nor is there any Lucanian flash-forward to the assassination of Caesar as just revenge for the murder of Pompey and for Rome's loss of liberty. It is Egyptian Ptolemy who is characterized in opposition to Roman Caesar as a cruel and licentious autocrat, and it is he who must be deposed and killed, climactically, on stage. With villainy thus unseated, no further war looms, and the opera ends triumphantly with joy for the lovers and for Egypt.

The pomp and ceremony, the passion and intrigues, the emotive arias of *Giulio Cesare in Egitto* were all very well received, and it was accordingly revised and revived by Handel many times both in London and elsewhere over the period 1725–37. A prologue and epilogue were added to the royal performance held in Hamburg in 1727 to honour the birthday of George I. Together they presented a display of 'The Joy and Happiness of the British Nation'. The architecturally elaborate scenic design for the prologue included a form of temple, in which the audience could see statues of Mars enthroned at front right, Minerva at front left. At centre back appeared a statue of the king, and leading the eye towards him were enthroned a series of nymphs signifying the blessings His Majesty's dominions were enjoying under the administration of their king (Figure 5.2a). The design for the epilogue displayed the city of London and the river Thames replete with ships and figures such as Neptune, and the finale to the opera was accompanied by the discharge of cannon and fireworks (Figure 5.2b). As with the excision of Lucanian condemnation, these framing devices celebrating the British monarchy effectively close down any possibility of irony in the final duet of the opera. The Egyptian episode is thus staged and sung as a self-contained story of young, impassioned, noble love which embraces fairest joy and

Fig. 5.2a Design for prologue to a performance of Handel's *Giulio Cesare*, in 1727 by T. Lediard.

pleasure (*la bella gioia ed il piacer*) for the Egyptian people, love, constancy and faith (*amor, costanza, e fè*) for Caesar and his Cleopatra.

The romanticized account of Julius Caesar's stay in Egypt obtains credibility and historical authority as a foreshadowing of the great love affair traditionally assumed for Cleopatra and Mark Antony. But it was partly as an attack against this kind of conflation that George Bernard Shaw wrote the anti-romantic history play *Caesar and Cleopatra*. Written in 1898, but first staged professionally in 1906, Shaw's play completely reconceives the episode so that it no longer involves the spectacular, erotic seduction of the Roman general. Instead, through the course of the play, lessons in political leadership are delivered by an unwarlike, world-weary elderly statesman to an infantile and sadistic girl of sixteen, in terms designed to evoke British imperial culture and to critique, most topically, its colonialist projects in the Sudan.

Fig. 5.2b Design for epilogue to a performance of Handel's *Giulio Cesare* in 1727, by T. Lediard.

Caesar is explicitly played as a man wholly unlike Antony, and that mismatch constitutes a major structuring device of the play, deliberately denying the audience the satisfaction of seeing young lovers embrace at the final curtain. Instead, in the closing moments of Act 5, Caesar turns to address Cleopatra:

> CAESAR: Come, Cleopatra: forgive me and bid me farewell;
> and I will send you a man, Roman from head to heel
> and Roman of the noblest; not old and ripe for the knife;
> not lean in the arms and cold in the heart; not hiding a
> bald head under his conqueror's laurels; not stooped with
> the weight of the world on his shoulders; but brisk and
> fresh, strong and young, hoping in the morning,
> fighting in the day, and revelling in the evening. Will
> you take such an one in exchange for Caesar?

CLEOPATRA: (*palpitating*) His name, his name?

CAESAR: Shall it be Mark Antony? (*She throws herself into his arms.*)

RUFIO: You are a bad hand at a bargain, mistress, if you will swap Caesar for Antony.

CAESAR: So now you are satisfied.

CLEOPATRA: You will not forget.

CAESAR: I will not forget. Farewell: I do not think we shall meet again. Farewell. (*He kisses her on the forehead. She is much affected and begins to sniff. He embarks.*)

THE ROMAN SOLDIERS: (*as he sets his foot on the gangway*) Hail Caesar; and farewell!

He reaches the ship and returns Rufio's wave of the hand.

APOLLODORUS: (*to Cleopatra*) No tears, dearest Queen: they stab your servant to the heart. He will return some day.

CLEOPATRA: I hope not.

(Bernard Shaw, Caesar and Cleopatra, 1898: Act 5)

Shaw makes of Caesar and Cleopatra two characters incapable of falling in love with each other. The Roman considers himself now too old for love, while the queen considers him too old, too bald and too thin. Throughout the play, she prefers cheap conventional dreams of romance in the strong, round arms of young, handsome Antony – an emotional self-indulgence, a submission to base passions, presented by Shaw as the antithesis of disciplined leadership.

In a new prologue composed for a 1912 revival of the play, and in a published response to critical reviews of a 1913 production, Bernard Shaw reproached his audiences for their expectation of romance (an expectation fed by the overwhelming pressure of repeated performances of Shakespeare's *Antony and Cleopatra*). He rejects the classical authority of Plutarch and Cassius Dio, and regards the Alexandrian episode as without erotic significance.

Antony, Shaw claims, let Cleopatra disgrace and ruin him, and yet returned to her like a needle to a magnet; Caesar was so little influenced by her that few people know he ever met her, and when he left her she had to go after him to Rome to get hold of him again. Although he extricates Julius Caesar from the romance of Greek historiography, Shaw does not then reimmerse him into the moral corruption of Lucanian epic. Instead, in *Caesar and Cleopatra*, he purifies the Roman statesman, returns him to the pristine condition of the self-authored Caesar of the Latin commentaries, and even elevates him into the Shavian conception of political greatness – a genius who exercises power objectively, without vengeance.

The text of *Caesar and Cleopatra* was published in 1901 in a collection which Shaw called 'Three Plays for Puritans'. The point, as Shaw explained in the preface, was to rescue British theatre from its current obsession with the vulgar theme of clandestine adultery, to free it from the 'deification of Love', and to produce edifying plays only intellectual puritans would appreciate. Yet the attraction of an amorous Caesar, or at least a Caesar susceptible to seduction, has been so strong that some erotic business was injected into the Technicolor film adaptation of the play (directed by Gabriel Pascal for the Rank studio and released in 1945), even though the film was made under the playwright's close scrutiny. Shaw himself prepared the scenario for a fresh scene, shot in the queen's sumptuous bedchamber in the palace at Alexandria as she prepares to meet Julius Caesar again the morning after his disembarkation. Sitting up on her bed, Cleopatra asks her nurse Ftatateeta, 'What will Caesar do with me?' The nurse, belying the otherwise faithfully anti-erotic flavour of the film's Shavian narrative, replies suggestively, 'Ask rather what you will do with him.' Pushing the reluctant queen towards her bath, the nurse also warns her charge that if she redden her lips, Caesar will not kiss them. Soft, light music begins to play in the background. The camera then lingers just for a tantalizing moment over the naked back of Vivien Leigh (who stars as Cleopatra), while she disrobes behind a gauzy curtain to enter the bath.

Released in December 1945, *Caesar and Cleopatra* was not a box-office success in the United Kingdom, where the national press and even Parliament expressed concern over the vast sums that had been expended unpatriotically on such cinematic froth during a period of wartime shortages. Desperate to recoup its heavy investment elsewhere, the Rank studio oversaw an advertising campaign for the American market that placed heavy emphasis on eroticism: Vivien Leigh as Cleopatra was 'the greatest woman in the history of romance and love'; Claude Rains as Caesar was 'a man who could conquer the world but found his match in a woman'. The 'deification of Love', by which Shaw claimed to be so appalled in the preface to the text of his play, was obviously an essential commercial device in the marketing of the big-budget film adaptation. But such advertising, and tie-ups with the sale of jewellery, clothing and cosmetics, sat uneasily with such an unerotic (and uncinematic) vision of Julius Caesar's meeting with Cleopatra in Egypt.

Nevertheless, Julius Caesar's triangular relationship with Cleopatra and with cinema became very close during the course of the twentieth century, especially across Hollywood's cycle of historical films, where the narrative focus was placed on Cleopatra, and her encounter with the Roman general in Egypt was played most frequently as a teasing prelude to a markedly more sensuous affair with Mark Antony (as in the now lost *Cleopatra* of 1917 starring Theda Bara, the 1934 *Cleopatra* starring Claudette Colbert, and the notorious 1963 *Cleopatra* starring Elizabeth Taylor).

So intimate has that association become that even an early twenty-first-century production of Handel's opera *Giulio Cesare in Egitto* has been staged as Hollywood homage. Under the direction of James Robinson, in its 2003–4 season, the Houston Grand Opera reset the love affair between Caesar and Cleopatra on an MGM soundstage – as a 1930s film musical in the making. A local newspaper reports on the Mount Parnassus seduction scene in Act 2:

> The clouds part, and fog rolls in, bringing with it a strolling chamber orchestra. Behind the clouds sits an art deco pyramid, striped in black and white. Stepping out of some Astaire – Rogers picture, chorus boys dressed in evening wear with top hats tap the front of the pyramid with the heads of their canes. The triangle breaks apart, leaving a bevy of beauteous chorines holding the pieces. There – in a star turn worthy of any queen of the silver screen – stands the resplendent Cleopatra.
>
> (D. L. Groover, *Houston Press*, 6 November 2003)

Caesar (sung here by the countertenor David Daniels) is seduced by a Cleopatra (soprano Laura Claycomb) costumed to resemble the Hollywood film star Jean Harlow: blonde, marcelled hair, long evening gloves, feather-trimmed cape, chevron-striped black-and-white halter-necked gown. As spotlights flicker behind her and confetti spills over the stage set, the watching Caesar collapses in an overexcited swoon. The Shavian epic film *Caesar and Cleopatra* is the exception to the rule that the sensual and the erotic should dominate in film versions of Caesar's seduction by the Egyptian queen.

The 1963 *Cleopatra* directed by Joseph Mankiewicz drew on, but modified even further, Shaw's staging of the Alexandrian episode. Julius Caesar (played by Rex Harrison) may be ageing and pedantic, but he is also virile and urbane. The queen offers him first Egypt's wealth, then her skittish charms, and finally her fertile body as source for the son whom Caesar longs for as an heir to his political ambitions at Rome. Another bedroom scene is here acted out, but in a more elaborate, explicit and knowing fashion than the brief scenario interpolated into the film adaptation of Shaw's history play. While sitting in her palace bedchamber upright, on a plain bench, fully clothed, drinking and eating modestly, and listening to a poetic recitation, Cleopatra is informed that Caesar is on his way. The queen (played by Elizabeth Taylor) accordingly orchestrates a titillating spectacle of her own flesh, posing supine and languid on a narrow couch, naked but for a piece of sparsely decorated, trans- parent fabric which covers her precariously. All around handmaids busy themselves dancing, playing exotic pipes, dipping grapes into wine cups or painting the finger- and toe-nails of their seductive mistress.

The 'intruder', Caesar, breaks in. The film at this point invites its spectators both to share with the Egyptian queen the clever prepa- ration of the erotic bait – a bedroom scene of fabulous proportions – and with the Roman conqueror the pleasure of erotic capture, for he (along with the camera) moves across the vast space to zoom in and take a good look at the voluptuous female body laid out before him. In reverse shot, we see that the Roman general is standing before the queen's canopied bed displayed invit- ingly behind and to one side of him. Sandwiched uneasily between narrow couch and empty bed, occasionally clutching his sheathed sword, the golden-armoured Roman speaks with Cleopatra of the perilous palace blockade. The scene ends with Caesar kissing the nearest of Cleopatra's handmaids, a fleeting substitute for sexual consummation with the queen, the desire for which her act has successfully aroused. The whole sequence hints at what the Houston operatic production reveals: Julius Caesar's encounter with Cleopatra is readily translatable into a mode of film spectatorship where a masculine gaze can be pleasurably sated by Hollywood's well-crafted, feminine eroticism (Figure 5.3).

Huge problems in its production, long delays in its release, vast

Fig. 5.3 Elizabeth Taylor (Cleopatra) and Rex Harrison (Julius Caesar)
relax on the set of *Cleopatra* (1963).

over-expenditure and much scandalized publicity concerning the
adulterous behaviour offset of its female star all appear to have
stimulated the incorporation of such self-reflexive strategies into the
1963 *Cleopatra*, strategies which invited the external spectators who
finally saw the beleaguered film to feel (like the internal spectators

Julius Caesar and Mark Antony) that they would be fully satisfied by the visual exhibition so carefully prepared for their pleasure. And, in fact, this self-regarding Hollywood depiction of Julius Caesar's stay in Egypt did have a significant impact on the original design and subsequent commercial success of the Caesars Palace casino-hotel which opened in Las Vegas three years later.

Begun in 1966, located at the time in striking isolation at the head of the Vegas automobile strip, set back from the road by an ostentatious driveway, Caesars Palace was first created as a themed architectural pastiche of imperial Rome in order to differentiate it from other roadside motels. It was named Caesars without an apostrophe to suggest that any gambler entering its grandiose casinos might become a Caesar and this his palace of pleasure, and both the name 'Caesars' and the architectural theme 'imperial Roman' were loosely conceived as an amalgamation of all the most celebrated Roman emperors and the whole age of empire. This modern American palace, however, was presented not as a reconstruction of original monuments from the ancient city but as a collation of Hollywood's simulations from the 1963 *Cleopatra* and other historical films set in ancient Rome; according to its original owner, the gambler Jay Sarno, guests were supposed to feel that they had passed through the cinema screen to become stars in their very own Roman epic of high living.

The lives they were most encouraged to emulate were those recently envisioned by Hollywood for Julius Caesar (who was, after all, Rome's ultimate high roller) and his Egyptian queen. Once even the signs on the toilet doors declared in Latinate script 'Caesars' and 'Cleopatras'. As late as 1998, media information packs included a photograph of Cleopatra standing on a terrace of the hotel in Vegas. Dressed in a show-girl version of Ptolemaic royal costume, she drops grapes into the mouth of a reclining Caesar, resplendent in his shining gold armour; a similarly attired Cleopatra was also led out on the arm of her beloved Caesar (this time bedecked in white and gold greaves, tunic, breastplate, epaulettes, and cloak) at the head of a procession of Roman characters in order to launch a New Year toga party for select high rollers held at Caesars Palace on 31 December 2000. For years and years, these costumed Cleopatras and their armoured Caesars have made an appearance every night to greet the patrons of the Palace.

As the targeted customers have changed over the last four decades from gamblers to family groups, so Caesars Palace has constantly expanded into an imperial 'set' so elaborate and immersive that the guests of its new corporate owners (Harrah Entertainment) have the opportunity to pass their entire vacation without leaving it. The hyper-themed environment may eventually cease to be a central part of the attraction, but for the time being at Caesars Palace the hotel suites, casinos, conference facilities, gardens, pools, nightclubs, sports colosseum, restaurants, bars, cafés, amusement rides and shops are all awash with playfully kitsch classicism: columns, pediments, architraves, arches, colonnades, fountains, statuary, friezes and mosaics. Now a casino-resort, it celebrated its fortieth anniversary in August 2006 appropriately enough with another toga party, and should you wish to make a reservation, you can take a virtual tour on the website around one of its Roman-themed nightlife settings: 'an exquisite replica of the vessel that carried Egypt's royalty along the Nile River in the times of Julius Caesar, Cleopatra's Barge is a vibrant nightclub featuring live music, DJs, an extensive cocktail list, and a truly unique floating dance floor'. A visit to Caesars Palace thus remains an invitation to become imperial Caesar or his queen Cleopatra for the duration of your stay.

In tandem with the local development of Caesars Palace, from the 1960s onwards Julius Caesar also increased his appearances in popular culture far more broadly as convenient shorthand in the language of advertising. Even the most lightly sketched image of the Roman statesman was instantly recognizable and, as we have seen, by now his life had accrued an extremely rich reception history: he was known as a connoisseur and a collector of high art, an extravagant spender, a refined consumer, a lover and a womanizer, all of which could be enlivened by racy hints of risk-taking and decadence. The advertising industry appropriated these associations to turn Julius Caesar into an inviting sign of consumption tied in to specific concepts such as power, luxury, sophistication and sensuality (as well as the concepts regularly attached to classical figures of quality, durability and high culture), and deployed to sell products ranging from cars to chocolates.

In the late twentieth century, a magazine advertisement for a company based in London displayed in its upper frame a figure identifiable as Julius Caesar by his scarlet cloak and golden laurel wreath, by his engineering skills and by his connoisseurship of bedroom furniture and fittings (Figure 5.4). In the lower frame, a photograph provided testimony to the incorporation of classical architectural symbols into the company's interior designs (columns, temple forms, entablatures and pediments). Tag-line and slogan (as well as logo) reinforced the transfer of values from past to present with their reference to 'elegance' and 'craftsmanship', and the authority of 'imperial' and 'decisions'. The reader of this set of images is offered the pleasurable sensation of membership of a sophisticated cultural community which understands the humorous juxtaposition of imperial tradition with modern technology, Julius Caesar with computer graphics, and the social coding of the furniture which that juxtaposition proposes. Caesar and the Roman past are utilized to create a future tense of anticipated consumption: with this bed, the advertisement suggests, you will be buying into Caesar's qualities (and, perhaps, his scandalous activities).

We may think that by now we have strayed a long way from the

Fig. 5.4 Advertisement for Fauchar furniture.

moral indignation towards Julius Caesar expressed in Lucan's Latin epic, but it was Lucan (and his medieval translators and adaptors) who first lovingly detailed the luxuries of Alexandria by which Caesar was seduced: Cleopatra's ornamented palace, her extraordinary banquets and her bejewelled body. In the context of the republican sympathies expressed by Lucan's narrator, the description of the sexual seduction, the Egyptian palace and the feasting are all an index of a supreme degeneration of morals; synonymous with oriental decadence, they are a stimulus to Roman social corruption. But while Lucan's adulterer was eventually transformed into the ideal courtly lover of medieval romance, Lucan's decadent Caesar has been more recently transformed into the ideal playboy of modern consumer culture. And as the context for the narration, musical performance or visualization of Caesar's relationship with Cleopatra shifts from a discourse of aristocratic and middle-class ethics to one of mass entertainment, the invitation to become like the charismatic Lothario whom Lucan's narrator so despised is addressed to us all.

6

TRIUMPHALISM

Rome, 46 and 45 BC

About twenty months stood between Julius Caesar's spectacular celebration of four triumphs through the streets of Rome in September 46 BC and his earlier Egyptian difficulties – hemmed in on the harbour island at Alexandria in January 47 BC. Caesar breaks off his narrative of the civil war at this delicate point, but the Caesarian corpus (a body of three anonymous works, which continue the Roman general's account on through the rest of the Alexandrian war to campaigns in Africa and Spain, written most probably by participating officers) enthusiastically catalogues subsequent events to the greater glory of their protagonist. He evaded danger in 47, the corpus tells us, by retreating to his ship from which, in turn, he jumped overboard and swam to safety as soon as he recognized that the overcrowded vessel was about to sink. Stimulated by such reverses, heartened by successes, Caesar and his troops soon managed to sail out and join up with large reinforcements arrived from the East, and thus overwhelm the boy-king's army in valiant combat. With the king drowned, and Caesar master of Egypt, he assigned the kingdom jointly to the younger brother and to Cleopatra 'who had remained loyally in his camp', disposed his troops, and set out for Syria (*The Alexandrian War* 20–33).

From June 47, after a nine-month stay in Egypt, Caesar picked up the pace of the Roman civil war against Pompey's sons and supporters. First he spent two months in the East, settling the Roman provinces and the client kingdoms which had formerly been disposed towards Pompey and extracting large payments from them as penalty. Advancing northwards from Syria, through Cilicia and Cappadocia to Pontus, he confronted the menacing pretensions of Pharnaces, King of Bosphorus, to extend his dominions southwards. Pompey had been victorious against the king's father Mithridates, but a legate of Caesar had recently been defeated by the son. In August 47, however, near the Pontic town of Zela, Caesar annihilated the king's army with astonishing rapidity despite being surprised by the enemy's frontal assault uphill (*Alexandrian War* 65–77). Thus the Roman dictator stamped his military authority on the East. Writing back to a friend in Rome, later sources add, the victor boasted of his lightning speed with appropriate brevity: 'I came, I saw, I conquered' (*veni, vidi, vici*).

Next Julius Caesar passed only four brief months on Italian soil, where he was largely occupied in the assembly of troops to fight in North Africa. Some veterans, demanding discharge and better reward, mutinied. Deputies sent by the general to placate them were violently rebuffed. The soldiers marched to Rome and attempted to scare Caesar himself with their demands. Despite his urgent need of them, he addressed the veterans as 'citizens', as if they had already lost their military status and with it the chance of great booty from the next campaign. Thus humiliated, they volunteered eagerly to serve again (Dio, *Roman History* 42.52–5). Having made a stand as a severely disciplined military commander, Caesar set sail for Africa in December 47.

For the next seven months, the dictator was embroiled in a difficult campaign against substantial senatorial forces which had assembled in Africa under the command of Pompey's son-in-law

Metellus Scipio, forces swollen in number by the support of Juba, king of neighbouring Numidia. Caesar held out for reinforcements while rendered vulnerable by the need constantly to foray for food and water. Then, boldly marching out and devising a daring blockade of the coastal town of Thapsus, he forced the opposition into pitched battle. In April 46, he finally achieved victory despite the hunger of his soldiers. The enemy's elephants he had put into panic with a constant hail of missiles so that they ran amok within their own ranks. But the dictator's troops could not be prevented from massacring their Roman opponents in the act of surrender. Chasing refugees from this defeat up to Utica, Caesar learned of the suicide of Cato, commander of that garrison and soon to be immortalized as symbol of a defunct republic. As the resistance of the Pompeians collapsed, the victor variously inflicted punishments and fines, distributed rewards, ordered executions and demonstrated clemency (*The African War* 79–98).

Julius Caesar returned to Rome in July 46. Two months later, having never before been feted by the whole city as a *triumphator*, he celebrated four spectacular triumphs in succession over the course of forty days. With the benefit of a massive outlay from his spoils of war, these triumphs were designed to surpass in duration, splendour and range any held by Pompey, and to give to Rome's citizens a tangible display of what the general and his soldiers had accomplished, on the basis of which he would now stake a claim to even greater political power.

The Roman triumph was a spectacular sacrament, undertaken on such a vast scale that its protocols were prescribed by law. Its patterns and purpose have been reconstructed from study of both documentary and material evidence for a whole assortment of triumphs, both republican and imperial. To celebrate a triumph was the greatest honour available to a Roman male citizen; it was available only if the victor had held a legitimate command against a fearsome opponent and the victory had augmented Rome's standing, involving large-scale losses for the enemy, and the capture and return to Rome of many prisoners and trophies. The whole community participated in prayers, sacrifices, processions, feasts and shows which glorified the *triumphator* as a man who had succeeded in battle by reason of his bravery and his god-given good fortune. The ceremonial parade passed along a set triumphal route through a special gateway into the city, wound round the circuses to the forum, and ended on the Capitoline hill before the temple of Jupiter, where offerings were made in gratitude to the god. Its choreography was equally preset: at the front the senators and other magistrates of Rome, then musicians, plunder, sacrificial bulls with gilded horns, prisoners of war, the general's bodyguard of lictors, the triumphant general himself, and at the rear his officers and troops, singing songs about him in a carnival atmosphere of celebration and derision.

The *triumphator* wore for the occasion a special costume: a tunic embroidered with palm motifs, a purple toga embroidered with gold stars, tall red boots, a crown of gold and precious stones, and a face painted the colour of blood. He carried special props: a laurel branch in his right hand, an eagle-headed ivory sceptre in his left. He rode into Rome in a special transport, a gilded chariot drawn by four horses. In all this, he departed far from the appearance of ordinary soldier or civilian in order temporarily to embody an ancient king of Rome or even the highest god of the city – Jupiter Optimus Maximus. As a consequence, the *triumphator* risked swelling up with excessive arrogance, so a slave rode behind him in the chariot and held over his head a gold wreath (borrowed from Jupiter's temple), while constantly declaiming, 'Look behind you; remember you are mortal.'

The Roman triumph was devised to parade the excellence of a victorious general, the courage of his soldiers, the military might of

Rome, its mission of conquest and domination, and the grandeur of its empire. Through the exhibition and distribution of booty, it spoke to its celebrants directly of community, national strength, safety, geographic centrality, prosperity and divine protection. And it also pinned these attributes of Rome onto the paraded body of the triumphing general. Yet there were a number of new or unusual features to the triumphs of Julius Caesar which distinguished them from those of the republican generals before him or the emperors after, imparting to them both magnificence and ambivalence, and giving a special direction to their reception.

On each of four days spread out at intervals, Julius Caesar rode into Rome guarded by seventy-two lictors to celebrate triumphs which he staged as victories won not in civil war against Romans, but in foreign campaigns fought over the territories of Gaul, Egypt, Pontus and Africa. Each of the processions which passed through the streets of Rome to the Capitol was differentiated from the others by the material that decorated the floats carrying the spoils: respectively, citrus wood, tortoiseshell, acanthus wood and ivory. Amid the music and the wafted perfumes, and before the arrival of the triumphant general and his marching legions, the ancient sources list in amazement parades of statues of rivers overcome (the Rhine, the Rhône, the Nile, even Ocean), replicas of edifices captured (the Pharos lighthouse), jingles pithily commemorating campaigns (the infamous 'I came, I saw, I conquered'), giant paintings of cities subdued (Marseilles) and enemies slaughtered (Achillas and Pothinus) or in flight (Pharnaces). And behind all this, prisoners of flesh and blood walked in chains: most conspicuously, the chieftain Vercingetorix for Gaul, the princess Arsinoë for Egypt, the royal infant Juba II for Africa. Only the first of these three was then led away – after a wait of six years – to be strangled in an underground prison cell.

Yet the same classical authors also catalogue causes of discomfort or offence to the Roman spectators of 46 (or even to themselves as they later record the events). The unprecedented number of lictors guarding the general in each of his triumphs was an insult (Dio, *Roman History* 43.19). The breakdown of his chariot before the Temple of Fortune, during the first triumph, was potentially such a disastrous omen that Caesar was constrained to alleviate it by finishing the journey up to the Capitol either humbly (on his knees up the stairs: Dio 43.21), or brilliantly (at night, accompanied on right and left by forty elephants bearing lamps: Suetonius, *Deified Julius* 37.2). To parade Arsinoë in chains – a woman and, once, a queen – was an unpleasant novelty that moved its witnesses to public pity, which then conveniently masked their expressions of grief over their own private suffering (Dio 43.19).

These problems were fully offset, according to the historian Dio, by the enormous number of Caesar's captives and achievements, both of which led the people to admire him greatly. Only brief mention is reserved in his account, however, for the gravest problem of all – the slaughter of Roman citizens during the African campaign. Yet, while victory over Pompey was at no point celebrated, and no Roman names were exhibited in the African triumph, a number of painted panels represented the gruesome suicides of the Pompeian generals who, from the official Caesarian perspective, had proved themselves traitors to the state by fighting in support of the barbarian Juba. Spectators could see Lucius Scipio wounding himself in the chest and throwing himself into the sea; Petreius killing himself at a farewell banquet; Cato, like a wild beast, ripping himself open (Appian, *Civil Wars* 2.101). While the purpose of such images may have been to demonstrate the consequences even to Romans of opposing Caesar, it is clear from the sources that he could not fully control responses to their display. Although the crowds applauded the deaths of Achillas and Pothinus, and laughed at the flight of Pharnaces, they groaned over the internal troubles which the Roman images evoked (Appian 2.101) – images which Caesar had seen fit to exhibit in the last, and the most threatening, of his four triumphs.

The final celebrations were equally distinctive and difficult to control. After the vast public banquet, there were gladiatorial combats, dances, stage plays, circus races and shows of horsemanship, athletic contests, fights with wild beasts, mock land and sea battles, and the first appearance in Rome of the giraffe. Spoils of war were distributed among the soldiers and male citizens in the form of money, grain or oil. Yet despite (or rather because of) all this, Julius Caesar was blamed: the vast number of deaths in these spectacles demonstrated only that he was not yet sated with bloodshed; their magnificence that countless sums were being squandered on such barbarous luxuries as a silk awning erected to protect spectators from the heat of the sun. Rioting broke out among the veterans, who were resentful of the citizens' share of the spoils. It did not stop until their general himself seized a soldier and delivered him up for execution. Two others were ceremoniously sacrificed by the priests and their heads put on display outside their general's official residence (Dio 43.24).

Worse was to follow. Within two months of his triumphs, Julius Caesar was compelled to return to Spain where the sons of Pompey had amassed a large army and revived the civil conflict. This proved to be the last and the most hazardous of all the general's campaigns. After months of marching and manoeuvring while the Pompeians refused to give battle, victory was finally snatched at Munda in March 45. *The Spanish War* (the third and last of the works belonging to the Caesarian corpus) fails to add – as do other later sources – that it was only after a long and ferocious struggle when, caught between a favourable moment and unfavourable terrain, Caesar had had to run right up to the panic-stricken frontline and ended up fighting for his life (Plutarch, *Life of Caesar* 56.3; Appian 2.104).

After months more of bitter conflict, with one son of Pompey dead and the other in flight, Julius Caesar finally returned to Rome to celebrate yet another triumph in October 45 BC.

Although the pageantry was not as spectacular as before, popular displeasure was even greater. The Roman triumph was already an equivocal ceremony. The only occasion when a general was legally permitted to enter the city at the head of his army, it marked practically and symbolically the boundary between military power and civil rule. It feted martial slaughter and drew attention to the fragility of the fame its triumphant general had earned. Julius Caesar's Spanish triumph was especially equivocal. However much Caesarian propaganda attempted to present and justify the war in Spain as a campaign against local rebels supported by Roman traitors, this triumph was understood and deplored as an explicit glorification of victory in civil war over fellow-citizens:

> This was the last war that Caesar waged; and the triumph that was celebrated for it vexed the Romans as nothing else had done. For it commemorated no victory over foreign commanders or barbarian kings, but the utter annihilation of the sons and the family of the mightiest of the Romans, who had fallen upon misfortune; and it was not meet for Caesar to celebrate a triumph for the calamities of his country, priding himself on actions which had no defence before gods or men except that they had been done under necessity.
>
> (Plutarch, *Life of* Caesar 56.4. Trans. B. Perrin, 1919: 573)

Within six months of parading before the Roman populace as a conquering hero, Caesar was assassinated.

The Roman triumph continued on into the imperial period, and would eventually become widely disseminated both as subject and as metaphor in Western literature, visual arts and state pageantry, but representations and re-enactments of Julius Caesar's triumphs are of particular interest because of the inherent ambiguities of the originals and because they were now located within an historical narrative where triumph was swiftly followed by catastrophic disaster.

After the end of the republic, the rituals of the triumph gradually sharpened focus on the veneration of the emperor's political authority and pretensions to divinity. In such a triumph, then, there was no place for a Christian except within the procession of captives. For, according to the early Church fathers, God is the supreme *triumphator*, and his followers win true glory and spiritual victory only through earthly humiliation and defeat. Accordingly, in the early Middle Ages, the Roman triumph was taken over for Christianity and transformed into an allegorical drama that celebrated, for example, the triumph of the seven virtues over the seven deadly sins. There were few exceptions to this general rule that only the Church could triumph, and even fewer instances of triumphs where Julius Caesar had any part to play.

One such exception occurred in 1237, after Frederick II, Holy Roman Emperor of imperial territories covering much of central Europe and Italy, won a decisive battle against a league of northern Italian cities which were fighting for independence. After his victory, the medieval ruler staged a triumphal entry into Cremona in the style and with the accoutrements of a Roman emperor: along with a parade of standards and insignia, an elephant from Frederick's menagerie drew into the city the captured *carroccio* of Milan (a wagon which bore into battle a cross, the relics of saints and sacred banners, all to symbolize the presence of divine protection), and chained to the wagon walked the leader of Milan's commune, accompanied by a large procession of other captives. In direct opposition to the authority of the papacy and in its full view, the emperor subsequently offered the *carroccio* to the commune of

Rome to stand on the Campidoglio (or Capitol) as material witness to the restoration under his leadership of imperial rule. The accompanying inscription informed its readers that this spoil of war 'makes plain the triumphs of Caesar'. Frederick II was shaping himself as the divinely appointed, legitimate successor to the founder of Roman empire and first emperor, Julius Caesar. In so doing, he also staged himself as Caesar triumphant. Frederick assumed the panoply of the Roman general better to keep it, and the imperial authority of ancient Rome which it represented, from the papal curia. Although not yet an antiquarian imitation of specific details, Frederick's strategy initiated the secular reanimation of the triumphs of Julius Caesar.

The representation of Julius Caesar triumphant in medieval iconography demonstrates the substantial historical imprecision with which his triumphs were viewed in this period, even where that representation was designed to illustrate the text of an historical chronicle of ancient Rome. A miniature from a late thirteenth-century manuscript of the *Historiae romanorum* or *Liber ystoriarum romanorum* frames its depiction of a triumph top and bottom with an explanation in Italian: 'How Julius Caesar subjugated the regions of the east and west' and 'How he returned to Rome with victory'. Remnants of the ancient choreography of the triumph are still discernible. A soldier heading the procession as it goes through a gateway of the city carries a war trophy; prisoners walk alongside a four-horse chariot; a winged victory crowns Julius Caesar with a wreath. But otherwise the image is a very loose approximation derived from a variety of surviving monumental models, such as the triumphal entry depicted on the arch of emperor Titus. The city itself repeats in outline contemporary urban architecture. The manuscript was written and illustrated in Rome and, arguably, commissioned by a Roman senator. The illustration's fusion of past and present supports the work's general project of articulating and legitimating the Roman commune's aspirations to regain the imperial power so evident in its classical history – the depiction of an ancient emperor heading triumphantly into the modern city is sufficient argument.

Julius Caesar appeared at the head of a procession of victims of all-conquering Love in Petrarch's vernacular poem *I Trionfi* (c.1338–1374). As we saw in the last chapter, the poem reshaped medieval allegorical drama along the contours of a Roman triumph so as to generate an epic narrative that proceeds to the victory of spiritual redemption. Chastity triumphs over Love and is in turn overcome by Death; Death may be overcome by those individuals who have earned Fame. In the fourth triumph, Julius Caesar reappears along with Scipio (as Roman men of action and well-known *triumphatores*) to lead the laurelled band of Fame's followers. But the commemoration here of military achievement touches on the ambivalence of the original Roman triumph and on those of Caesar in particular. The fame which the original ritual bestowed on its protagonists is in this new metaphoric context recognized to be utterly fragile, and the pursuit of it becomes the greatest of human vanities. For, in the processional form of Petrarch's poem, Time next triumphs over Fame, and Time in turn is overcome by Eternity (with its promise of salvation for the virtuous). Julius Caesar does not have the virtue to advance beyond Fame's temporary triumph and, moreover, seems just to be beaten into second place by Scipio, whose triumph for victory over Carthage receives extensive attention in Petrarch's Latin epic *Africa*, where he is also hailed as a hero of republican liberty.

Across Petrarch's works, however, it is possible to discern a duality towards Caesar. At first condemned as the original tyrant, Caesar is gradually reinstated in the later works as symbol of legitimate government, because he is newly understood as instigator of a desired national unity and Italy's imperial expansion. Thus later visual representations of Petrarch's *Trionfi*, when read individually rather than as part of an overarching narrative, can appear to stabilize the triumph of Fame as a permanent pictorial glorification of those who have performed great deeds. An enormous tapestry of the early sixteenth century, woven in Brussels, displays on its left the chariot of Death drawn by four bulls over which the figure of Fame flies, and on the right Lady Fame triumphant on her chariot drawn by four elephants; these are surrounded by ancient heroes, at whose centre stands the Roman general Julius Caesar.

Pageantry became an essential feature of politics in the Renaissance. All the states, courts and major cities of Europe used it as a dramatic and persuasive mechanism for relaying their identity, integrity and authority to participating citizens and to foreign observers. From the late fourteenth century, such pageantry began regularly to include elements of the Roman triumph, driven by the new humanist engagement with *renovatio*, or the renewal of classical antiquity. Autocrats, in particular, abandoned Christian humility to appropriate the triumph back from the Church and transfer to themselves its historic glorification of the fearless, divinely sanctioned individual, military might and territorial ambition. In a fusion of Roman custom, Christian allegory and local festal tradition, the medieval ritual of the city-entry was transformed into a triumph of absolutism.

In its early stages the triumphal entry did not draw directly on historical accounts of particular Roman models but on their more recent metaphoric evocation, such as in the *Trionfi* of Petrarch and pictorial renditions of his poem. But the entry did change in form away from the medieval presentation to the ruler as audience of allegorical religious tableaux, better to match the Roman focus on the procession itself as vehicle for symbolism. The political drama of the city-entry was now staged as a Roman triumphal procession with a classicizing *mise en scène*, Roman props, and even on occasion the appearance of Julius Caesar himself as a player.

Two examples may suffice. In 1443, the king of Aragon made a ceremonial entry into Naples. He entered the city he had besieged, centre of the only kingdom in Italy, in military triumph as its new sovereign Alfonso I. The procession was choreographed as an amalgam of sacred and profane symbolism. The Spanish *triumphator* rode into the city in a gilded chariot drawn by the requisite white horses and, recalling the delicate silk awning provided by Julius Caesar in his original triumphs but now diverted from the protection of spectators to that of the protagonist himself, a canopy of cloth of gold was held over him by a whole host of nobles. The king was escorted by knights, priests, musicians and city worthies to finish his journey at the cathedral, where he attended a *Te Deum* – appropriate substitute for the Roman sacrifice to Jupiter on the Capitoline hill. And instead of prisoners to precede him, there rode the seven virtues on horseback. This being one of the first Renaissance triumphs to sustain the Roman theme, an actor provided explanations of the allegorical figures paraded before the crowds (such as Fortune and Virtue) – an actor wearing the toga and laurel crown of Julius Caesar. Only the actor wore a laurel crown. Alfonso had refused it, claiming with ostentatious humility that he dared not compare himself with the mighty Roman, but perhaps aware of the ruinous political ambition that had been paraded in the dictator's triumphs.

Julius Caesar again figured as performer, though in a more confident role, when Borso d'Este, Duke of Ferrara, Modena and Reggio, entered Reggio Emilia ceremonially in 1452. There, again in a fusion of sacred dramatic allegory and profane triumphal procession, he was welcomed at the city gates by its patron saint and received its sceptre and keys from a circle of cherubim. Triumphal chariots bore along allegorical figures such as Justice and Charity, and the procession ended at the cathedral, where the apostle Peter placed a laurel crown on the Duke's head. And Julius Caesar, accompanied by seven nymphs or virtues, bestowed his blessing on the Italian *triumphator*. No hesitancy then for the Duke in assimilating himself to the Roman dictator. And, in a rhetorical strategy to be repeated over and over again in the records of such events, the court chronicler bolstered one purpose of the event by comparing the Italian triumph's protagonist unequivocally to sovereign Caesar.

This taste for the revival of the Roman triumph expanded beyond the streets of (especially) Italian cities into every sector of the visual arts including, perhaps most curiously, the decorative panels of wedding chests. And, towards the end of the fifteenth century, this taste became ever more antiquarian and archaeological, drawing on the classical texts newly rediscovered by humanist scholars and their more systematic archaeological interest in the material remains of Roman ritual, so that the specificity of Julius Caesar's triumphs began to re-emerge.

The Triumphs of Caesar, painted at Mantua by Andrea Mantegna over a period of some seven years (c.1485–92), are particularly significant. They constitute the first known post-classical attempt at an accurate visual reconstruction of the Roman triumph and, furthermore, a noteworthy departure from the medieval and early Renaissance conventions for depicting Julius Caesar, where he had generally figured in fresco and tapestry cycles as merely one member – however significant – of a group of 'nine worthies' or 'famous men' (see Chapter 1). The processional sequence of nine life-size painted canvas panels, now in the Orangery at Hampton Court Palace, is exclusively concerned with the particularities of Julius Caesar triumphant.

Mantegna's series is possibly incomplete, as its procession ends with the *triumphator* and not, as was the Roman custom, with his parading army. It has also suffered considerable damage and a history of drastic restoration and repainting. Yet it still depicts in escalating succession and extraordinary detail a parade of standards, pictures and replicas of towns captured, statues of gods, siege equipment, tablets and military trophies, spoils of silver and gold vessels, sacrificial oxen, trumpeters, elephants, prisoners and much more. Finally, in the last panel, Julius Caesar makes his entry seated on a highly decorative two-wheeled cart (Figure 6.1).

In his depiction of Julius Caesar's triumphs, Mantegna appears to have drawn on contemporary antiquarian studies of the Roman ceremony, such as Flavio Biondo's *Roma triumphans* (1457–9) and Roberto Valturio's *De re militari* (1460), alongside the classical account by Suetonius. At first glance, the processional sequence appears to be specified as the first, Gallic triumph, since Panel 2 includes in its parade the inscription 'for conquered Gaul', but

Fig. 6.1 *The Triumphs of Caesar* (c.1485–92), A. Mantegna. Panel 9: Caesar on his Chariot.

instead Mantegna merges all five triumphs into one supreme event. In Panel 5 we can spot the elephants and candelabra Suetonius allocated to the Gallic triumph, but the slogan '*veni, vidi, vici*' of the Pontic triumph in Panel 9; an Ethiopian in 1, spoils from the East in 4 and 6, Greek captives in 7, a Phrygian musician in 8, an Hispanic standard in 9. But the painter omits the images of Pompeians slain which were originally paraded in Caesar's African triumph and sustains a difference throughout between the appearance of soldiers and captives, thus eliding some of the troublesome, civil-war dimensions to Julius Caesar's triumphalism.

Mantegna also incorporated elements from other Roman triumphs, familiar from the main classical texts which by now were all in print and, most probably, in the Mantuan court library. For example, from Plutarch's account of the opulent triumph of Aemilius Paulus against the Macedonians are borrowed some of the spoils in the first few panels and the grouping of the Greek captives in Panel 7. Other features appear to be influenced by Mantega's knowledge of ancient artefacts and architecture: his reconstruction includes a column and a triumphal arch which recall imperial triumphal monuments still surviving in the city of Rome, such as Trajan's column and the triumphal arches of Titus and of Constantine. So this Julius Caesar triumphant stockpiles for himself all the best features of other Roman triumphs (whether republican or imperial) to become the Roman *triumphator* par excellence. And most of Caesar's troublesome dimensions can be painted over.

In this novel blend of literary and figurative traditions, and of classical and modern materials (classical artefacts in a state of romantic decay, a Petrarchan triumphal cart, fifteenth-century weaponry), touches of barbarity as well as nobility of purpose are discernible. Some critics have suggested that the painter translates the terrible vexation over the Spanish triumph described by Plutarch (quoted above) into a visual representation of aural dissonance. In Panel 3, a towering, angled structure of military spoils is so loosely held together by wooden supports and knotted thongs that it conveys of itself the dreadful racket of clanging metal its movement will create. Others note that whereas the first six panels are choreographed as a forward surge, Panel 7 changes to a much slower pace as it focuses in on a pack of captives shuffling across a more claustrophobic, urban landscape. The panel doubly invites its viewers to feel pity: pity for the captives who pointedly include women and children, breast-feeding babies and their nurses; pity with the internal spectators, tiny in scale and trapped uncomfortably behind a window grating. *The Triumphs of Caesar*, viewed in this way, take on the hue of a sombre tragedy.

The pressure to adopt a gaze which moves in narrative sequence from first to last panel, however, allows the viewer of *The Triumphs* to loiter only for a moment on such pathetic details. The vast series progresses inexorably away from the portrayal of the somewhat alien and menacing characteristics of a distant ritual in Panels 1 to 7 towards scenes, in Panels 8 and 9, which better merge with the current festive processional form of the High Renaissance. It also presents Julius Caesar's claims to supreme authority in relatively reassuring terms. Already in Panel 7 he is formulated as no despot: above his huddled captives is borne the inscription 'for the liberator of the city'. In Panel 9, he appears in civic toga not military armour, seated not standing, serene not forbidding, even as his supreme power is expressed spatially – raised up, alone, high above the others (Figure 6.1). And as viewers scan each panel in turn, their gaze is persistently directed up towards the Roman *triumphator* by many an admiring backward glance from the celebrants who process before him.

The context of the production and display of *The Triumphs of Caesar* also encourages a reading of the panels as a glorification of military force and political absolutism, as an instructive depiction of the presumed occasion when the whole of Rome gave sanction to its general's assumption of dictatorial powers. Mantegna's work had been commissioned by the Gonzaga family to decorate the public halls of their palace in Mantua. Although it did not contain their portraits, its themes were highly pertinent to their interests. For example, Francesco Gonzaga (who became the Marchese in 1484) shaped himself as a valiant soldier-prince and evinced considerable zeal for wars in which he could enlarge his subject territories. Saluted by the court poet as a 'new Caesar', he might now be understood to embody or even rival the militant qualities of the old Caesar in his possession and on public display in his palace.

The Gonzaga had further cause to look upon a depiction of the triumphant parade of Julius Caesar's supremacy as an instrument for their own legitimation (and to expect that it would so be seen by others), since in 1433 they had seized Mantua as their own imperial dominion and established themselves as its dynastic rulers. A painted Caesar triumphant, therefore, might provide the Gonzaga with a glorious historical precedent (however short-lived the original might have been) for their own usurpation of power and imperial claims.

Straightaway *The Triumphs of Caesar* began to accrue their own fame, until they were one of the most celebrated and copied artworks of the sixteenth and early seventeenth centuries. The Gonzaga gave away prints as gifts of state, and later other governments and rulers also came to display the paintings (or copies of them) as a metaphoric legitimation of their rule. Xylographies (multi-block woodcuts) increased the circulation of Mantegna's triumphant Caesar even further, and from such woodcuts other versions were adapted and exhibited as drawings, engravings, friezes, paintings, tapestries, dishes and caskets. By this means, Julius Caesar's visual ascendance as the definitive *triumphator* was secured for centuries (with Scipio now demoted to second place), and it stimulated the transformation of the royal entries of the late Renaissance into thoroughgoing re-stagings of the Roman sacrament of the triumph, Julius Caesar's in particular. Each re-staging became a form of ceremonial initiation – a retracing of the Roman dictator's steps in order to lead to closer identification with him.

Such re-enactments were at first concentrated in Italy, where the ritual had originated, and where different modes of government (some republics, one kingdom, many principalities, the unique papal states) vied with each other in the style and magnificence of their civic pageantry as in all else. Even the warrior pope Julius II (1503–13), who aspired to the creation of a papal empire out of the unification of the peninsula's disparate territories, staged himself as a perpetual *triumphator*, an imperial Caesar.

At the same time, however, the Roman triumph was appropriated by Italy's foreign invaders – such as the French kings Charles VIII and Louis XII or the Holy Roman Emperor Charles V – and replayed to its subjected peoples in an intimidatingly militant form. Always the 'new Caesar' processed through the streets of the subjugated Italian city in his chariot or cart (often dressed in a form of imperial Roman armour), accompanied by his troops and representations of towns and castles taken, actual spoils of war, Latin inscriptions (such as '*veni, vidi, vici*'), and appropriate personifications of his virtues and those of his kingdom (such as Fortitude, Justice, Temperance). From Italy, the re-staging of Caesar's triumphs then spread to other European countries, and often became embedded into complex royal entry festivals, such as the supremely elaborate and copiously recorded entry into Rouen in 1550 of Henri II, King of France.

These royal entry festivals were by now far more complex than a top-down celebration of political power, military might and territorial expansion; rather, they constituted a form of reciprocal trade whereby a city exchanged its public affirmation of a sovereign's authority in return for his recognition of its rights and liberties. Thus the entry at Rouen first involved a long triumphal procession which filed past the king as spectator, seated on a platform shaped like a triumphal arch. Then the king joined the end of the procession as protagonist to enter into the city past a series of *tableaux vivants* designed to flatter, entertain and educate him in the virtues by which it was hoped that he would rule over his citizen-subjects. The city authorities employed scholars, poets and artists both to design the events and, subsequently, to record them in an idealized narrative of the entry richly illustrated with woodcuts, so that a permanent record might survive of their ceremonial contract with the king (such as Figures 6.2a and b).

Fig. 6.2a Bearers of standards and trophies, from the entry of Henri II into Rouen in 1550.

After the king received obeisance from an initial cortège which included members of the monastic orders, trade guilds, civic officials and the king's own officers and troops, there followed a dramatic reconstruction of a Roman triumph that closely followed

Mantegna's visual aesthetic of Julius Caesar triumphant (via a direct
dependency on a series of woodcuts of *The Triumphs* made by
Jacques de Strasbourg in 1503). Legionaries and their captains
dressed in Roman style preceded a series of three symbolic chariots surmounted by Fame, Religion (or Victory in some accounts)
and Good Fortune, in between which paraded trumpeters crowned
with laurel, bands of armed men bearing trophies and spoils such as
amphorae, cups and vases, and banners representing fortresses of
Boulogne recently captured from the English (Figure 6.2a), as well
as a sacrificial lamb, animals dressed as caparisoned elephants and
slaves as bare-foot oriental captives. The goddess Flora and her
nymphs threw flowers before the hooves of the caparisoned horses
dressed as 'unicorns' which drew the third and final chariot (Figure
6.2b). On it an effigy of the king, with representations of four of
the royal children in front of him, sat on a throne dressed in royal
robes, a sceptre in one hand. In marked imitation of Mantegna's
depiction of Julius Caesar, Good Fortune, straddling her customary

Fig. 6.2b The Chariot of Good Fortune, from the entry of Henri II into Rouen in 1550.

wheel held an imperial crown over the king, his hair styled –
according to one account – '*à la césarienne*'. Immediately after followed the dauphin on horseback, fifty men at arms representing the
Norman barons, infantry, children of honour and gentlemen of the
royal household, until finally the king left his platform to join the
procession and enter Rouen escorted by princes of the royal house
and a guard of archers. On route, Henri was presented with a series
of spectacular tableaux beginning, just outside the city walls, with
a Brazilian village at war and ending with the Elysian fields of a ter-
restrial paradise. Thus the king's own ideology of military combat
and conquest is celebrated in the Caesarian triumph but in the
course of the narrative tableaux is left behind, to be replaced ultimately by a civic vision of peace and concord.

Of all the triumphs of the new Caesars staged across the states of
Europe in the course of the sixteenth century and beyond (and
revived yet again in the early nineteenth century to give a glossy
sheen of classical dignity and importance to the empire of the
Napoleons), perhaps one deserves a final mention for the relative
singularity of its focus and the degree of confidence with which it
appropriated Julius Caesar. Cardinal Cesare Borgia crossed his own
Rubicon into secular life in Chapter 4, above. In February 1500,
returning from military campaigns in Romagna, he staged his own
entry into Rome in triumph as Duc de Valentinois, victorious
general of the papal armies. Choreography and content evoked the
ancient ritual prescriptions. On the first day, the procession into the
city included a parade of papal infantry in full armour, and a hundred grooms and mace-bearers to act as the Duke's bodyguard
while wearing, embroidered in the middle of their doublets in
thread of silver, the legend CESAR. After the cavalry, the Duke
himself entered the city followed by carts full of spoils. They rolled
past the Castel Sant'Angelo, where huge banners floated alluding to
Cesare's exploits on the battlefield. Saluted there by a salvo of

artillery fire, the general then completed his journey to the Vatican, to attend a service held by his father the pope. The second day, a similarly spectacular but allegorical procession followed. Eleven decorated carts bore tableaux concerning the exploits of the original Caesar, including his crossing of the Rubicon. In the last sat Caesar himself, enthroned, and crowned with the laurels of victory. Cesare accompanied this second procession on horseback to arrive, for a second time, at the Vatican. In this case the represented Caesar was made to retrace the steps of the living Caesar, the old to ape the new. An eyewitness aptly concluded in his diaries that on this occasion the ancient model had found its precise rapport (not to say its transcendence) in reality.

7

LIBERTY AND TYRANNY

Government, 49–44 BC

Julius Caesar's mode of government was the subject of hot debate right from its violent beginnings. As it became ever more authoritarian, the presentation of his political legitimacy was gradually countered by at first guarded and then, eventually, lethal opposition. The conspiracy to assassinate him was built on philosophical questions: Which is the best mode of government? Is monarchy tolerable? Before, during and immediately after the assassination, liberty was proclaimed against the tyranny Caesar embodied. Ancient writers subsequently wrestled with the difficulty of distinguishing between the merits of the dictator's government and of his murder. Once his government was understood, with sufficient hindsight, as the initiation of a sharp turning point in the history of Western culture from republic to imperial monarchy, so Caesar's political actions came to provide fundamental historic models to imitate or to shun. Julius Caesar took his place in Western political discourse and action as a call to revolution, an instrument of monarchic or dictatorial legitimation, a justification of repression, a precedent for assassination.

Yet, paradoxically, the Roman general's hold on government was short and fragile. Not the five years from crossing the Rubicon in January 49 BC to assassination in March 44, if account is taken of his prolonged absences from Rome on campaign, in constant civil war, across the extremities of the Roman empire. Perhaps between five and six months from last triumph (the victorious return from Spain in October 45 BC) to bloody death, if viewed in terms of the tranquillity of a sovereign (Velleius Paterculus, *Roman Histories* 2.56.3) or mastery of the world (Napoleon, *Précis des guerres de César*, 1836: 207). Not even that, according to some modern historians, for in that brief period military revolt against Julius Caesar's government scarcely ever ceased.

Whatever the political programmes and aspirations attributed to Julius Caesar by conspirators or supporters, later imitators or detractors, no evidence survives to suggest that the Roman general overtly laid claim to the destruction of the republic, the creation of a monarchy or the institution of a new order. At first, liberty was a watchword on both sides. After crossing the Rubicon, Caesar articulated his aims as being partially political, but also personal. In his own commentary on the civil war, he justifies his invasion as needed

> to defend himself from the insults of his foes, to restore to their position [*dignitas*] the tribunes of the people who at that conjuncture had been expelled from the state, to assert the freedom [*libertas*] of himself and the Roman people who had been oppressed by a small faction.
>
> (Julius Caesar, *Civil War* 1.22.5. Trans. A. G. Peskett, 1914)

Here Caesar takes as his own catchphrase the restoration of *libertas* (or the freedom of speech and action that was marked as a defining characteristic of the Roman republic, setting it apart from the tyranny of the earlier regal period), although he aligns it with the restoration of *dignitas* (that of the tribunes and, first and foremost, his own).

Yet the liberation asserted by the dictator, and stamped on his coinage of the period, could be understood otherwise: as a petty desire to prevent his opponents from terminating the glorious career he had, in his view, merited. The reassuring appeal to *libertas* and the statement of small-scale, negotiable grievances might also be read as a strategic contrast to the grand claims of Caesar's enemies. With the errant general declared an enemy of the state, his opponents could present themselves as representatives of constitutional authority, fighting a patriotic war for the preservation of liberty and the republic (both understood in limited, aristocratic terms), a war that permitted no negotiation with traitors.

Less than three months after the Rubicon crossing, the dreadful prospect of tyranny was already an anguished theme of Cicero's private correspondence, although in one such letter it was doubly hedged – written in Greek, and presented as an increasingly dramatic set of questions of principle. For example:

> If one's country is being tyrannized, what are the
>   arguments in favour of helping it by verbal means
>   and when occasion arises, rather than by war?
> Is it statesmanlike, when one's country is under a tyranny, to
>   retire to some other place and remain inactive there, or
>   ought one to brave any danger in order to liberate it?
> If one's country is under a tyranny, is it right to proceed
>   to its invasion and blockade?
>   (Cicero, *Letter to Atticus* 9.4.2. Trans. M. Grant, 1960)

A more concise, concrete version might read: Should I write about Caesar's illegal seizure of power or join Pompey's army and fight against it?

While Julius Caesar's opponents sustained and gradually fortified their denouncements of tyranny and appeals to liberty, *libertas* does

not seem to have sat so well with the dictator. As his military cam-
paigning against Roman citizens became more bloody and his
political powers departed further and further from republican tradition, it was soon supplanted in his propaganda with such concepts
as security and clemency. Yet even *clementia*, which Caesar took up
as a key policy, attracted controversy or, at the least, some suspicion.

Clemency often figures in the recorded conduct of the dictator
and in complimentary representations such as his coinage and senatorial decrees (whether of temples or thanksgivings). In September
46 BC, for example, Julius Caesar acceded to a request to recall and
restore a senator who had fought against him and was his most
prominent surviving enemy. Not having spoken in the senate for
two years, Cicero opened a speech of thanks fulsomely: 'It would
be quite impossible to refrain from commenting on this remarkable
leniency, this unaccustomed and indeed unprecedented clemency,
this unique moderation on the part of a ruler whose power is
supreme, this unbelievable and almost superhuman wisdom' (*pro
Marcello* 1, trans. M. Grant 1969). Yet while the ruler in question
regularly depicted himself, in the *Civil War*, demonstrating generosity towards his defeated opponents, he did not describe his
policy in terms like those of Cicero. Under the republic, clemency
was a virtue to be exercised by the Roman state and her generals on
the state's behalf. The beneficiaries were to be either foreigners
defeated, captured or killed in Rome's wars of expansion, or sub-
jects living in the provinces. Now the dictator was exercising it as
an individual towards his fellow citizens, binding them to him in a
demeaning debt of gratitude (because it could never be sufficiently
repaid). Cicero's emphasis on the absence of custom or precedent in
Caesar's act of recall, the reminder that this is a supreme ruler's
unexpected moderation (not, by implication, the cruelty or anger
usually manifested by a tyrant), may thus carry some bite.

If Julius Caesar had a coherent programme for government in

mind, there is no surviving description of it. The closest approximation is a passing, pithy reference Caesar makes to what might be achieved if, during the early stages of the civil war in 48 BC, negotiation with Pompey could be brought to a successful conclusion: tranquillity for Italy, peace for the provinces, security for the empire (*Civil War* 3.57.4).

The laws and measures the Roman dictator passed – concentrated largely in the period from April 46 to March 44 – have long been subjected to close scrutiny and debate. Do they constitute limited, ad hoc responses to some of the political, social and economic problems besetting the republic or a cohesive package of radical reforms? Should they be read as the outcome of short-term self-interest or long-term vision? For example, Caesar took steps to improve Rome's food supply, reduce debt, monumentalize the city with public building programmes, expand membership of the senate in terms of eligibility and quantity, increase the number of magisterial offices, distribute to his veterans and to the urban poor land on which to settle, grant rights or citizenship to provincial towns, reorganize provincial administration and establish Roman colonies overseas. In doing so, was he rewarding his own supporters at home and abroad, increasing their number and securing his own authority over a failing republic, or working to relieve the conditions of the city's poor, turn the Roman senate into a national body, manage better the distant parts of the growing empire and give its diverse peoples a new, imperial cohesion?

At least in the immediate aftermath of the assassination, no one suggested that the dictator had found an answer to the difficulties of government. His grieving friend Gaius Matius is reported by Cicero as saying 'if he despite his genius did not find a way out, who will find one now?' (Cicero, *Letters to Atticus* 14.1.1). Even where critics have all acknowledged the lasting and beneficial effect of Julius Caesar's administration, his motives can still be called into question. In 46 BC, he initiated the overhaul of the old lunar calendar which consisted of 355 days plus the irregular insertion of others in alternate years. Many extra days were now added to the civic year so that it would no longer drift ahead of the seasons. From January 45, the year was now to last 365 days with an additional day inserted every fourth year. These revisions have since undergone only a few minor modifications and otherwise remain in force, but their political advantage for Caesar has also been noted. Now even time itself was to be governed by the dictator, given a new precision and, thus reordered, enclose within an apparent naturalness the autocracy it was measuring.

Most controversial of all, however, were the mechanisms by which Julius Caesar governed. After his invasion of Italy and armed seizure of power, the Roman general restored a semblance of constitutional scruple and republican administration by orchestrating his appointment to a number of temporary dictatorships (understood traditionally as emergency military commands) interspersed with election to a succession of consulships. Yet, simultaneously, he controlled Roman armies and the state treasury, appointed governors abroad, fixed the candidacies for office at home, directed the votes of the popular assembly and often used the senate merely to ratify prior decisions, regularly preferred personal decrees over public legislation, employed a large staff of private advisers and, when absent at war, continued to rule through his agents.

In the African campaign of early 46 BC, on the battlefields where propaganda stakes were at their highest, Caesar's soldiers were the recipients of pamphlets encouraging them to liberate the senate and the people of Rome from tyranny such as this. From April of that year, political criticism focused around the dead Cato. Critics such as Cicero and Brutus acclaimed Cato's suicide in the theatre of war and eulogized the conservative republican as an exemplary stoic and political martyr. A relatively safe first stab at Caesar, 'praise of Cato' subsequently developed into a widespread rhetorical code for assaults on European and American autocrats. Sufficiently stung, the Roman general, even as he was involved in further military action in Spain, prepared a rebuttal of such works. Couched not as a defence of self against accusations of tyranny, but as an *Anti-Cato*, the work comprised a catalogue of toxic, personal abuse.

Victory in Spain in March 45 BC, the ostensible end to civil war, and the disturbing celebration in October of a triumph over fellow Romans, together signal an even more authoritarian direction to Julius Caesar's government and the start of more direct demonstration against it. The senate decreed the erection of a temple to the goddess *Libertas* (whose function it was to protect her worshippers against political servitude to foreign enemies or domestic tyrants), and the casting of a statue of the dictator as a new liberator from tyranny. This and the bestowal on Caesar of the honorific title *Liberator* are best read not as propagandist strategies initiated by the dictator himself, but as overtures to him at the apparent closure of the civil war, reminders of his as yet unfulfilled pledge 'to assert the freedom of himself *and* the Roman people'.

Caesar seems instead to have favoured a self-image as Saviour of Rome from ruin, as new Founder and as Father (*parens patriae*). The last of these three honorific titles conveniently transposed the supreme authority which the Roman general had captured militarily into the more comfortable realm of the domestic. The political parity and reciprocity expected between citizens of a republic were now radically revised, naturalized, and preserved in terms of the hierarchical love of a father for his children and the children's respect for, and duty to, their father. Thus infantilized, Julius Caesar's 'children' were required, from early in 44, to pray annually for the welfare of their 'father' alongside that of the state with which he was elided.

Such attempts to stimulate familial sentiment and religious devotion were conspicuously contradicted, however, by the designation of Julius Caesar as dictator for life in February 44 BC. Modern historians concur that this new step, along with other magistracies, honours and titles (such as the hereditary use of *imperator*), amounted to a shocking rupture with the republican constitution, or at the very least its extension to breaking point. According to traditional practice, the dictatorship was a temporary military appointment and its use restricted to state emergencies. Caesar's new office was to be permanent and unhampered by collegiality, annual renewal or accountability. Moreover, it was soon to be carried out from a great distance. For, bypassing the republican tradition of free elections (however notional), the Roman general fixed senior appointments for the next two years at home and abroad, in anticipation of a grand military expedition which he was planning to lead to Parthia within a matter of weeks.

Whether or not he aspired to become another Roman king, or was seeking purposefully to found a monarchy inspired by those of the Greek East, Julius Caesar's accumulated powers now seemed to harbour a strong resemblance to those of royalty. And the countermoves of his opponents surface in the ancient sources on Caesar's last weeks in the form of an escalating catalogue of public, physical incidents when his rumoured regal ambitions were both whetted and contested. Already some six months before the climactic assassination, Cicero had piled kingship on to the accusation of tyranny in his private critiques of the dictator, because it implied a return to the abhorrent political condition at Rome's mythic origins, a terrible time of subjection out of which the republic of citizens had gloriously been born.

In the aftermath of Caesar's murder, interpretation of the momentum of his last months of government openly and sharply divided between progress (towards further war, even greater military glory, territorial expansion and the growth of empire) criminally cut short by purported friends, or decline (towards oppressive kingship, humiliating servitude, the destruction of the republic) deservedly cut off by noble tyrannicides. The reception of Julius Caesar's assassination will be considered in the next chapter; here we might note that within Cicero's philosophical works, and with an eye to the rise of Mark Antony as Caesar's political successor, the author now bluntly indicts the Caesarian mode of government.

In *de officiis* (*On Duties*), written in late autumn 44 BC and addressing the obligations to the state of the next generation of Rome's elite (and of his son in particular), Cicero presents the appalling case of the man who is prepared, in pursuit of power, to ignore all that is right and decent. Identified only obliquely as the dead Caesar, he is nonetheless described extravagantly as a man who longed to be (and became) king of the Roman people and master of all nations, and who mistakenly saw advantage for himself in tyrannizing his country:

> In the attempt to rescue him from that delusion there must be no limit to our reproaches and appeals. Who, in God's name, could possibly derive advantage from murdering his country? Of all murders that is the most hideous and repulsive: even when its perpetrator is hailed, by the citizens he has trodden underfoot, as 'Father of his Country'.
>
> (Cicero, *de officiis* 3.83. Trans. M. Grant, 1960)

Here it is tyranny (not tyrannicide) that counts as murder, and murder of the foulest kind. Julius Caesar is no father to his country but, on the contrary, its assassin. And, while he may have been deluded enough to imagine that treading Rome's citizens underfoot gave him the advantage of obtaining the prize of absolute power, in fact he gained no advantage at all. For to that position accrues great hostility, much disloyalty and little friendship. It is a life of torments, anxieties, constant terrors, plots and dangers. Having used

Rome's armies to crush Rome's people, having converted into his own personal servitude a nation once accustomed to freedom and rule over others, he grew to be most profoundly hated by very many (*de officiis* 3. 84). By his annihilation of law and freedom, then, Caesar became not father but master, Rome's citizens not children but slaves. And from those slaves was secured not love for their 'father' but hatred for their master. Of course, the truth of what Cicero says about Julius Caesar as tyrant, king and slave-master appears to be guaranteed by the dictator's recent dramatic downfall.

In contrast, when Julius Caesar's grand-nephew Octavian accepted the terms of the dictator's will (becoming son and heir), he immediately assumed his adoptive father's name and changed his own in order to be called 'Caesar, the son of Caesar'. It was precisely from this inheritance, after all, that he initially derived his popular backing, his soldiers, his finance and his claim on power. By January 27 BC, after the murder of Cicero, the suicides of the conspirators Brutus and Cassius on the battlefields of Philippi, the defeat of Antony (Octavian's rival to the succession) in 31 BC in a sea battle off Actium, and the transformation of Julius Caesar into a god, Octavian had become *Imperator Caesar Divi Filius Augustus* (in approximate translation, 'Commander-in-chief, Caesar, Son of God, Venerable').

Use of 'Caesar' as a family name (and a claim on power) was continued by all the Roman rulers of the Julio-Claudian dynasty. Although replaced under the Flavians by 'Augustus', it was eventually restored as a designation for absolute power over the Roman empire. Likewise *imperator* – originally a temporary title by which a Roman general was acclaimed for a glorious victory, then an honorific name bestowed on Caesar – developed eventually into an official designation for a political office meant to exceed even the authority of kings, namely chief of the empire (or 'emperor'). During the reign of the emperor Trajan, moreover, acknowledgement of the Roman general as 'first of the Caesars' appears to have become regularized. And, as first Caesar, the divine Julius would also be newly conceived as the crucial pivot between republicanism and monarchy; no longer the instigator of a failed attempt at sovereignty, but founder of empire and first emperor.

Surviving into the Middle Ages as a name and a political office, Caesar gave a shape to the Antichrist in ecumenical literature and dramatized the virtues (and sometimes the vices) of earthly sovereignty in secular epics and chronicles. In the fourteenth century, he was sacralized by Dante as founder of a divinely sanctioned empire now needing restoration, and in the fifteenth, at the same time as his name was taken up and lauded by Europe's ruling dynasts to give historical authority to their political ambitions, he was demonized as the quintessential usurper and tyrant, symbolic foil for the expression of a modern Italian republicanism. The battle lines of the bitter political struggle between, for example, the autocratic Visconti princes of Milan and the republican city of Florence were partially drawn up in terms of supporters or opponents of Caesar. Now under the scrutiny of humanist scholars, Julius Caesar's statecraft was often carefully distinguished from his literary and military brilliance as a model for the abolition of republican liberties; consequently, according to Machiavelli, the Roman's mode of government was an example which ought not to be followed by the princes of sixteenth-century Italy.

In the seventeenth and eighteenth centuries, Julius Caesar continued to give flesh and blood to the abstract categories of political thought, and drama to the explication of political ideologies. Distasteful embodiment of usurpation and tyranny for the English parliamentarians of the seventeenth century and some of the Enlightenment philosophers of the eighteenth, his name and his person were then vividly invoked during the American and French revolutions as Roman history was restaged, and new Brutuses rose up against their modern sovereigns.

Any of these and many other moments in the reception of Julius Caesar's mode of government deserve close attention, but my concern here begins in the nineteenth century when, in tandem with the identification of some European leaders as Caesarist, the Roman statesman helped define a new conception of government and 'Caesarism' came into being as a new political term. Caesarism is more or less understood as rule by an individual who seizes power from an elected government, establishes an authoritarian, centralized regime, is sustained by the military, and claims a democratic legitimacy. It became a key term in the political discourse of rulers, practising politicians, political philosophers and analysts, social theorists and historians, and by the century's end had entered the vernacular of political debate. Simultaneously, there developed a dispute over the utility of the term. Is there any intellectual benefit in looking to the Roman past to understand the European present? Does the regime of Julius Caesar really provide a helpful parallel for the new political formations of Europe's nation states? The process of applying or disavowing the term Caesarism, of bringing up or denying parallels between modern rulers and the Roman dictator, became of great importance to the political actors of nineteenth- and twentieth-century Europe, and a key instrument for understanding and evaluating not only modern governments but the original government of Julius Caesar himself.

At the beginning of the nineteenth century, as a populist soldier and statesman, Napoleon Bonaparte compared and encouraged the comparison of his government with that of Julius Caesar (as witnessed in Chapter 4, above). Whether admired or despised, analogy between the Roman and French generals was then regularly deployed by propagandists, intellectuals, artists and novelists throughout the nineteenth and twentieth centuries, and stimulated a reassessment of Julius Caesar's historical importance in the light of Napoleon's achievements.

Seizing power from the First Republic's national assembly in the *coup d'état* of 18 Brumaire 1799, the French general swiftly attained supreme power. Initially entitled First Consul, and authorized to hold office for ten years, Napoleon Bonaparte already had access to the licence of military dictatorship: the decisions of the First Consul did not require the backing of his two subordinates. Three years later, by an overwhelming plebiscite, he was elected First Consul for life, and in 1804, also by plebiscite, was granted the hereditary title of Emperor of the French. From then until 1815, he engaged in constant warfare across Europe to assure the hegemony of his empire. In his use of Roman history to represent himself, his passage to power and the formation of his French empire, the modern emperor was aware of the different attractions of Caesar and of Augustus as models. Augustus offered durability and the lesson to proceed discretely and in small stages to absolute power, refusing exceptional offices unless presented as the will of the people, and always declining the title of king (as it brought the risk of assassination). But Augustus could not offer the reputation of extraordinary military acumen, leadership on the battlefield or glorious territorial conquests.

Already in 1800, Napoleon's brother Lucien circulated a pamphlet which became a primary text for the construction of a tight relationship between the French and the Roman generals. *Parallèle entre César, Cromwell, Monck et Bonaparte* opens: 'There are some men who appear in certain epochs to found, destroy or repair Empires. All yield beneath their influence.' Despite its title, the work dismisses all comparisons between Napoleon I and previous historical figures as superficial, malevolent or mad, except for Julius Caesar. Napoleon is Caesar's equal as general, because they both terminated civil wars, triumphed throughout the known world, conquered barbarous peoples, and are immortalized across Italy, France and Africa. But Napoleon is Caesar's superior as politician, because Caesar overthrew the just party (1800: 10). The Bonaparte message is that the modern French empire will incorporate both the empire of Caesar and the republic of Brutus (as defender of civic order and hero of the French Revolution). In rousing alarm, the pamphlet concludes with a direct appeal to the French people to wake up: great men are subjected to greater hazards than the vulgar and, at any moment, the tranquillity which Napoleon has given to them as a gift may vanish.

After Lucien's brother had indeed succumbed to the hazards great men suffer, in exile on the island of St Helena, he passed some of his time annotating a copy of Julius Caesar's commentaries and dictating an analysis of Caesar's military campaigns. In *Précis des guerres de César* (published in 1836), Napoleon now interlinks more closely his own fate with that of the Roman dictator. The concluding eulogy of Caesar as statesman is a mechanism for implicit, self-justifying autobiography. The perpetual dictator's authority was legitimate because the senate, torn apart by earlier civil wars, was only a sham, the veterans merely served the interests of their generals not the republic, and the deliberative assemblies could no longer govern. The person of Caesar was, therefore, the guarantee of the supremacy of Rome over the universe and of the security of Roman citizens of all parties (1836: 212–13). Brutus, now transformed into an opponent of democracy, obliterated the interests of the country and the will of the people when he struck Caesar down.

Napoleon's critics both at home and abroad read Roman history differently; comparison with Julius Caesar only exposed the French emperor as a usurper and a military dictator, set on replacing republicanism with despotism, needing grandiose military victories to shore up his claims to absolute power, destined by history to fall. Nonetheless, celebratory depictions of Napoleon and Caesar as a close pair of supreme leaders framed and permeated the regime, and brought with them a radical rehabilitation of the Roman dictator after the dominance, in the fifteenth to eighteenth centuries, of the discourses of republicanism in which Caesar's government had been deplored. It is in this new context that the term 'Caesarism' emerged.

A sustained theory of Caesarism was first developed by Auguste Romieu in a short predictive polemic called *L'ère des Césars* (*The Age of the Caesars*, 1850). An ardent admirer of Napoleon Bonaparte, Romieu abhorred liberal democracy on the grounds that it deprived the nation of strong leadership. The historical sequence in which first Julius Caesar violently attempted to install a new mode of government at Rome (a monarchy based not on continuity and religion, but on military force alone), and then Caesar Augustus succeeded, was born from the necessity of the times (1850: 34). The Caesars came because they had to come (1850: 39). At present, history repeats itself. Napoleon I has been the harbinger of a new Caesarism. Now that he like Julius Caesar has fallen, there will again be a succession of military commanders, a state of civil war and then, finally, Caesarism will be properly installed.

The *coup d'état* launched by Napoleon's nephew Louis in December the following year appeared to confirm the truth of Romieu's prediction that the age of the Caesars had arrived. Consequently, Romieu's book attained very wide circulation, in many editions, even outside France, and 'Caesarism' quickly took on fashionable status as a handy label for and description of the government of the Second Empire, and as a theoretical term for a new, modern type of regime that political analysts agreed had arisen in France after the coup of 1799 and again after the subsequent coup of 1851. The nephew, they observed, had pursued a similar route to power as his uncle, and as Julius Caesar before both of them. Louis Napoleon seized control from the national assembly of a republic by military force. He invested executive power in himself as the holder of supreme office, and drastically reduced popular participation in government whilst establishing an enormous base of popular support. He sought legitimacy through plebiscites. As Napoleon III, he re-established the office of French emperor, and attempted further to expand the empire.

The new political concept of 'Caesarism' gained explanatory force because the novelty of Louis Napoleon's regime was considered to reside in the exercise of absolute power by a leader who shored himself up on ostentatiously populist foundations, while Julius Caesar was believed to have based his military dictatorship on the will of the people (rather than on law or tradition). So Napoleon III was designated a new French Caesar: military demagogue or democratic monarch. The designation was rendered especially effective because Napoleon III explicitly took both his uncle and his uncle's Caesar as models from the very moment he fashioned his coup as 'opération Rubicon' (see chapter 4, above).

During the course of the regime, between 1851 and 1871, its apologists used the term 'Caesarism' positively to signify a classical legitimacy and to justify the coupling of authoritarian leadership with popular support ostensibly to stem the complete breakdown of political institutions, check revolution, restore order, and ensure peace, prosperity and the glorious extension of empire. More often than not, however, 'Caesarism' was used negatively. Conservative opponents, confronted by Louis Napoleon's plebiscitary regime and their own fear of acquiescing to the demands of the unpropertied classes for involvement in politics, utilized 'Caesarism' in their political vocabulary as a credible means of conjoining democracy distastefully with dictatorship: the unthinking masses look for powerful leadership which, in turn, proceeds to deal with them directly and thus destroys the traditional institutions of reflective government.

Other opponents on the left saw 'Caesarism' as a means to mark the government of Napoleon III as illegitimate, to name a military dictatorship which claimed popular sovereignty but violently repressed opposition, and to herald the arrival in modern Europe of a new kind of tyranny. Others still rejected altogether the historical parallelism implied by the use of the term 'Caesarism', on the grounds either that it bestowed on Louis Napoleon's regime undeserved importance and grandeur or that it misunderstood history. Within months of the coup, Karl Marx denounced 'the eighteenth Brumaire of Louis Bonaparte' as no glorious repetition of Roman history but merely its degraded re-staging as farce (as we have seen in Chapter 4), and in the preface to the second edition of his celebrated work, published in 1869, urged the elimination of 'Caesarism' as a superficial political analogy made by schoolmasters, one which falsely elided two very different class struggles, ancient and modern.

The new French Caesar himself, Napoleon III, stepped into this controversy with the publication, in 1865 and 1866 respectively, of two volumes of his own unfinished biography *Histoire de Jules César*, which (as we saw previously) took the Roman dictator from birth as far as the further bank of the river Rubicon. Explicit reference to Napoleon I often surfaces in this partisan narrative and, in the preface to the first volume, the author dramatically aligns the murder of Julius Caesar with his uncle's captivity and exile; the appalling treatment of these two privileged and providential beings could not destroy their popular causes without comeback, causes only temporarily overthrown by a league disguised under the mask of liberty.

In order to make Julius Caesar worthy of comparison with Napoleon Bonaparte, Louis must elevate and sustain him above the somewhat ambivalent position at which he had been held at the start of the century, as well as paint him in Bonapartist colours. For the brother Lucien in 1800, the Roman was brilliant as a general, more suspect as a statesman, not quite the match for the potentiality of Napoleon Bonaparte. For the nephew Louis in 1865, Caesar was the people's choice, the guide of civilization, an ambassador of fate, terminator of civil war, steadying helmsman of a storm-tossed ship of state, instigator of a more stable, stronger, more just government. But according to the concluding paragraph of the second volume, tragically, the Roman's work had been left unfinished:

> It is not given to a man, in spite of his genius and his power, to stir up the waves of the masses as he pleases; however, when he appears, appointed by public acclaim, in the middle of the storm which has put the ship of state in danger, then he alone can steer its course and guide it to harbour. Caesar was not then the instigator of that profound perturbation of Roman society, he had become the indispensable pilot. If it had been otherwise, when he vanished all would have been put back in order; on the contrary, his death delivered the whole universe to all the horrors of war. Europe, Asia, Africa were the theatre of bloody struggles between the past and the future, and the Roman world did not find calm again until the inheritor of his name made his cause triumph.
>
> (Louis Napoleon, *Histoire de Jules César*, 1866: 516–17)

In this particular rhetorical manoeuvre, Julius Caesar becomes Napoleonic in order to make Napoleon appear indisputably Caesarist. The nephew – also the inheritor of a name which authorizes power – then marks himself out as Augustus to his uncle's Caesar. Like Romieu before him, Napoleon III attempts to predict and secure the future by narrating the progress of the Roman past.

Even with this imperial intervention, not everyone was persuaded that the age of the Caesars had now arrived. In the same year as publication of the first volume of the French emperor's history of Julius Caesar, on 11 March 1865, the British satirical magazine *Punch* carried a cartoon in which an imposing statue of a garlanded Julius Caesar looks out sternly over the seated figure of emperor Napoleon III, who is trying to blow up a balloon figure of Napoleon I to match the more majestic proportions of the Roman general (Figure 7.1). Louis, characterized disparagingly as 'an ambitious boy', boasts in Franglais, 'I sall make 'im so big as you!' The image encapsulates a hostile sense of the pretensions of the Caesarian comparison; Louis is an infantile adult, Napoleon is a flimsy, distorted and over-stretched balloon, only Caesar is a sturdy and virile statue. The caption 'Nullus Aut Caesar' ('Nobody or Caesar') recalls the motto of another overly

NULLUS AUT CÆSAR.

Louis (*An Ambitious Boy*). "AH HA! MON AMI! I SALL MAKE 'IM SO BIG AS YOU!"

Fig. 7.1 'Nullus aut Caesar', *Punch* (11 March 1865).

pretentious ruler, Cesare Borgia, who in the final analysis became nobody rather than Caesar. The *Punch* cartoon suggests the same fate awaits Louis and his Caesarist ambitions. And, indeed, within six years France was to face humiliating defeat in the Franco-Prussian war, the emperor was exiled to England, and the course of French history tore apart both the Roman parallel and the Napoleonic thesis that Caesarism brings the people security and even happiness.

Even before the publication of Napoleon III's history of an infamously Bonapartist Julius Caesar, the German politician and historian of classical antiquity, Theodor Mommsen, was working to extricate the Roman statesman from any connection with Napoleon Bonaparte, to elevate him high above the Napoleonic dynasty and to protect him from any taint with which his modern imitators and their detested Caesarism might otherwise infect him. In his monumental history of Rome, *Römische Geschichte* (narrated over five books and published between 1854 and 1856), towards the end of his last book, where he is outlining the transition from the old republic to a new military monarchy, Mommsen launches into an unrelenting encomium of the dictator. Across eleven pages, the author judges Julius Caesar to be not only pivotal in history but also profoundly balanced in character; the Roman was gifted with both mighty creative power and a most penetrating intellect, the highest energy of will and the highest capacity of execution, filled with republican ideals yet born to be a king, culturally both Roman and Hellenistic. The inclusiveness of his personality thus made of Julius Caesar 'the entire and perfect man' (5.313).

The born ruler whom Mommsen envisages would never have resorted to the brutality of the 18 Brumaire. His impulse was to social reform, and he ruled the state as a democratic monarch not, in the manner of Napoleon, as a tyrant:

Caesar, from the outset and as it were by hereditary right the head of the popular party, had for thirty years borne aloft its banner without ever changing or even so much as concealing his colours; he remained democrat even when monarch. As he accepted . . . the heritage of his party, as he displayed the bitterest, even personal, hatred to the aristocracy and the genuine aristocrats; and as he retained unchanged the essential ideas of Roman democracy, viz. alleviation of the burdens of debtors, transmarine colonization, gradual equalization of the differences of rights among the classes belonging to the state, emancipation of the executive power from the senate: his monarchy was so little at variance with democracy, that democracy on the contrary only attained its completion and fulfilment by means of that monarchy.

(Mommsen, The History of Rome. Trans.
W. P. Dickson, 1913. Volume 5: 324–5)

According to Mommsen, Julius Caesar was a unique and visionary political genius; only he appreciated the utter dishonesty of Roman politics and understood its sole remedy to be the strong rule of a benevolent dictator. He laboured for the rebirth of the nation, which was fortunate enough to be represented by a man in whom it was entitled to have infinite faith.

A teleological conception of history permeates this narrative of the collapse of the Roman republic and Julius Caesar's part in it. Drawing on the philosophy of world history articulated by Hegel in his lectures at the University of Berlin between 1822 and 1831, in Mommsen's *History of Rome* it is destiny that the republic, not Caesar, should fall. For the idealist philosopher Hegel, Alexander the Great, Julius Caesar and Napoleon were all great men of history, not just conquerors of Asia, Gaul and Europe respectively, but genuine radicals demolishing old structures and erecting new. All were profoundly cognizant of the historical needs of their age. And in Caesar's case, the world-historic end by which he was propelled was to advance the Roman state from the lie that was the republic and do so through the imposition of his undivided sovereignty. For the classical scholar too, the Roman state as victim of an illiberal, incapable, aristocratic oligarchy had necessitated rescue in the form of Julius Caesar's monarchy.

Yet, in Mommsen's view, this did not mean that presumptuous French imitators should be set beside the Roman Caesar:

> It is true that the history of past centuries ought to be the instructress of the present; but not in the vulgar sense, as if one could simply by turning over the leaves discover the conjunctures of the present in the records of the past, and collect from these the symptoms for a political diagnosis and the specifics for a prescription; it is instructive only so far as the observation of older forms of culture reveals the organic conditions of civilization generally – the fundamental forces everywhere alike, and leads and encourages men, not to unreflecting imitation, but to independent reproduction. In this sense the history of Caesar and of Roman Imperialism, with all the unsurpassed greatness of the master-worker, with all the historical necessity of the work, is in truth a sharper censure of modern autocracy than could be written by the hand of man.
>
> (Mommsen, *The History of Rome*.
> Trans. W. P. Dickson, 1913. Volume 5: 325–6)

In this well-known addendum to the second edition of his work, published in 1857, the German historian argues that the life of Caesar which he has been narrating offers an indictment of modern Caesarism, not a justificatory analogy or political prescription for it. While the violent actions of the Roman general were necessary in the specific historical circumstances of oligarchic absolutism and Rome's slave society, in contemporary conditions of increasing capitalism and Europe's urban, industrial society, unreflecting imitation of such actions constitutes usurpation and tyranny. Modern states require their own distinctive forms of liberal-democratic government. Caesarism (both as governmental form and political term) is a hideous mockery of the Roman statesman's programme, and the author ends his chapter on the transformation of ancient republic into military monarchy pointedly, by entitling the dictator 'the first, and withal unique, Imperator Caesar' (5.442).

In many different editions, and in translations which began to appear within a few short years of its first publication, *The History of Rome* swiftly became one of the most widely read and influential works on Julius Caesar of the nineteenth century. However, the insertion of an explicit rejection of Caesarism into the second edition constitutes the author's unsuccessful attempt to stem contemporary readings of his narrative as an advocacy of Caesarism, if not for France then certainly for Germany. Readers had been encouraged by the vivid rhetorical devices with which Mommsen sought to relate the history of the Roman republic's collapse to the political life of the nineteenth century (by, for example, the modernity of his language and comparisons), and by his own well-known political activism, to understand the work as an 'instructress of the present', as a tract for their times.

A revolutionary journalist during the upheavals of 1848, and then a liberal politician, Theodor Mommsen had supported the formation of a unified German nation out of the previously loose federation of principalities, and opposed the Prussian aristocracy as an obstacle to the liberalization and modernization of Germany. Now his account of the overthrow of the Roman senate (characterized as the necessary demolition of the authority of a corrupt and reactionary aristocracy) was comprehended as an invitation to its 'independent reproduction' in the overthrow of the conservative squirearchy of Prussia. But many of his readers also began to understand his eulogistic characterization of Julius Caesar as giving shape to the ideal leader for a modern, dominating Prussia – militaristic, pragmatic, anti-constitutional, populist and reformist.

Although 'Caesarism' was a term bound up at first with Bonapartism, and the populist, authoritarian rule of Napoleon III in particular, after the double downfall of the French Caesars its use became less restricted and more widespread. Whilst in the taxonomies of political scientists it would be deployed to mark out and explain plebiscitary domination as a subset of tyranny, 'Caesarism' continued to have a place in the popular political discourse of the late nineteenth century loosely to characterize modern autocratic regimes, such as that established by Otto von Bismarck, prime minister of Prussia from 1862, imperial chancellor of the new German empire or Second Reich from 1871 to 1890. Thus, despite Theodor Mommsen's sustained and staunch opposition throughout his political life to the domestic authoritarianism of Bismarck, the classicist's history of revolution, military monarchy, imperial expansion and the strong, dominating leadership of a man of action came to be read as nationalistic longing, fulfilled (for good or ill) in the powerful Reich established by the chancellor's iron hand.

When the German states were victorious in their war with France, king William I of Prussia was proclaimed emperor of Germany and assumed the suitably imperial title of Kaiser; but it was his chancellor, as founder of the Reich and leader of the newly unified German nation-state, who was more commonly described as a Caesarist ruler, and the style of government which he established as Caesarism. At the turn of the century, for example, the renowned sociologist Max Weber discriminated in his political writings between types of Caesarism. In his view, the best form – and that which deserved emulation in Germany – consisted of plebiscitary leadership embedded within a dynamic parliamentary and demo-cratic system, such as might be found in a British prime minister or an American president. Bismarck's government, in contrast, had been a profoundly detrimental form of Caesarism. Conducted out-side parliamentary structures, it had accordingly failed to modernize Germany and promote the new state to the level of a world power.

In Weber's analysis, Bismarck had been a Caesarist on a number of counts. Masked by a legitimate monarch, he had illegitimately acquired quasi-dictatorial authority: transferring the powers of the political parties, parliament and cabinet to a Reich executive under his direct authority; accumulating offices in his own person (chan-cellor, prime minister, foreign minister, minister of finance). He had severely limited the powers of his parliamentary opponents in the Reichstag while simultaneously seeking popular acclamation by appealing directly to the electorate. And, during the 1870s and 1880s, he had acquired a personality cult, a Caesarian myth of charismatic leadership, a unique, heroic stature as unifier and founder of the German nation.

The characterization of the German chancellor's rule as Caesarism took on especial vitality during the early 1870s, in rela-tion to his authoritarian control over Germany's domestic development and his violent conflict with the Catholic Church in particular. In 1870, as part of an offensive against the growth of sec-ularism and liberalism, the Vatican Council proclaimed the infallibility of the pope in matters of faith. Such interventions stim-ulated forceful responses, such as the powerful critique of the Catholic Church published in 1874 by the British statesman and recent prime minister William Gladstone. In Germany, Bismarck initiated a virulent and systematic *Kulturkampf* ('struggle for civi-lization') against the Catholic Church and its political representative, the Centre party. Repressive legislation, for example, included the introduction in 1871 of a new offence under the penal code according to which clerics could be prosecuted and imprisoned if, during religious services, they preached about matters of state in a way that might 'endanger public order'; and, in 1875, the requirement of a civil ceremony for marriage. In the counter-rhetoric of the Church, these moves served to demonstrate that the disease of Caesarism – the illegitimate primacy of state over church, the civil over the spiritual – was on the rise in Germany. In 1873 the Archbishop of Westminster and titular head of English Catholicism, Henry Edward, dramatically attacked Bismarck and his government for controlling the actions of the Church in Germany and for persecuting Catholics. Prussia, he claimed, is rejecting the Church of God and replacing it with the deification of Caesar. Divine Caesar and the Vicar of Christ are two persons and two powers between whom there can be no peace.

A cartoon in the American political magazine *Harper's Weekly* for 16 January 1875 translates the *Kulturkampf* into ancient Roman (and New Testament) terms under the caption 'Amphitheatre Flavius, Rome, MDCCCLXXV. Caesar Having Things Rendered Unto Him'. On the far right, down below in the arena, the diminutive figures of Gladstone and a soldier embodying Germany physically abuse the pope and pull his crown of religious office down over his face. On the left, and filling most of the image, the giant figure of Bismarck sits enthroned, caricatured by means of his whiskers, his corpulence and his infamous love of food and drink, while dressed and situated as a Roman emperor enjoying the spectacle of his Christian persecutions from the luxury of an imperial box. Set in the 'amphitheatre Flavius', however, the cartoon discloses the degree to which the designation of the autocratic German chancellor as a modern 'Caesar' has lost much of the word's precise bond with the first Roman Caesar, Gaius Julius.

Although Bismarck often appeared in a general's uniform at sessions of the Reichstag, he had won the rank through political rather than military triumphs, while after 1870 he ceased to pursue an aggressive or expansionist foreign policy. Although military seizure of power was constantly threatened as a means of crisis management, none took place under Bismarck's leadership. Constitutionally he was no dictator, but instead was dependent for his appointment on the Prussian king. Nor did he ever attempt to identify himself with Julius Caesar or have himself written into the life of the Roman general, as had the recent French Caesars.

Nevertheless, for several decades to come, many German intellectuals and writers – often looking back nostalgically at Bismarck as founder of Germany and its empire – expressed yearning for a new Caesarist saviour, even quite specifically a German Julius Caesar, who would crush damaging dissent and lead their nation into world power or *Weltpolitik*. Thus, at the very outset of *Caesar: Geschichte seines Ruhms* (1924), a breathless narrative of the fame of Julius Caesar through the ages from Cicero to Nietzsche, the historian Friedrich Gundolf declared:

> To-day, when the need of the strong man is felt, and when – the hagglers and babblers having lost their popularity – sergeants and corporals are resorted to instead of leaders; when, particularly in Germany, the guidance of the people is entrusted to any striking talent in the military-economic field, so long as it can occupy office or show literary ability; and when parsons of social tendencies and generals of unsocial tendencies, or giants of acquisition and industry, as well as rabid petty bourgeois individuals, are considered statesmen – we should like to recall to the minds of those of hasty judgment the great man to whom the supreme authority owes its name and for centuries its guiding thought: Caesar.
>
> (F. Gundolf, *Caesar*. Trans. J. W. Hartmann as
> *The Mantle of Caesar*, 1929: 9)

For Gundolf, the history of the reception of Julius Caesar on which he is about to embark should have an important political function in helping to 'animate the atmosphere in which deeds of insight shall be accomplished', and to 'recruit adherents for the heroes that are to come' (1929: 9).

When his account of Western responses to the Roman 'strong man' is complete, Gundolf then aligns himself with Friedrich Nietzsche as someone who has been summoning up history and its departed spirits in order to mould present-day life (1929: 302). And both in his conclusion and throughout his work, he sustains a depiction of a quasi-mythic, Nietzschean Julius Caesar, the lordliest of statesmen, fit to stand shoulder to shoulder with the modern incarnation of that ancient ideal – Napoleon. According to this history of his reception, Julius Caesar will now bequeath the mantle of his greatest characteristics and achievements to the superhuman commanders Nietzsche had demanded for the future – those few heroes able (unlike the hagglers, babblers and petty corporals) to arrest decline and restore the herd of men to their humanity. Readers of *Caesar: Geschichte seines Ruhms* will now be able to recognize, appreciate and support them when they come.

It was not in Germany, however, but in Italy that a twentieth-century Caesar had already emerged – a leader who identified closely with Julius Caesar, legitimated his government as Caesarian and was ultimately derided as a mere sawdust Caesar, a comic actor without substance, no match for the monumental solidity of the Roman dictator whose statues still rose high over the streets of modern Rome. While Adolf Hitler was to draw largely on Germanic myth and history, Spartan structures of government and a Hellenic aesthetics to create historical support for National Socialism and the cult of the *Führer* as leader of a racially pure Germanic people, Benito Mussolini drew systematically on ancient Rome and Julius Caesar to launch, sustain, and strengthen the

Fascist regime and the dictatorial style of leadership he developed in the course of the 1920s and 1930s.

After the initial invocation of Julius Caesar and his crossing of the Rubicon as illustrious precedent for the 'March on Rome' of October 1922 (see Chapter 4), the exploitation of Caesar as both general and statesman was embedded within the Fascist doctrine of *romanità* – which argued for continuity between modern Italians and their Roman ancestors, for a contemporary Romanness. A tight bond between Roman past and Fascist present was articulated and authorized by popular histories of ancient Rome composed by classical scholars, research projects and publications produced by state-sponsored institutes and journals, archaeological excavations and monumental exhibitions. Designed to shape a collective, national identity for Italy's disparate masses, to stimulate popular enthusiasm for the regime and its Duce, and to predicate a glorious imperial destiny, this highly partisan historical memory of republican and, especially, imperial Rome was expressed rhetorically in political speeches and broadcasts, displayed visually in monumental public architecture and sculpture, paraded theatrically and quasi-mystically in military and civilian iconography, gestures and ceremonies, and taught intensively throughout the school curriculum. Within this cultural landscape of Fascist *romanità*, Julius Caesar made a pervasive appearance.

In the course of the regime, Mussolini himself contributed a whole series of personal interventions in order to sustain the close identification between himself and Julius Caesar, the Black Shirts and the Roman legionaries, with which he had initially legitimated and inflated the March on Rome. In October 1923, as we have seen, the first of many annual commemorations of the Fascist 'seizure' of power had culminated with the party leader ritually laying a laurel wreath on Julius Caesar's altar in the Roman forum. This public act was augmented from 1933 by the order to honour

Julius Caesar every Ides of March by placing spring flowers at the feet of his newly erected statues. Such strategies laboured to invest the chief venerator with the same qualities as the venerated: first as virile general and principled revolutionary, later as dynamic leader and founder of empire. Widely read interviews with the Italian dictator, such as that undertaken by the German biographer Emil Ludwig in 1932 and published that year in Italian translation as *Colloqui con Mussolini*, drew attention explicitly to the personal investment of il Duce in the Fascist adoration of Julius Caesar. In a vivid account, Ludwig recalls that for Caesar, and only for Caesar, Mussolini demonstrated a profoundly religious admiration. The author also relays some of the tone as well as the content of the comments made by Mussolini about his hero:

'Caesar's murder was a disaster for mankind.' Then he added in a low, but strangely agitated voice: 'I love Caesar . . . The greatest of all men who have ever lived.'

(E. Ludwig, *Three Portraits: Hitler, Mussolini, Stalin*. 1940: 73–4)

Within the context of the discourse of *romanità*, of historical continuity between Fascist present and Roman past, veneration by Mussolini merges with veneration required by Mussolini and with identification between dictator and *duce*, such that homage to Caesar might be construed as homage to Mussolini and – as we shall see – defamation of Caesar's mode of government as defamation of Fascism.

Although Mussolini's own ideology of Caesarism was rather vaguely articulated – a superman is needed, a new Caesar, to seize hold of the state, to give form and will-power to the inchoate masses, to create a new nation – he also contributed to current debates about its definition and value as a modern mode of government. In December 1933, for example, he warmly reviewed in the Fascist newspaper *Il Popolo d'Italia* a political study by the historian and philosopher Oswald Spengler, *Jahre der Entscheidung* (*The Hour of Decision*). The German author had published, more than a decade earlier, a sensational and polemical work of prediction entitled *Decline of the West*, in which he had argued that history is cyclical and regularly repeats an organic pattern involving three phases: growth from a primitive prehistory of tribes and their chieftains, maturation into a culture of nations and states, decay down to civilization and the shapelessness of mass politics, and then a return to primitivism. Just as the civilization of ancient Rome (artificial, vulgar, urban) stepped on the corpse of Greece's cultural eclipse, so now the West is following the same sequence of decline from culture to civilization. Within our contemporary civilization, following the patterns of ancient history, Caesarism will feed off the corruption of mass democracy and, although it will not be able to stop the eventual decline, it should significantly impede it. For the despotism of a great ruler will mark the return of authority, duty, honour; it will give shape to the masses and furnish a new unity.

While *Hour of Decision* was centrally concerned with Spengler's disappointment with National Socialism, and had little to say about Italian Fascism, Mussolini was evidently impressed by reference to himself within the work as a master-man, lord of his country, ruling alone, seeing everything. Embedded within this brief accolade, Spengler adds that dictatorship (meaning, presumably, Fascism's variety) is Caesarism at its most perfect, dictatorship not of a party, but of one man against all parties, even his own.

Like the French Caesars of the nineteenth century, Mussolini also contributed to the literary reception of Julius Caesar, not historiographically as in the analysis of the Roman general's wars by Napoleon I or the monumental biography by Napoleon III, but dramatically in collaboration with the playwright Giovacchino Forzano (although at the time the personal involvement of the

Duce was not explicitly acknowledged). Their propagandist play, simply entitled *Cesare*, was first performed in 1939. The first act opens with Julius Caesar on the brink of revolution against corrupt democratic opposition, and ends with his courageous decision to cross the Rubicon and save Rome. In the second act, he triumphs over barbaric Egyptians, is hailed as a god by Cleopatra, and establishes Rome as an imperial power. Tragically, in the final act, the treachery of his self-serving enemies cuts him down just as he is planning further glorious conquests for the benefit of his people. Throughout, Julius Caesar is characterized as a more-than-human hero, necessarily solitary, wise and clement.

The grandeur of the leader was matched by the grandeur of the performances, first in Rome, then Milan and other major Italian cities, and then Budapest and Berlin. Aided by generous state support, they involved casts and sets on a spectacular scale all working to stage a great classical past that, by implication, was being re-staged – if not bettered – in the Fascist present. As one modern critic has put it, audiences were effectively brought together in a collective act of worship at the altar of Fascism and, it should be added, of its new Caesar, who was present on the first night to hear the enthusiastic applause.

Early political awareness, even outside Italy, of this constant emphasis on Fascism's Caesarian government and its Caesarist dictator is disclosed by a cartoon which appeared on 14 February 1926 in the satirical weekly *Kladderadatsch*, published in Berlin. Constitutionally, Mussolini was not the head of the Italian state; that position belonged to the Italian king Victor Emmanuel. The relative authority of the king and his prime minister is here expressed as a superficial conflict between the respective role models in whose clothing they have dressed themselves up (Figure 7.2). Under the title 'Roman carnival', the king poses in the garments and the gesture characteristic of Napoleon Bonaparte, while Mussolini appears triumphantly as a garlanded and togate Caesar. In one hand il Duce firmly grasps an umbrella shaped along the contours of the fasces (the axe and bundle of rods which symbolized the absolute authority of Roman magistrates and had become the ubiquitous emblem and supposed etymological source of the Fascist party). In the palm of his other hand, he holds up the diminutive figure of the Italian sovereign, whose ridiculous imitation of the French emperor so ill-suits him that his face is obscured by his Napoleonic hat. The cartoon image mocks the conviction with which the 'baby king'

Fig. 7.2 'Römischer Karneval', designed by O. Garvens for *Kladderadatsch* (14 February 1926).

appears to be telling his colossal prime minister: 'You are absolutely right, Mussolini. Caesar was great, but Napoleon was greater still!' The designer Oskar Garvens suggests, however humorously, that identification with Julius Caesar has been an act successfully performed by a sharp-eyed Mussolini to increase his political stature at the expense of the blinded king.

Criticism of Julius Caesar's mode of government was not completely unheard of during the dictatorship of Mussolini. One of the regime's biggest and most enduring cultural undertakings was to finance the publication of the vast *Enciclopedia Italiana* – a monumental taxonomy of Fascism's worldview. Over thirty volumes, produced under the supervision of the political philosopher and apologist for Fascism Giovanni Gentile, and written with the collaboration of a host of prestigious scholars, were issued over a ten-year period between 1929 and 1939. An entry on the doctrine of Fascism appeared in volume 14, published in 1932, where, after various definitions of the Fascist state as absolutist, totalitarian, corporatist and nationalistic, there follows a whole section dedicated to 'the traditions of Rome'. Picking up on Mussolini's public speeches, in which he had regularly proclaimed ancient Rome to be Fascism's point of origin, its mode of orientation, its symbol, myth or dream, the encyclopaedia entry draws attention to the exaltation of ancient Rome and her values as one of Fascism's driving forces.

Yet in volume 9, published in the preceding year, the initial historical entry on Julius Caesar constructs a political biography for the Roman dictator as an audacious military genius who nonetheless was a greedy, cruel and unscrupulous demagogue. And in establishing an absolute and theocratic monarchy, he acted against both tradition and history. Written by Mario Attilio Levi (a Fascist who held the highest credentials, having been a party member even before the March on Rome), the entry on Caesar cannot have been designed as an indirect attack on Mussolini, for that on

Mussolini (which the same author supplied) appears to set the illegality, rupture, decadence and failure ascribed to Caesar's short
dictatorship against the legitimacy, continuity, growth and success
ascribed to the Duce's. Love of Caesar as Fascist paradigm was sufficiently strong, however, to provoke virulent criticism in the pages
of *Il Popolo d'Italia* of the disjuncture Levi had effectively created
between the Roman and the Italian leaders. Supporters of the
regime's rhetoric of Caesarism were insistent that Julius Caesar
must be recognized as the first Black Shirt.

Political analogy or identification with Julius Caesar was always
problematic, as Levi seems to have recognized. Criticism of the
Roman dictator's government by now had a long and rich history.
Caesarian government was all too regularly viewed as usurpation
followed by tyranny. It did not last for long, it failed to establish an
imperial monarchy, it ended in bloody assassination – and the assassins had even been glorified. A solution arrived in May 1936: with
the proclamation of a new Italian empire, the chief obstacle to the
construction of a correspondence between Mussolini and the
emperor Augustus vanished. Between 1937 and 1938, a vast exhibition was held in the capital devoted to the presentation of Italy's
inheritance of empire from ancient Rome. Conveniently attached
to a national celebration of the bimillennium of that emperor's
birth, it was entitled *Mostra Augustea della Romanità*. Within the vast
halls of the exhibition space, only a single room was reserved for the
display of Julius Caesar's skill and his schemes (military ingenuity
linked to plans and projects to order the state, embellish civil life,
found empire and pacify the world), while eight displayed the
attainments of his adopted son (the assumption and completion of
that inheritance).

So strong was the attraction of Julius Caesar, however, that other
methods continued to be found to lessen the difficulties of political assimilation between the ancient and modern leaders. In 1941,

for example, some five years after war in Ethiopia and the declaration of empire, the biographer Nello Lombardo chose both to whitewash the Roman general and to elevate the Duce a little above his Roman model. The introduction to Lombardo's parallel lives, *Cesare e Mussolini*, addresses the youth of imperial Italy and declares explicitly that the ensuing biography of Caesar will ostracize the 'malice' expressed by some of the ancient and modern sources, rendering him the ideal forefather of their race. That strategy gives the author scope to list a whole series of 'truly impressive' analogies between the two brilliant dictators in which Mussolini often surpasses the achievements of his Roman precursor: while Caesar conquers immense territories and prepares other conquests in the East, only Mussolini passes into history with the title 'Founder of Empire'; while Caesar merely plans the draining of the Pontine marshes, Mussolini realizes the age-old dream and founds new cities on the site. Now that, in effect, the Fascist leader takes on not only the best features of the conquering Roman general but also those of the general's adopted son, the climax of Lombardo's catalogue can even delineate a mysterious physical resemblance between the two heroic soldiers of his title, supported by the juxtaposition of their faces on the cover of his book: 'the same energetic and strong-willed profile, the same hawk-eye and the same magnetic glance, the same physical good looks' (1941: 10).

The fundamental importance of Julius Caesar and Caesarist government to Fascist doctrine was matched by the centrality of Caesar and Caesarism to discourses of anti-Fascism. Antonio Gramsci, the celebrated Marxist theoretician and leader of the Italian Communist Party in parliament from 1924 until his arrest and imprisonment in 1926, found it necessary to grapple with the concept of Caesarism as part of his attempt to understand the failure of Italy's liberal institutions and the triumph of Fascism. In his prison notebooks (composed over the period 1929 to 1935, but unpublishable in Italy until after the overthrow of the regime and the end of the Second World War), Gramsci defined Caesarism as an outside intervention (by, for example, a dictator or charismatic leader) over a struggle between progressive and reactionary forces which are so balanced against each other as to be heading towards their mutual destruction. Caesarism had arisen in Italy because of a longstanding weakness of the state – the absence of a stable hegemonic or consensual relation between the ruling class and social groups within the general population. This twentieth-century Caesarism had first emerged in the organization of coalition government (rather than in the person of a military leader) and, when Mussolini came to power constitutionally as the appointed head of government within a parliamentary coalition, then moved through diverse stages until it reached a purer and more permanent form in the latter half of the 1920s. Evolving naturally out of the weak structures of the liberal state, Italian Fascism rapidly developed into a purer form of Caesarism which activated coercive sectors of the state apparatus (such as the military and the police) in conjunction with the ideological and cultural apparatus of the mass media, mass communication and mass mobilization, to produce political, economic and social regression. Mussolini's revolutionary and populist claims are thus undermined (although in necessarily coded form) and the rise of his brand of Caesarism is made to signal a crisis of authority and the degeneration of free, republican politics.

While Gramsci sought to critique the Caesarism of Fascism, others sought to demolish Fascism's Julius Caesar. Writing in exile from Italy in 1933, the popular historian and outspoken political commentator Guglielmo Ferrero introduced *The Life of Caesar* (1933) as a work of anti-Fascist historiography. This highly critical biography of the Roman statesman had first appeared at the beginning of the century as the opening volumes of his mammoth narrative of ancient Rome's greatness and decline (*Grandezza e*

Decadenza di Roma). Ferrero recalled that in his original assessment of Caesar his purpose had been to overturn the nineteenth-century, romantic exaltation of the Roman dictator as a 'hero-usurper' and 'saviour-tyrant' – a Caesar who had been manufactured only to act as a suitable older brother for the tyrant of genius Napoleon and, in so doing, to advocate Caesarism. Thirty years on, he now observes with intense concern that his reappraisal had carried only temporary conviction. Romantic illusions about the Roman 'Archdestroyer' have been reawakened and now they must once again be crushed (along with those about Napoleon). Once again, for Ferrero, Julius Caesar is a pragmatic general, an intelligent writer, a gifted and driven character, but no great statesman. Rather than a doctor for his country's ills, Caesar was the purposeless opportunist who advanced its destruction.

Similarly, the following year, in the dissident journal *La Cultura*, the young classical historian Piero Treves perilously attacked the current 'mania' for Caesar, the stultifying atmosphere of heated and verbose adulation in which Italians are now forced to live:

> If Napoleonic historiography aimed at the adulation in Caesar of . . . Caesarism, today's Italian adulation of Caesar celebrates in him the conqueror, the founder of autocratic empire, 'the man of the Rubicon'. Really the word most often repeated and, alas, least clear is another, aspiring and solemn, indeterminate and fascinating: revolution. Caesar, crossing the Rubicon illegally, setting himself against Rome and the Senate, accomplished a revolutionary act: with his army he destroyed a republican and representative state; in its place he made another rise, conciliatory, dictatorial: 'the strong state', as it is generally called. This is the thesis in vogue.
>
> (P. Treves, *La Cultura*, November 1934: 129)

For Treves, as he goes on forcefully to argue here, the current vision of the revolutionary Caesar and his strong state has scarcely any justification in historical truth.

Outside Italy, from the mid-1930s, attacks on Fascism began to undo the coupling of Mussolini and Julius Caesar. Some years after his expulsion from Italy by the regime, the American journalist George Seldes published a systematic deconstruction of its myths under the memorable title *Sawdust Caesar* (1935). The dirty secret of Italian Fascism was that it merely constituted an inchoate movement in search of a programme, and its leader an opportunist in search of an image. Mussolini invites us to compare him with world-conquerors such as Julius Caesar, but the Italian dictator steps into that role 'as an actor into his makeup' (1935: 370). Mussolini is a mediocrity, a man of straw and sawdust. As such, the book's final paragraph bitterly proclaims, he should be swept away with ease.

To ridicule Mussolini's identification with Julius Caesar in this way would have been an extremely dangerous enterprise in Italy while the Duce was still alive. But soon after he was executed on 28 April 1945, Enrico Gianeri published a heavily illustrated and impassioned history of caricatures of the Italian leader that had appeared in the foreign press during the course of the regime yet been utterly suppressed at home. With the declared intention of unmasking Mussolini as a criminal who over twenty-five years usurped power, poisoned a generation, ruined the country and threw the world into the worst of wars, the volume carried the title *Il cesare di cartapesta* ('The Papier-Mâché Caesar') and included among its many examples a political cartoon from the satirical magazine *Simplicissimus* under the title 'Cesare Mussolini'. Elsewhere in the polemical work, Gianeri reminds his Italian readership that Mussolini had desired to be Caesar and took pleasure whenever servile paintbrushes and chisels represented him in classical style, adorned with a laurel crown. In the German cartoon of 3 May 1926, the Italian dictator does indeed salute his troops on shipboard attired in laurel wreath and full Roman military costume. But he also sports a clown's bulbous nose.

Since the end of the Second World War, the spectre of Caesarism has been discerned in the evident expansion of the powers of the president of the United States of America. While Max Weber, at the beginning of the twentieth century, had identified American 'leadership-democracy' as a positive and vibrant form of Caesarism which deserved imitation in Germany, most political analysts of the USA's system of government, if they have identified the presence of presidential Caesarism at all, have decried it as a perversion of the nation's founding republican principles. And, correspondingly, no US president has dared (in the manner of a Napoleon or a Mussolini) candidly to advocate Caesarism or to dress their authority in the dictatorial costume of Julius Caesar.

Yet in 1957 the French critic Amaury de Riencourt generated substantial, alarmed public debate when he revived the by now somewhat moribund concept of Caesarism and placed it at the heart of a startling prediction about the future of the USA and its consequences for the world. He asserted that the United States of America now stood in the same relation to Europe as ancient Rome had once stood to Greece. The adoption by modern America as well as ancient Rome of the twin strategies of democratic growth and imperial expansion proved decisive. Just as Roman civilization had been destined to overwhelm Greek culture and master the world, so American civilization was now destined to triumph over a declining European culture and dominate the world of tomorrow. For the ancient and the modern civilizations the consequence was (or now would be) loss of liberty, centralization and the arrival of Caesarism: 'Our Western world, America and Europe, is threatened with Caesarism on a scale unknown since the

dawn of the Roman empire' (1957: 5). Hence de Riencourt suc-
cinctly entitled his grim political prophecy *The Coming Caesars*.
The argument borrowed its organic and biocyclical philosophy of
history from Spengler (civilizations trample over cultures and then
ossify and decay into lethal tyrannies until the cycle begins again).
At the same time as history is cyclical, however, it is also paradoxically apocalyptic (expanding democracy leads to imperialism
which in turn destroys republican institutions and concentrates
absolute power in a single Caesarian ruler, leading to nuclear holocaust and the end of history).

Modern American Caesarism will not be heralded abruptly by a
military coup, de Riencourt clarifies, nor will it initiate civil war or
defy the constitution. Instead it will emerge, or rather it is emerging, slowly from a gradual concentration of power in the office and
the person of the chief executive (1957: 11). This process of concentration is already under way because democracy's drive towards
war and foreign expansion has necessitated the enhancement of the
powers of the executive over congress. Moreover, the free people of
the United States are surrendering their authority to one autocratic
master voluntarily, for the masses (being democratic and egalitarian)
are feminine and, therefore, positively seek out the masculine and
paternal leadership of a Caesar.

After running through the history of the failing Rome republic
and its astonishing similarity to that of the United States to date, and
after depicting Franklin D. Roosevelt as the first real 'pre-Caesarist'
president because he most nearly established dictatorial rule, de
Riencourt concludes:

> [T]he President of the United States is the most powerful
> single human being in the world today. Future crises will
> inevitably transform him into a full-fledged Caesar, if we do
> not beware. Today he wears ten hats – as Head of State, Chief

Executive, Minister of Foreign Affairs, Chief Legislator, Head of
Party, Tribune of the People, Ultimate Arbitrator of Social
Justice, Guardian of Economic Prosperity, and World Leader of
Western Civilization. Slowly and unobtrusively these hats are
becoming crowns and this pyramid of hats is slowly metamor-
phosing itself into a tiara, the tiara of one man's world imperium.

(The Coming Caesars, 1957: 330–1)

What function can such parallels between past and present serve?
For the brother of Napoleon Bonaparte, comparison with Julius
Caesar would wake up his French readers to the grave dangers
their dear leader faced. For Friedrich Gundolf, an account of the
enduring importance of Julius Caesar would help German readers
to recognize and support their saviour-heroes when they came. In
the alarmist context developed by de Riencourt, however, parallels
between the actions of the Caesars and the presidents of the United
States provide warning beacons to shed light on the bleak destiny of
the world. Or, a little more optimistically, the step back into
Roman history which the author offers is, in his own metaphor, an
opportunity to wake up and see properly the road we have all been
sleep-walking along (1957: 6), and also to adjust our path before it
is too late (1957: 356). Armed with our knowledge of historical
cycles, we may be able to prevent or modify the worst features of
American Caesarism and save ourselves from the holocaust.

Not surprisingly, de Riencourt's thesis of Caesar in the White
House immediately generated considerable debate. Political conservatives rejected his Roman analogies as robustly as they denied
his bold predictions for America's future place in the world. The
political philosopher and libertarian Frank Meyer, in an issue for
that same year of National Review (a magazine of conservative
and, more recently, neo-conservative opinion of which he was a
co-founder), objected that this young Frenchman's thesis ignored

an essential characteristic of American political life, namely its Christian vision of the innate value of the person and of his free-dom under God. Confident of the difference between Christian Americans and the iron, soulless administrators of Rome, Meyer boldly proclaimed that Americans would indeed determine the fate of the West, but on their own terms: any future American era of Western culture will be 'not Caesarist, but free' (1957: 233). Few critics since have been prepared to argue for a thoroughgoing historical correspondence between ancient Rome and modern America, but moments of political extremity or military crisis in the USA and in world politics have often witnessed a return to de Riencourt's original and flamboyantly dramatic use of Julius Caesar – namely, to paint a minatory vision of the future of the American presidency, of the United States, and of the world.

During the Vietnam war, for example, the front page of the *National Review* on 3 May 1966 carried the legend: 'Imperial America: A look into the future'. Inside, the Catholic philosopher and conservative political theorist Thomas Molnar, while acknowl-edging national resistance to the historical analogy, accepted without hesitation that by now the United States had become an imperial power like Rome, and that Americans were the new Romans. Like the reluctant Romans before them, the United States had been compelled to take on conquests in the East and provide protection in the form of a *pax Americana*. But empire *needs* a single power centre (to permit quick decisions and fast action): imperial responsibility inevitably brings with it increased centralization. So, if the United States has grown like Rome from small agrarian republic to world empire, then will its Chief Executive also become an imperial Caesar?

Molnar catalogues an extraordinary number of correspondences between modern American presidents and Julius Caesar (or, at times, less specifically, the Caesars) in order to pinpoint inevitable domestic consequences of international growth. Caesar and the new-type President empty traditional institutions of their power (the Roman Senate, the American Congress). They are charismatic figures who promise but only partly deliver the demands of the newly important masses. They both constitute commander-in-chief of the armed forces; it is they who decide troop movements (from Gaul to Egypt, from Germany to Vietnam). For their double role as chief administrator and military protector, they are compensated by considerable privileges (a crown for Julius, four mandates for Roosevelt). They curb the legislative arm of government, contain popular discontent (free grain distributions, anti-poverty funds), and accrue a large expert staff which duplicates all forms of government and whose political existence is tied to their leader alone.

Molnar's conclusion demonstrates the function the Roman equivalence is again made to serve as the predictor of catastrophe:

> Caesar leans on popular, radical elements, makes concessions, keeps the balance among pressure groups and grabbing hands. But on one point he cannot yield to the domestic left: on military matters, since the second chief support of his office is armed protection of the nation. Thus evolves the Deal: popular demands are satisfied, the poor and the proletariat are cared for by free grain and circuses; but the military budget is also approved, the foreign bases and allies are well supplied, the foreign potentates are flattered and kept in power, the legions and divisions splendidly equipped. The price is ever-climbing budgets, higher taxes, and built-in inflation.
>
> The end of the story? Caesar reaches for absolute power, and absolute power corrupts Caesar first, the public and its morality next. Priests or television screens divinize his Image. Eager, famished enemies appear at the gates . . .

(T. Molnar, National Review 18.18, 1966: 411)

The author rounds off his essay with a reassurance to his readers that these thoughts on a Caesarian presidency are merely an intellectual exercise and that none of his predictions might come true. It is scarcely meant to quell the alarm his preceding analysis was clearly designed to generate.

Although in his account of 'Imperial America' Molnar made no direct reference to the then current president of the United States, the Democrat Lyndon B. Johnson, the date of his article is significant. Only a year earlier, Johnson had authorized ground war in Vietnam at the same time as he undertook sweeping policy innovations at home with a view to constructing a 'Great Society'. Criticism of the president's policy in Vietnam, of his military strategies and their cost in men and money, escalated in the early months of 1966, with televised hearings of the Senate Foreign Relations Committee, newspaper articles and nationwide demonstrations against the war. Even in the face of all this criticism, Everett Dirksen (leader of the Republican party in the Senate) remained a staunch advocate of Johnson's supreme constitutional authority – as commander-in-chief and 'holder of the sword' over and above Congress as 'holder of the purse'. But in May of that year, he called for a comprehensive debate about the situation in Vietnam and attacked Johnson's secrecy at a time when ground engagements and air strikes were both on the increase.

Thus a political cartoon in the *Washington Post* on 10 June 1966, only a month after the publication of Molnar's Roman speculations, displays on its left a short bespectacled senator dressed in simple Roman tunic and boots. He holds a cigar in one hand and raises up a scroll in the other on which is written: 'Dirksen accuses administration of lack of candor on Vietnam' (Figure 7.3). On the right, a tall President Johnson swathed in an enveloping toga and Roman sandals, and wearing a laurel wreath, finds himself backed against a pillar. The caption over the president's head reads 'EV TU?'. The

"Ev Tu?"

Fig. 7.3 'Ev Tu?'. A 1966 Herblock Cartoon. *Washington Post* (10 June 1966).

familiar Latin tag *et tu, Brute?* ('also you, Brutus?') which Julius Caesar famously cries out in Shakespeare's play as he gives in to death at the hands of his most trusted companion, is here misspelt in order to be pronounced 'you too?' It identifies the modern confrontation as one between a perplexed Caesar and an American Brutus who, though once loyal, has finally been pushed to the brink.

In the twenty-first century, prolonged war abroad has again encouraged this critique of American empire – that it leads to domestic Caesarism and may even lead to global apocalypse. Until 11 September 2001, most American conservatives had expressed distaste for the concept of an imperial America. After the attacks on the Twin Towers, many political pundits of the New Right were emboldened to take up the trope of historical destiny and to claim provocatively that the United States was the new Roman empire. Meanwhile, neo-conservative policy-makers and governmental advisers sought (on the grounds of an unavoidably aggressive and expansionist foreign policy) to restore the prerogatives of the chief executive to the levels of the so-called 'imperial presidency' of Richard Nixon, which were lost after the scandal of Watergate. To criticize this new development, one obvious rhetorical strategy adopted by sectors of the international and domestic media was to pursue multiple and adverse parallels between the empire of ancient Rome and modern American imperialism, and between Julius Caesar's mode of government and this new, more arrogantly imperial presidency.

Such critiques began to gather momentum in the lead up to the invasion of Iraq. In his address to the United Nations on 12 September 2002 (the day after the first anniversary of 9/11), George W. Bush effectively declared that, if the UN was not going to act against Iraq, the United States would do so alone. A spate of articles in both the British and the American press subsequently compared the US president with the Roman emperors, sometimes specifically with Julius Caesar. The day after the address, for example, Robert Fisk (Middle East correspondent for the British newspaper the *Independent*) observed that, seated in the UN General Assembly, surrounded by green marble fittings and a backcloth of burnished gold, the president was able to enjoy the furnishings of an emperor, 'albeit a diminutive one'. Suggesting that Bush's speech was tantamount to a declaration of war against Iraq, the journalist concluded his newspaper article dramatically: 'What was the name of that river which Julius Caesar crossed? Was it not called the Rubicon? Yesterday, Mr Bush may have crossed the very same river.'

Similarly, towards the end of 2002, condemnation of the American president's increasingly Caesarian style appeared in the progressive monthly *Harper's Magazine*. Under the title 'Hail Caesar', Lewis H. Lapham (longstanding editor of the magazine until 2006) contrasted his personal experience of fierce, nationwide opposition to the invasion of Iraq with the sycophancy of most of the national news media and the subservience of both Senate and Congress:

> After the pretense of a debate that lasted less than a week, Congress on October 11 invested President George W. Bush with the power to order an American invasion of Iraq whenever it occurred to him to do so, for whatever reason he might deem glorious or convenient. Akin to the ancient Roman practice of enthroning a dictator at moments of severe crisis, the joint resolution was hurried into law by servile majorities in both a Senate (77–23) and a House of Representatives (296–133) much relieved to escape the chore – tiresome, unpopular, time-consuming, poorly paid – of republican self-government. The sergeants-at-arms didn't take the trouble to dress up the occasion with a slaughter of sacrificial goats or the presentation of a bull to Apollo, but the subtext of the vote could be understood as a submissive prayer: 'Our President is a Great General; he will blast Saddam Hussein and rescue us from doom. To achieve this extraordinary mission he needs extraordinary powers, so extraordinary that they don't exist in law . . . Great is Caesar; God must be with him.'
>
> (L. H. Lapham, *Harper's Magazine*, December 2002: 9)

Here again Caesar appears as a natural consequence of and counter to the neo-conservative embrace of empire. Comparison of George W. Bush and Julius Caesar works to create a striking and sensational narrative. Traditional democratic institutions abdicate their power. An untrustworthy and bellicose leader usurps their authority. In a time of crisis, the country turns to dictatorship. A single individual amasses extraordinary powers. War is declared illegally. Troops march blindly across forbidden borders into an invasion which will bring with it historic, and most probably disastrous, consequences.

After the invasion of Iraq in 2003, adverse comparison of George W. Bush with Julius Caesar and critiques of his mode of government as Caesarism rapidly escalated. While congressional oversight of war (both in Afghanistan and Iraq) was diminished and the executive's powers of domestic surveillance and prosecution increased, both left and right hotly argued over the merits of the label Caesarism and over comparison with the Roman dictator (as well as, far more commonly, the terms empire and imperialism) in books and newspapers, on radio and television, on the websites of a wide range of political groups, and most recently in weblogs.

As foil for Western traditions of republicanism, Julius Caesar has come to symbolize the moment of greatest danger to the Roman republic. He was its ruin. His self-interested ambition led him to usurp senatorial authority by arms. His designs on monarchy led to the establishment of the rule of emperors. His escalation of the expansion of empire and the centralization of power led ultimately to Rome's fall. Caesar has been index and embodiment of a devastating turning point in political history. Caesarian analogy makes possible and plausible an especially vivid representation of contemporary American politics. It paints a portrait of its foreign policy in the bright reds of a bloody imperialism, its president in the deep purples of a ruthless tyranny. It constructs this moment, at the beginning of the twenty-first century, as equal in historical significance to that when the Roman republic collapsed and the Roman empire was born. It ennobles those politicians and pundits who utilize it with the *gravitas* of a brave American Cicero or Cato, and links them back to their own nation's Founding Fathers as new guardians of that republican legacy.

A new twist to the Caesarian comparison appeared to develop during the course of President Bush's second term of office. Now that the war in Iraq had been so prolonged and its pacification proven so difficult, now that the details of illegal torture, secret prisons and substantial domestic surveillance had emerged, when financial costs were so high and the loss of personnel so substantial, when domestic support for the president and the war was rapidly diminishing and Senate, Congress, and the Supreme Court were all beginning to reassert their political authority over and against the Administration, then George W. Bush was criticized not for being like Julius Caesar but for being no match.

On 22 October 2005, *The Economist* carried an article warning of the waning of this imperial presidency:

> This autumn's most gripping television series, HBO's *Rome*, tells the story, in deliciously graphic detail, of how Julius Caesar tightened his grip on power in the capital of the world's greatest empire. In the new Rome, on the banks of the Potomac, exactly the opposite is happening: George Bush's iron grip on power is loosening, as more and more Washingtonians join the revolt against the imperial presidency.
>
> (*The Economist*, 22 October 2005)

Just as Mussolini was eventually reduced to the status of a 'sawdust Caesar', so George W. Bush in the eyes of his critics became a general not brave or brilliant on the battlefield, a statesman not eloquent or cultured, an imperial leader destined paradoxically not to instigate a modern empire which would endure for centuries. Instead, small both in stature and historical grandeur, he was proclaimed a terrifying 'wannabee Caesar with nukes'. At the start of the twenty-first century, the specifics of Julius Caesar's mode of government and the concept of Caesarism no longer hold a major place in political theory, but they sustain a vital life in popular political debate. Regardless of the relative validity of the denunciations catalogued above, in the latter part of Bush's presidential career comparisons between Roman dictatorship and his imperial presidency suggested (as we shall see again at the close of the next chapter) that while he was no longer replicating Julius Caesar's political rise, he might well repeat the fall of Caesar's political authority.

8

ASSASSINATION

The Ides of March, 44 BC

The most famous and the most resonant of all events in the life of Julius Caesar is his murder on the Ides of March 44 BC. The dictator was assassinated in the senate house, at the feet of the statue of Pompey, only days before he was due to embark on a grand military expedition to Parthia. Julius Caesar, as we have seen throughout this book, could lay claim to fame on numerous counts: charismatic leadership, triumphant military acumen, aggressive imperial expansion, revolutionary risk-taking, ostentatious romance (or, at least, physical entanglement) with an Egyptian queen, novel statescraft that twinned populism with dictatorship. It was a life parts of which Caesar memorialized in his own surviving commentaries and which many other ancient writers rewrote from diverse and polemical perspectives. Classical scholars, however, speculate that ancient assessment of Caesar's achievements in comparison to those of his rival Pompey, the earlier dictator Sulla or the long-lived emperor Augustus might have been diminished had he died abroad on a battlefield, injured by a Parthian missile. Instead, assassination in the Roman senate house, at the dagger-tip of leading politicians, some of whom had been close friends, the startling success of the murder plot and the extraordinary failure of its political rationale, all add garish colour to an already colourful life and substantially increase its dimensions to grand, tragic proportions. Now, too, Caesar's wounded corpse can embody the disintegration of the republic, and the story of his sudden end and its devastating consequences stage, in the most sensational terms, an historic shift to empire and imperial monarchy. And, in whatever way the story is retold, its audience is invited to reflect on the life as a whole and consider the justice of its abrupt conclusion.

Even in the ancient world, Julius Caesar's assassination and the actions which led up to it demanded close scrutiny. In the first surviving outline of his life, embedded in a biography of Augustus by the Greek courtier Nicolaus of Damascus, Caesar is characterized almost exclusively by the manner in which he died. The fullest narratives of his murder, all written at least a century after the event, may be relatively consistent with each other in matters of substance, but they differ in aspects of chronology, detail and emphasis. The killing of the Roman dictator had to be reconstructed from conflicting reports which would have been deployed originally as propaganda in the debates, and then the wars, which ensued between the Caesarians and the assassins. Clearly it attracted embellishment, even a high degree of fictionalization, as well as moral evaluation.

In the later sources, in the biographies of Plutarch and Suetonius and the histories of Appian and Dio, the portrayal of Caesar ranges from great (if flawed) statesman criminally butchered by treacherous friends and favourites to arrogant, self-serving, aspirant king from whose grasp the tyrannicides attempted to liberate the state. It is partly this range which has made the assassination of Caesar such a useful mechanism in subsequent centuries for exploring a number of key political questions: How and when should you differentiate between public image and flesh-and-blood person, between political actions and their motivation? When should you place duty above friendship? How far should you tolerate autocracy? To what limits should you go in support of civic freedom? Most importantly, in what circumstances might it be justifiable to depose a leader?

Between them, the ancient sources build up a tense and vivid narrative of distastefully inflated honours (because both divine and regal) decreed by the senate or people, and readily accepted by the dictator, and of shockingly public gestures towards kingship, a series which accumulates speed and intensity between Julius Caesar's victorious return to Rome from Spain in October 45 BC and his murder in March the following year. Over the course of those few months, as a result, Caesar falls further and further into disfavour and the conspirators are goaded into their fateful act.

Already in 46, after the dictator's victory in Africa, the senate had allocated him a place in Jupiter's temple on the Capitoline hill. Facing Jupiter's statue, one of Caesar was to be mounted on a globe (symbolizing his mastery of the world) and placed in a triumphal chariot. An inscription would proclaim him a demi-god, the self-proclaimed descendant of the mythic union between the goddess Venus and the royal warrior Anchises. After victory in Spain against the sons of Pompey, however, fresh honours were conceived to display in religious terms the unique political supremacy Julius Caesar had achieved. The distinctions now awarded raised the Roman general above mortal stature towards that of a living god and introduced to Rome an official cult of the ruler.

The senate decreed that a statue of Caesar be erected in the temple of the Italian divinity Quirinus inscribed 'to the unconquerable god', and another set up on the Capitol between those of the ancient kings and Lucius Junius Brutus (Rome's liberator from kingship). Other statues of Caesar were decreed for both Roman and municipal temples and for important public locations in the capital, statues which styled him as conqueror, liberator, saviour, founder. He was granted spatial, temporal and corporeal distinction

from his fellow Romans: he was to sit on a gilded throne for sessions of the senate or court; his opinion was to be stated first, even
before that of the consuls; his person was declared sacrosanct and
inviolable; on official occasions, he might wear a laurel wreath, triumphal costume, and the purple mantle and tall red boots of the
kings of old. His distinctive trappings and his likeness were to be
ritually displayed and paraded before the people: his gilded throne
and gem-encrusted crown were to be conveyed into the theatre like
the chairs of the gods; his triumphal statue was to be taken from its
shrine in the temple of Jupiter, placed on a special litter and carried
alongside images of the gods in the religious procession held at the
circus. Games, festal holidays, sacrifices, prayers and oaths were
instituted to honour Caesar's heroism, commemorate his past military victories, celebrate his birthday, demonstrate loyalty and secure
his safety and welfare (interlinked now with that of the state). For
the first time in the history of the republic, coins would be minted
bearing the image of a living Roman. The month in which Caesar
was born, *Quinctilis*, would have its name changed permanently to
Iulius. Finally, a temple would be dedicated wholly to the new god
divus Iulius and to his Clemency, and with a temple would come an
appointed priest, Mark Antony. The decree of Julius Caesar's deification was to be inscribed in letters of gold on silver tablets, and put
on display at the feet of Capitoline Jupiter. Divine Caesar was now
to be addressed directly as 'Jupiter Julius'.

The ancient biographers and historians who catalogued these
escalating honours dispute whether they constituted awards made
by servile flatterers pandering to Caesar's grandiose ambitions, or
devious strategies devised by his opponents in order to stimulate
popular revulsion and provide a pretext to kill him. They concur,
however, that the dictator was unwise to allow or take pleasure in
such excessive honours, and that their acceptance did indeed arouse
or intensify hatred towards him, because they were too great for

mortal man (Suetonius, *Deified Julius* 76.1) or proclaimed him openly to be a monarch (Dio, *Roman History* 43.45). That hatred was finally rendered both open and deadly, when Julius Caesar began to behave like a king or appeared publicly to be testing attitudes to his own coronation.

The first of three swift steps leading up to murder is launched when the Roman senators, preceded by the consuls and other magistrates, all formally dressed in their robes of office, arrive in a body to deliver their decrees of extraordinary honours directly and publicly to Caesar. The dictator fails to rise, merely extending his hand as if greeting a group of private persons – a political gesture that speaks to its observers of insulting haughtiness, a passion for royal power (Plutarch, *Caesar* 60; Suetonius, *DJ* 78.1; Appian, *Civil Wars* 2.107; Dio, *RH* 44.8). The gravity of this error is marked by narrative dalliance over the question of its origin (Is it Caesar's heaven-sent fatuity or the malicious advice of another?) and the hasty apology which followed (frailty induced by epilepsy; an attack of diarrhoea).

The second step is taken as a consequence of Julius Caesar's ill-treatment of two tribunes. In January 44 BC, a new gold statue of the dictator standing on the rostra is suddenly found to be adorned with a diadem, that is a crown of laurel bound with a white ribbon, insignia of Hellenistic monarchy. The tribunes order that the ribbon be removed from the wreath and thrown away, and that the perpetrator be hunted out and imprisoned. Shortly after, when Caesar is entering Rome ceremoniously on horseback, he is hailed king by some members of the crowd. He responds as if it is merely a case of mistaken identity: 'I am not King, I am Caesar.' But when the same two tribunes initiate a prosecution of one of these royal enthusiasts, the dictator summons a meeting of the senate and accuses the tribunes of conspiring to cast on him the odium of royalty. He orders their expulsion from office and their dismissal from the senate, even though they are sacrosanct just as he is.

While the Roman biographer Suetonius acknowledges in passing a pro-Caesarian interpretation of these events (Caesar became
angry with the tribunes because – 'as he asserted' – they had
deprived him of the opportunity to reject the unwelcome title of
king), he lays emphasis instead on an anti-Caesarian interpetation
(Caesar was affronted that his deliberately instigated intimation of
regal power had not been well received), and the author calls it at
the outset an act of even greater insolence than the last (*DJ* 79.1).
The Greek historian Dio, however, argues that these public gestures
towards kingship had been orchestrated by the conspirators further
to embitter the people, and even Caesar's friends, against him. But
even he has to admit that the dictator was now cast into disrepute
because he had only attacked the tribunes and not those whom he
should have hated for calling him king (*RH* 44.9–10). In any case,
the narrative of Julius Caesar's career comes full circle: the man who
claimed that he was crossing the Rubicon to restore tribunes now
deposes them.

The third and final step leading up to murder is taken the next
month, February 44 BC. Julius Caesar watches the fertility festival of
the Lupercalia seated on his gilded throne high up on the rostra.
Appearing now in public as dictator for life, he wears for the first
time his golden crown and the ceremonial costume of the ancient
Roman kings. Mark Antony, consul, priest and festival participant,
climbs up to place a diadem on Caesar's brow, to the noisy displeasure of the crowd. When Caesar rejects the diadem, they
applaud. Antony tries twice more, and twice more Caesar refuses it,
ordering instead that it be taken to Jupiter in his temple as the one
true king of the Romans. The earliest detailed account of Caesar's
'coronation' at the Lupercalia, written by Nicolaus of Damascus,
considers a number of distinct explanations for this event too:
Caesar's overly arrogant trial of his royal powers? An ambitious
political gesture undertaken by Antony without Caesar's prior

consent? An opportunity staged by Caesar to denounce once and for all such initiatives? But all the later sources are here in agreement that this act was Julius Caesar's failed political experiment, a public rehearsal for monarchy which went disastrously wrong. Even Dio states that it provided proof of the dictator's true desire for the title of king, no matter how much he had pretended otherwise (*RH* 44.11). And this certainly works very well as the conclusive step up to murder. In the narrative of Caesar's death, supplying the final insult, it is not a statue but the living person who is crowned, not by persons unnamed but by a consul, not once but three times.

At last, the ancient accounts have reached the who, when and where of assassination. For the conspirators (who number anywhere between fifteen and eighty in the sources), Julius Caesar's now manifest passion for kingship can be made the spur (or the noble pretext concealing ignoble motives). In Rome's constitutional mythology, kingship was set in sharp opposition to the city's republican ideals. Its mythic founder Romulus had been killed when he descended into abhorrent tyranny; the republic was formed at the moment when the heroic Lucius Junius Brutus expelled the royal house of the Tarquins from Rome. Its aristocrats were so thoroughly educated in Greek and Roman narratives concerning abuses of power and glorious tyrannicide that the killing of a tyrant might seem a sacred civic duty. As chief and noblest conspirator, Lucius' descendant Marcus Junius Brutus possesses exceptional ancestral suitability, and is prodded into the task by reminders of his family history. Speed and location are then added to the dramatic narrative of political assassination. A rumour is rife: an official oracle has predicted that Parthia can only be conquered by a king. Accordingly, at the next meeting of the senate, due to take place on the Ides of March in a purpose-built hall attached to the great theatre of Pompey, the title of king will be advocated for Julius Caesar (even if it is only to apply outside Italy).

Many of the specific details concerning Julius Caesar's last bloody moments are most likely to have been preserved and embellished by his camp-followers, as the stabbing of the dictator could easily be moulded into a tale about the vulnerability of the single victim, the cruelty of his numerous killers, and then the profound shock and grief of a people bereft of their leader. But much else in the ancient narratives remains open to interpretation. The portents and disturbances of nature which frame the assassination may mark a double-edged destiny. If, for example, the day before the Ides a tiny 'king' bird (or *avem regaliolum*) flew into Pompey's senate-hall carrying a sprig of laurel, was pursued by other birds from a grove nearby, and was torn to pieces by them (as Suetonius, *DJ* 81.3), is the incident a signal from the gods that they approve or that they condemn the murder of Julius Caesar? Either way, they invest Caesar's death (and, therefore, his life) with cosmic importance, and the narrative of murder is propelled forward by a sense of inexorable fate.

A similarly ambiguous effect is created both by the intimations of danger the dictator receives (he is warned a month earlier by the seer Spurinna to beware the Ides of March), and by his own various pronouncements on death (he refuses to retain a bodyguard because 'it is better to die once than to be always expecting death'; on the eve of the Ides, he tells his dinner companions that it is best to die 'unexpectedly'). Do these gestures, the sources speculate, indicate a brave indifference to death or an arrogant contempt for it, a poignant awareness of what is to come or an exhausted acceptance (as Suetonius, *DJ* 86.2 and 87)? For Plutarch, an inner, pitiable drama of slaughter is framed by an outer description of its location that displays strong republican overtones. Caesar goes to his death on 15 March 44 BC in the grandest edifice of republican

Rome (an edifice which had been built by his rival Pompey) and he ends up collapsing against the blood-drenched pedestal of Pompey's statue: it is as if some divine power had drawn the dictator there in order that he be punished for Pompey's death (Plutarch, *Caesar* 66.1), as if Pompey himself has the satisfaction of presiding over his fallen, quivering enemy (66.7).

The killing itself is several times placed in suspense. The day gets late and still Caesar has not arrived. When he does, his entry into the senate-hall is delayed by various petitions, potential disclosures of the conspiracy, unfavourable omens and prophetic warnings. When finally the senators rise to greet his approach, he has already been cautioned again cryptically by the seer Spurinna ('The ides have indeed come, but they have not yet gone': Suetonius, *DJ* 81.4). And, in the highest tragic irony, he clutches in one hand a scroll he has been prevented from reading, a scroll that specifically indicts the conspirators.

The narrative of the actual assassination falls into three broad stages: a supplication, the savage stabbing and the confrontation with Brutus. The supplication by Tillius Cimber for the recall of his exiled brother may have been originally decided upon by the conspirators to provide a conclusive demonstration of Caesar's humiliating autocratic rule: the senator would fall to his knees, others would clasp Caesar's hands or kiss his chest and head, the dictator would reject the request, Cimber would pull Caesar's toga from his shoulders to launch the assault. All or most of this is so described in the classical biographies and histories, but the disorganized butchery which Plutarch recounts as having followed immediately after probably has its origins in the camp of Julius Caesar's successors. Caesar, after Casca's first misjudged dagger thrust and his own brief attempt at self-defence, 'hemmed in on all sides, whichever way he turned confronting blows of weapons aimed at his face and eyes, driven hither and thither like a wild beast, was entangled in the hands of all; for all had to take part in the sacrifice and taste of the slaughter' (Plutarch, *Caesar* 66.6, trans. B. Perrin 1919). The hunting metaphor suggests horrifyingly that the conspirators have dehumanized the Roman dictator and reduced him to prey or meat. The sadistic particulars of the hunt jar with their setting in the senate-house and betray this killing as a bogus sacrifice.

For later readers of the classical accounts, the unpleasant rhetorical conjuncture of assassination and a hunt is exacerbated if Plutarch's account of the murder is merged with other versions. Then, whilst the assassins look upon a beast, Julius Caesar catches sight of close friends, perhaps even family. At the climax of the assassination, Caesar is confronted by Brutus and despairs. While Shakespeare was to give him the Latin tag *Et tu, Brute?* ('Also you, Brutus?'), some early reports which Suetonius and Dio had encountered claimed for him in his dying moments an intimate exclamation in Greek, καὶ σύ τέκνον; ('Also you, child?'). It would appear that, soon after the murder, attempts were made to construct the event as the gross betrayal of a father-figure, or even as parricide, for Brutus had always been highly favoured by Julius Caesar and, conveniently, rumours had even circulated that he was Caesar's illegitimate son. Similarly, the dignity with which the dictator tries to die (he uses his toga to cover his head and feet) is pitifully counterpoised in Suetonius' biography by the shameful details that his body suffered twenty-three stab wounds, lay abandoned for some time as the whole senate fled, and was finally carried home on a litter by three slaves, with one arm hanging down (Suetonius, *DJ* 82.3).

Like Julius Caesar's mode of government, his murder was the subject of violent controversy from the moment it was committed and led to more than a decade of further civil war. Although the assassins immediately represented themselves to the Roman

populace as their victorious liberators, and a few days later were formally thanked and pronounced honourable and patriotic citizens by
a seemingly conciliatory meeting of the senate, and although the
office of dictator was now abolished, Mark Antony (as Caesar's
successor in political authority) ensured that none of the dictator's
decrees were repealed and that he would receive a state funeral in
the forum – an honour reserved for Romans who had demonstrated the highest service to the republic.

The ceremony was carefully orchestrated: a solemn torch-lit
procession, a gilded shrine modelled on the temple of Venus,
within it an ivory couch decked with purple and gold coverlets, the
shocking display of the bloody, torn toga and a rotating wax image
of the corpse pitted with stab wounds. When Caesar's funeral
couch was finally brought down into the forum, Suetonius tells us
that two divine beings appeared suddenly and

> set fire to the couch with torches. Immediately the spectators
> assisted the blaze by heaping on it dry branches and the
> judges' chairs, and the court benches, with whatever else
> came to hand. Thereupon the musicians and the masked pro-
> fessional mourners, who had walked in the funeral train
> wearing the robes that he had himself worn at his four tri-
> umphs, tore these in pieces and flung them on the flames – to
> which veterans who had assisted at his triumphs added the
> arms they had then borne. Many women in the audience
> similarly sacrificed their jewellery together with their chil-
> dren's golden buttons and embroidered tunics. Public grief
> was enhanced by crowds of foreigners lamenting in their own
> fashion, especially Jews who loved Caesar for the friendship he
> had shown them, and came flocking to the Forum for several
> nights in succession.
>
> (Suetonius, *Deified Julius* 84.3–5. Trans. R. Graves, 1957)

The funeral rites triggered widespread resentment against the liberators – a resentment which was fed by the public disclosure of Caesar's generous bequests to the people of both money and gardens. The liberators were soon forced to flee the city, and by August the country. As contemporary witness to news of the cremation and the unofficial cult of Caesar, the rioting and the assaults on the properties of the liberators, and as direct observer of the rise of a new despot to take Caesar's place, Cicero acknowledged in private correspondence the manifest failure of the assassination's political rationale, even as he lauded the assassination itself: it was a deed undertaken with manly courage but infantile understanding (*Letters to Atticus* 14.21.3).

As to the moral virtue of killing Julius Caesar, Cicero was not in doubt. In his philosophical work *de officiis* (*On Duties*) composed late in 44 BC, Julius Caesar is obliquely presented as tyrant and aspirant king. But a tyrant is not human; he is a ferocious beast in human form. Just as we would have no compunction in removing a limb if it were lifeless, so tyrants are equally without human life and ought to be severed from the body of humanity (3.32). A correspondent of Cicero's, Gaius Matius, protests that he cannot raise himself to such philosophical heights. It is not a question of country and tyranny, humans and beasts, limbs and amputations in his letter to Cicero, but of friendship: although, he says, he did not approve of what Julius Caesar was doing, he had to stand by a friend over whose destruction he now grieves (Cicero, *Letters to Friends*, 11.28).

Such debates about the assassination themselves became deadly, however, as they were forced to become more pragmatic, when the Caesarians began a war of vengeance against the liberators and the longer and more intense struggle began between Mark Antony and Octavian to inherit Caesar's autocratic powers. Courageously, in a bold and ferocious warning to Antony, Cicero presented Julius

Caesar's assassination as a wonderful lesson which brave men would put into action without delay – a warning which was not delivered directly as a speech but widely circulated as a polemical pamphlet:

> Your ambition to reign, Antony, certainly deserves to be compared with Caesar's. But in not a single other respect are you entitled to the same comparison. For the many evils which Caesar inflicted upon our country have at least yielded certain benefits . . . Do these facts never occur to you? Do you never understand the significance of this: that brave men have now learnt to appreciate the noble achievement, the wonderful benefaction, the glorious renown, of killing a tyrant? When men could not endure Caesar, will they endure you? Mark my words, this time there will be crowds competing to do the deed. They will not wait for a suitable opportunity – they will be too impatient.
>
> (Cicero, *Second Philippic* 2.117–18. Trans. M. Grant, 1960)

But by the end of the following year, it was Cicero not Antony who was dead, killed on the orders of the Caesarians, his head and hands cut off and displayed in the forum on the speakers' platform.

The killing of Julius Caesar ceased to be a blunt instrument with which to threaten the rulers of Rome once the suicides of the chief conspirators on the battlefields of Philippi in 42 BC effectively brought the Roman republic to an end. And once Octavian had defeated Antony at the battle of Actium more than a decade later and transformed himself into the venerable 'Augustus', founder of an imperial monarchy (a mode of government which proved even more autocratic than the dictatorship of Julius Caesar), the murder could scarcely be described in public as one that deserved immediate imitation. Even Lucan's epic poem on the civil war between the Roman dictator and Pompey, which describes the murder in passing as the fitting punishment of a Roman tyrant and a warning to them all (*Civil War* 10.343–4), stops short of advocating openly the assassination of the current emperor Nero. In contrast, the first extant narrative of the dictator's death by Nicolaus of Damascus is embedded in a biography of the next Caesar (Augustus) and, while it is still too close to the conspiracy and murder to bestow on them epochal repercussions, their description as a botched coup against a politically incompetent and naive victim at least takes on a cautionary note – as a lesson in how to avoid rather than how to commit assassination.

Generally, however much imperial writers may criticize Julius Caesar's violations of the Roman constitution and distinguish him from subsequent Caesars, if they address the morality of his murder, they deplore it. The Roman senator and historian Cassius Dio, for example, after cataloguing the careful appointments the dictator made in anticipation of a welcome campaign against the Parthians, opens the next book of his Roman history with condemnation of Caesar's jealous and here unnamed 'slayers', who unlawfully and impiously deprived Rome of the stability it had at last acquired:

> but a baleful frenzy which fell upon certain men through jealousy of his advancement and hatred of his preferment to themselves caused his death unlawfully, while it added a new name to the annals of infamy; it scattered the decrees to the winds and brought upon the Romans seditions and civil wars once more after a state of harmony. His slayers, to be sure, declared that they had shown themselves at once destroyers of Caesar and liberators of the people: but in reality they impiously plotted against him, and they threw the city into disorder when at last it possessed a stable government.
>
> (Dio, *Roman History* 44.1.
> Trans. E. Cary, 1916)

Equivocation emerges most conspicuously, as Christopher Pelling has argued, only when the assassination of Julius Caesar is incorporated into a narrative centred around the chief conspirator Marcus Junius Brutus. Among his biographies of great soldiers and statesmen, Plutarch recounts both a *Life of Julius Caesar*, in which the murder is located close to the end of the story, and a *Life of Brutus* in which the murder occurs before the halfway point. Tyrannicide is a noble deed. Brutus' ancestor Lucius was honoured with a statue set among those of the kings when he rid Rome of the royal house of the Tarquins and established the republic. From the perspective of these two Brutii, disinterested tyrannicide admirably confronts arrogant ambition, republicanism courageously opposes kingship. Yet, at the opening of his *Life of Brutus*, Plutarch contrasts the humanity and temperamental balance of Marcus with the steely resolution of his ancestor, who was able to kill his own sons without hesitation because they had conspired to restore the kings to Rome:

> The Brutus who is the subject of this Life took pains to moderate his natural instincts by means of the culture and mental discipline which philosophy gives, while he also exerted himself to stir up the more placid and passive side of his character and force it into action, with the result that his temperament was almost ideally balanced to pursue a life of virtue. So we find that even those men who hated him most for his conspiracy against Julius Caesar were prepared to give the credit for any redeeming element in the murder to Brutus, while they blamed all that was unscrupulous about it upon Cassius, who, although a relative and a close friend of Brutus, was neither so simple in character nor so disinterested in his motives.
>
> (Plutarch, *Life of Brutus* 1. Trans. I. Scott-Kilvert, 1965)

The biographer proceeds to develop for Brutus both a major part and a moral dilemma in killing the dictator.

Initially, this humane idealist is reluctant to participate in the conspiracy because it represents a choice between public good and private loyalties, between country and a friend, benefactor and saviour (and, according to the rumour reported early in the *Life*, possibly even father). Tortured by the choice between patriotism and gratitude, Brutus is finally goaded to participate by the more self-interested and devious Cassius. At the culminating moment, when the slaughter has commenced, Caesar finally ceases to resist and yields his body up to the blows when he catches sight of his friend (and, possibly, son) closing in on him, dagger drawn. Presented in this way, we are given the opportunity to appreciate the terrible difficulty Brutus faced, the splendid selflessness of his choice, but also the tragedy for Brutus and for Caesar of this betrayal.

It was with these two *Lives* above all, and the *Life of Antony*, that William Shakespeare engaged to construct his tragic presentation of the assassination in his play *Julius Caesar* (1599), not directly but at two removes: via *The Parallel Lives of the Most Noble Greeks and Romans*, which had been published twenty years earlier by Sir Thomas North as an English version of a French translation by Jacques Amyot of the original Greek. Plutarch's biographies had achieved widespread circulation in the West by the end of the sixteenth century, once his text had been rendered more accessible first in Latin and then vernacular editions. His subtle equivocations about the murder were then appropriated and adapted by Shakespeare for a play which has become the most celebrated, the most familiar and the most influential representation in Western culture of the assassination of Julius Caesar. Over and above all other examples, the play is the prism through which Julius Caesar is now most commonly perceived, a Caesar whose life is defined first and foremost by its end.

Shakespeare's tragedy stages a heated debate about the assassination and then explores its catastrophic consequences. In a form of
rehearsal for the deadly assault on Caesar's person, the tribunes in
the play's opening scene order the removal of flattering trappings
from his images, because it is necessary thus to pluck the 'growing
feathers' from this bird of prey who soars above his fellow Romans
and keeps them all 'in servile fearfulness' (1.1.72–5). Brutus specu-
lates that once Caesar is crowned king and has ascended to the top
of ambition's ladder, he may scorn 'the base degrees' and only look
up to the clouds. The chief conspirator concludes, 'Then, lest he
may, prevent' (2.1.21–8).

The physical weakness, age and vulnerability with which
Shakespeare endows his Roman ruler place on the stage a neat
counterpart to the frailty of the English nation's current government. At the time of the play's first production in 1599, the
childless, ailing autocrat Elizabeth I had been on the throne for
more than forty years. Dispute over the succession, conspiracy and
rebellion were all in progress or imminent, generating fears that if
the Tudor monarchy were overthrown, civil war might follow.
Furthermore, from John of Salisbury in the Middle Ages right up to
the seventeenth-century parliamentarians, the paradigm of Julius
Caesar was constantly deployed in debates about tyrannicide.
Shakespeare's tragedy and English political philosophy share use of
both the Roman example and the vocabulary of tyranny (at
1.2.133–6, for example, Cassius compares great Caesar to a colossus,
in a simile which was elsewhere used to identify tyranny as a huge,
empty, overwhelming construct and one, therefore, liable to topple).
By the end of the sixteenth century, such debate had gained sufficient strength to challenge the authority of oppressive monarchy like
that imposed by Queen Elizabeth, to explore the advantages of
republicanism and, even, to consider the compensations of regicide
(if recast in terms of the removal of a wicked tyrant, rather than a

good, true king). In staging Roman history, Shakespeare's *Julius Caesar* elides Tudor present with Roman past and permits – while eluding censorship – explicit accusations of tyranny, urgent pleas for tyrannicide, the display of a bloody political assassination, deadly repression and bitter civil war.

Julius Caesar encourages its audiences to consider how you distinguish an arrogant tyrant from a just king, how you distinguish envious murderers from heroic patriots, and how you distinguish bloody murder from noble assassination. But nowadays most critics agree that its defining features (temporal disruptions, ambivalent characterizations, a binary structure and probing self-reflection) prohibit the retrieval of simple answers from within the text itself.

Disturbingly, the distance between historical past and its present reconstruction is both dissolved by the exploitation of disruptive anachronisms and reinforced to the point of alienation. The anachronistic clock which, in Act 2, infamously strikes for the conspirators on the morning of the murder alerts its auditors in the Globe Theatre to a specific connection between the regimes of Julius Caesar and Queen Elizabeth: namely, a dispute over the calendar's mismatch with the seasons, and the proclamation of controversial state (or, in the latter case, papal) edicts to adjust time which is out of sync. The political vocabulary of kings and commoners is interspersed with that of patricians, praetors and plebeians; chimney-tops and doublets mingle with trophies and the entrails of augury. Yet such suspension of difference works only to expose the dissimilarities which are most disconcerting. Contemporary debates about the legitimacy of tyrannicide hinged on a fundamental distinction between 'tyrant' and 'king', but the terms are interchangeably distasteful in the Elizabethan play as in republican Rome. And, ironically, Julius Caesar himself is presented at his most alien when he utters the only line of Latin contained in the play: *Et tu, Brute?* (3.1.77).

Characters and actions in *Julius Caesar* are as double-edged as the play's time-keeping. Cassius, the instigator of the conspiracy, holds to the conviction that Caesar is indeed a tyrant (1.3.103) because his fellow Romans have sheepishly permitted him to usurp their authority and now they endure a self-made bondage. Shakespeare's Caesar possesses some of the traits which political philosophy attributed to tyrants (imperiousness, insolence, obstinacy, fearfulness) and is described by means of conventional bestial metaphors: he is the wolf to the Romans' sheep, the lion to their hinds, a nascent serpent which needs killing in the shell. Yet this constitutes a perception of 'Caesar' as a public position, an incarnation of great power which the dictator himself compares not to lowly beasts but to the firmament's shining northern star (3.1.60). The man of flesh and blood is, in contrast, aged, physically frail, indecisive and trusting. In the absence of any extended soliloquies for Caesar, the theatre audience sees, but is not granted intimate access to, that more private and vulnerable figure.

In the last four centuries, many directors, actors, audiences and critics have performed and viewed Shakespeare's Brutus as a faultless embodiment of Roman civic virtue and republicanism. Yet, at the beginning of Act 2, the reluctant conspirator has serious difficulty in justifying the assassination to himself. He is here unconcerned with the restoration of the republic or civic liberty, but only with speculation about the aspirant king, who is not yet an unreasoned tyrant in practice, but may be in the making. Moreover, his idealistic concern to demonstrate the purity of the conspiracy's intentions ultimately brings ruin on his country for, later in the same scene, Brutus dismisses Cassius' practical proposal to kill Antony as well as Caesar, on the grounds that once they have cut off the head there is no need also to hack the limbs. Audiences familiar with the history of the Roman republic will be all too conscious of the naivety of this argument. He then adds:

> Let's be sacrificers, but not butchers, Caius.
> We all stand up against the spirit of Caesar,
> And in the spirit of men there is no blood.
> O, that we then could come by Caesar's spirit,
> And not dismember Caesar! But, alas,
> Caesar must bleed for it. And, gentle friends,
> Let's kill him boldly, but not wrathfully;
> Let's carve him as a dish fit for the gods,
> Not hew him as a carcass fit for hounds.
> And let our hearts, as subtle masters do,
> Stir up their servants to an act of rage,
> And after seem to chide 'em. This shall make
> Our purpose necessary, and not envious;
> Which so appearing to the common eyes,
> We shall be call'd purgers, not murderers.
>
> (Shakespeare, *Julius Caesar* 2.1.166–80)

Brutus recasts the killing as dispassionate, ceremonial sacrifice; his metaphors attempt to fix the conspirators not as butchers but as priests, who will slay an animal and serve it up to the gods in a ritual of state purification. And then, emphasizing the appearance over the substance of moral rectitude, he urges that the assassins – subtle masters of their every gesture – subsequently give out the impression that they regret what they have just done.

After the dictator's murder at the opening of Act 3, before Brutus instructs the assassins to walk out into the marketplace waving their weapons over their heads and crying 'Peace, freedom, and liberty!', he seeks to make the killing into a sacrifice by urging that they besmear their swords and bathe their hands up to the elbows in Caesar's blood (3.1.105–10). Critics have long observed that in performance such a visual parade of Caesar's blood, along with the constant display of his mutilated corpse, would provide tangible, grotesque reminders of the moral disorder in Brutus' attempt to direct events. As in Plutarch's narration, so in the London theatre, we are invited to reject the staging of Caesar's assassination as holy sacrifice and reinterpret it as after all a brutal hunt. Antony soon provides the counter metaphors to sustain such a reinterpretation. Speaking directly to the mutilated corpse, in the very presence of the assassins, he plays on the pun that Caesar was 'a brave hart', one who was brought to bay by hunters now marked crimson by their spoil (3.1.204–10). After the conspirators have left the senate, Antony styles them precisely in the terms Brutus had attempted to silence with his metaphors of sacrifice – as butchers (3.1.255). Finally, in the next scene set in the forum before the plebeians, Antony tantalizingly proclaims from the pulpit that the commons would kiss dead Caesar's wounds and dip their napkins in 'his sacred blood' if only they heard his generous bequests to them (3.2.132–9). It is as if Brutus and his fellow conspirators have slaughtered not a ceremonial beast but a blessed martyr, whose blood becomes not a banner of civic liberty but a cherished holy relic.

It is not Caesar but the conspirators who butcher, and it is not Caesar but his successors who cruelly condemn Romans to death. Julius Caesar may be the tragedy's eponymous hero but his appearances are few, often brief, and confined to the first half of the play. This binary structure effectively demonstrates, as Brutus also discloses in his speech above, that Shakespeare's drama does not centre on the man of flesh and blood but on his spirit or, perhaps, his public image as 'Caesar'. Brutus slays the bleeding body but the murder empowers its disembodied name as vengeful ghost. No reliable source of government takes the dictator's place. Caesar was ambitious, the conspirators resentful, the rest of the senate feeble, the plebeians open to persuasion and his successors vindictive and vicious. The play closes with a civil war still unfinished.

The Shakespearean distinction between the body of Julius Caesar and his deathless image embeds a strong sense of the dictator's construction and reception into the tragedy itself. The play reflects upon the linguistic fashioning of Caesar undertaken by both the dictator himself and his contemporaries, upon his narration in history, and even his performance as political theatre. Shakespeare's Caesar frequently speaks about and perceives himself in the third person. He constructs himself and is constructed by the other Roman characters as a public figure distinct from the private self. Through the grandiose rhetorical style of this tragedy, its public proclamations, abstract debates and declamatory speeches, 'Caesar' is staged as political utterance and the assassination as simultaneously an historical act and a theatrical performance.

Cassius attempts to articulate a tyrant Caesar out of the glossary of tyrannicide, while Brutus seeks to stage murder as sacrifice. While ritually washing themselves in Caesar's blood, both conspirators self-consciously predict a future performance history for the fateful play they are themselves acting out:

> CASSIUS: Stoop, then, and wash. How many ages hence,
> Shall this our lofty scene be acted over,
> In states unborn and accents yet unknown!
> BRUTUS: How many times shall Caesar bleed in sport,
> That now on Pompey's basis lies along,
> No worthier than the dust!
>
> (Shakespeare, *Julius Caesar* 3.1.111–16)

As Romans engaged in a killing of undoubtedly enormous consequence, the conspirators predict its translation from the glorious history they are now trying to manufacture into other languages and cultures, and its re-enactment as theatrical entertainment. As players in the Globe Theatre, they self-reflexively predict the success of Shakespeare's *Julius Caesar* and its endless repetition on the Western stage.

Metadramatic strategies such as these have contributed significantly to the fulfilment of the second prediction. The play's representation of the assassination of one of the most famous leaders in Western history, its ideological flexibility, and its own engagement with the fashioning of history and the theatricality of politics have all ensured its central place in the Western dramatic canon and helped popularize the drama of Caesar's death as persistently relevant to the time in which it is performed. Since its first presentation in London's Globe Theatre in 1599, Shakespeare's *Julius Caesar* has achieved world-wide recognition and continues to be called back on to the stage or read as part of the school curriculum of many countries. Historians of Shakespearean theatre even boast that it has been published in more editions and more copies than any play in any language. My focus here will be on some episodes in the long and rich production history of *Julius Caesar* in the United States of America, because its staging there has been tied explicitly and often to large-scale questions about national identity, domestic government and foreign policy. In the US, Shakespeare's rendition of the dictator's death and its aftermath has been played or understood as a contemporary tragedy about revolution, dictatorship and war.

The first recorded performance on North American soil of Shakespeare's *Julius Caesar* took place on 1 June 1770 at Philadelphia's Southwark Theater. Advertised as never before acted in America, the production was now incorporated into the repertory of the American Company at a time of pronounced resistance to British colonial rule. A thorough education in Greek and Latin, as well as a broader cultural engagement with antiquity, had supplied colonial statesmen with many classical models for rule, resistance and revolution. But the Roman republic in particular was idealized as a model of government for the New World of the eighteenth century. As American resistance developed into revolution and then into open war, Julius Caesar came to epitomize the greatest political villainy (the rise of tyranny and the destruction of · republics) and Great Britain was styled in political debate as Caesar to America's Rome (that is, a corrupting, pernicious influence).

When, for example, the British government passed an act which for the first time would levy tax directly from the colonies without the consent of their assemblies, the revolutionary leader and famed orator Patrick Henry passionately protested against the degeneration of George III's rule into tyranny. In a celebrated speech, delivered in May 1765 to the delegates of the colony of Virginia's House of Burgesses, he declared that the British king might profit from the knowledge that 'Caesar had his Brutus'. Although required to apologize for such treason by the Speaker, reports of Henry's speech were widely circulated and stimulated radicals in other colonies to similar or even greater acts of defiance. In their increasingly seditious rhetoric, American intellectuals came to revere Cato and Cicero as noble statesmen who had courageously sacrificed their lives in vain resistance to the Roman dictator's rise to autocratic power, and passionately identified with Brutus and Cassius as having heroically assassinated Caesar in order to save their republic.

Alongside the works of classical authors, the text of Shakespeare's *Julius Caesar* was also much read by the eighteenth-century revolutionaries, and rousing sayings of the conspirators were extracted from it for preservation in commonplace books or for circulation in letters and political pamphlets, such as 'Cassius from bondage will deliver Cassius' (1.3.90) or 'There is a tide in the affairs of men, / Which, taken at the flood, leads on to fortune' (4.3.217–8). In the revolution's early years, for example, Abigail Adams used to send heartening letters containing quotations from the play to her husband John (one day to become the second president of the emergent nation), and even signed them 'Portia', that is as principled Shakespearean character and wife of a tyrant-slayer. Thus *Julius Caesar* was first performed in the New World as a call to arms to fight for American liberty against English tyranny.

On 31 May 1770, the *Pennsylvania Journal* carried a notice of the next day's premiere sandwiched between offers of reward for the capture and return of a runaway slave and a black horse, advertisements for starch and hair powder, and sales pitches for tracts of land or spaces on ships sailing to Bristol and the Barbados. The notice advised that the play contains:

> The noble struggles for Liberty by that renowned patriot, Marcus Brutus: the death of Caesar in the Capitol, the remarkable orations of Brutus and Antony, upon that occasion. The first shewing the necessity of his death, to give Freedom to the Roman People; the latter to enflame their minds, and excite them to a commotion, in which the orator succeeds, and is the cause of the civil wars.

Yet severe alterations to the received text were required in order to reshape the tragedy as a stirring work of revolutionary sentiment able to inculcate (in the words of the play's producer Francis Gentleman) 'one of the noblest principles that actuates the human mind, the love of national liberty'. As a strategy which would be regularly repeated in later productions in the United States and elsewhere, the text was cut or rewritten, and whole incidents omitted which might be thought to detract from Brutus' heroic achievement. These are usually thought to be the scenes in which Cinna the poet is killed without cause by the vengeful Roman mob (3.3), where Caesar's successors tick off enemies to be slaughtered (4.1), and when Caesar's apparition appears to taunt Brutus (4.3). So reconstituted, a performance of the tragedy might then aim to call upon all loyal Americans to play the part of a Brutus – to act out the role of new liberators who, in their distinct context, might this time succeed in overthrowing tyranny and turn England's colonies into a new nation, an enduring American republic. Together Julius Caesar and Shakespeare provide enhanced historical legitimacy and cultural authority, as well as forceful rhetoric and imitable dramatic action, for this kind of propaganda which could now advocate revolution and war in an easily decipherable code.

It is perhaps no surprise, therefore, that from the time of the war of independence until well into the nineteenth century Shakespeare's *Julius Caesar* was not performed on the English stage, whereas the play was immediately co-opted into the cultural life of the new American nation. On stage, at school and in the political arena, the tragedy became a key means to bind America's new mode of democratic government to that of the Roman republic and to stimulate the republican ideals of political liberty and civic virtue on which the Founding Fathers had drawn to establish their nation. And, whatever the complexities of the original text's politics, it was almost invariably performed, read and cited until the twentieth century as a re-presentation in the past of America's even more glorious (because victorious) struggle for liberty and the death of tyranny.

By the mid-nineteenth century, *Julius Caesar* was fast becoming the most commonly taught Shakespeare play in American high schools, and its performance was undertaken with fanfare on the frontiers and as a gala in the larger cities. In New York's Winter Garden Theater, on the 25 November 1864, the three Booth brothers took the stage together in a lavish benefit performance which was briefly disrupted by a fire in the building next door. The fire was generally believed to have been one of many arson attacks launched that night by Confederates wishing to bring the Civil War, now in its third year, home to the Unionist North. Family witnesses reported that, in heated debate over breakfast the next morning, brother Edwin declared for President Abraham Lincoln, while John Wilkes (a star in the South) violently opposed him on the grounds that the President was grown so powerful he would soon be crowned king of America. Within months, on 14 April 1865, John Wilkes Booth shot Lincoln at a theatre in Washington. Subsequent newspaper reporting of the assassination – the first of a president of the United States – could conveniently add extra drama to the already dramatic deed by dressing it, and the Shakespearean actor turned assassin, in the rhetoric of a Caesarian tragedy. But John Wilkes had not merely in delusion merged his art with life; he (like many others) saw President Lincoln as a domestic Caesar in need of his tyrant-slaying Brutus.

At the time of the constitutional debates of 1787–8, many American politicians and intellectuals had expressed their alarm that a presidential Caesar could be created by the structures of government now being put into place. Opponents of federalism's centripetal and hierarchical organization criticized the scope it gave the executive branch to abuse power and, in particular, warned that the joint office of president and commander-in-chief constituted an accumulation of powers comparable to those of a monarch or a military despot. In sum, and invoking a colonial memory of the hated Julius Caesar, the war of independence had expelled tyranny only to invite it back in. When once the United States turned to empire-building, Caesarism became a regular term of abuse to be hurled at presidents who appeared to be menacing demagogues, autocrats or imperialists (for modern examples, see Chapter 7, above). Lincoln too was subjected to such attacks, particularly during the course of the Civil War of 1861–5, when he centralized government even further and regularly violated the law. The Republican President appears to have represented himself defensively as a Brutus-figure in the mould of the revolutionaries and the Founding Fathers: working to protect the nation 'conceived in Liberty', preserve the republic from destruction by new tyrannies, save the Union, emancipate the slaves. Yet he often attracted accusations of Caesarism, while his opponents in the South began to issue calls to follow Roman history, to resist his usurpations of power, even to assassinate him.

During the height of the Civil War, on 24 October 1863, the *Southern Illustrated News* (a weekly newspaper published in Richmond, Virginia, for a brief two-year period) carried on its front cover – as it did every week – a sketch of a Confederate general alongside an article praising his role in the war. On the back cover appeared a cartoon reproduced from the London *Punch* carrying the title 'Brutus and Caesar' and subtitled 'From the American Edition of Shakespeare' (Figure 8.1). The scene is elucidated within the newspaper. An Ethiopian banjo-player ('dis child') has fallen asleep while singing about the Civil War. Rather than wake him, Brutus/Lincoln asks for his copy of Shakespeare's plays with citations from which the President was known to entertain his staff (here specified respectively as the US Secretaries of State and of War): 'Where is the noble work whence I cull anecdotes and jocund jests, wherewith to announce my statesmanship, making smooth Seward smile, stiff Stanton scowl?' Instead there arrives the 'black spectre' of Caesar, who declares, 'I am dy ebil genus, massa LINKING.'

From the British perspective, through its radical incongruities (the caricature of a black slave as majestic Caesar, the stars and stripes for a toga, a perplexed Lincoln in tunic and sandals, the distortion of Shakespearean verse into the imagined argot of the Negro), the cartoon derides the Roman posturings of American

Fig. 8.1 'Brutus and Caesar', *Southern Illustrated News* (24 October 1863).

statesmen, the Americanization of Shakespeare and the appropriation of *Julius Caesar* as a play about contemporary American politics. But, in its new context, for the citizens of the Confederacy, the cartoon ridicules any suggestion that Lincoln is an heroic, Shakespearean Brutus in the most viciously racist and, therefore, pertinent terms. Here an embodiment of slavery (rendered more convincing by the common use in the South of 'Caesar' as a slave name) comes back to haunt Brutus/Lincoln, and readers can gratify themselves that, in repeating the course of Roman history and the plot of Shakespeare's tragedy, the 'hero' will lose the civil war and die in the next and final act.

For John Wilkes Booth, the President was without question an American Caesar and he the true American successor to Brutus. On the evening of 14 April 1865, after he had leapt down onto the stage and fired his pistol up into the presidential box, Booth waved his weapon (in adaptation of the directions given by Shakespeare's Brutus to his fellow conspirators after Caesar's murder) and cried out to the audience '*Sic semper tyrannis*. The South is avenged.' To Southern politicians and partisans alike, their bond with the Roman republic seemed tighter than that of the North: after all, they too were governed by a privileged oligarchy whose aristocratic power was built on ownership of land and slaves, an oligarchy who were now being brought to ruin by the North's authoritarian, repressive government. In the first part of his pronouncement, the Shakespearean actor was quoting the state motto of Virginia (in English translation 'so always tyranny [is brought to an end]'). The Latin motto appeared on the state seal whose obverse displays a tyrant crushed under the heel of armed Virtue. Booth, who had once briefly served in the Virginia militia, was thus responding to Southern protests against the President's violations of the constitution by activating its republican ideal of always crushing tyranny. In anticipation of the assassination, he even named the day to himself as 'the Ides'.

John Wilkes also continued to keep a diary while on the run, vividly revealing the intimacy with which he had taken on the heroic version of Brutus' assassination of Julius Caesar, thus to sanitize and endow with a noble moral authority his act of murder:

After being hunted like a dog through swamps, woods, and last night being chased by gun-boats till I was forced to return wet cold and starving, with every man's hand against me, I am here in despair. And why? For doing what Brutus was honored for.

(Quoted from T. Derrick, Understanding Shakespeare's Julius Caesar, 1998:128)

Shakespearean phraseology then infested the shocked accounts of the assassination which were published in both Northern and Southern newspapers. The Republicans organized a three-week long funeral pageant which took President Lincoln's embalmed body – its face still disfigured by the bullet wound – on a special train around the major cities of the North. The witnessing of the mutilated body by millions of spectators was seen by one senator sympathetic to the Confederate cause as another example of the cunning despotism of the Federal Union: a political trick akin to 'the crafty skill of Mark Antony in displaying to the Roman people the bloody mantle of Caesar'.

Thus, in the nineteenth century, Shakespeare's Caesar was infamously appropriated to dress up an American president as a despot and Shakespeare's Brutus to stage that president's assassination as a noble drama. Most commonly, though, such political appropriations have been acted out as theatre rather than reality. In the twentieth century, the most celebrated and influential performance of Shakespeare's tragedy in the United States, the version directed by Orson Welles in 1937, presented Caesar's assassination memorably as a swift series of increasingly alarming events, punctuated by sharp contrasts of light and darkness and jarring sound effects, bluntly staged, dressed in present-day costume, all devised to evoke the format of a current-affairs radio broadcast, documentary film footage or a living newspaper. Both the modernist style of this production (which was pointedly entitled in its advertising *Julius Caesar: Death of a Dictator*) and the context of its consumption as theatre invited audiences to understand it as an urgent warning and a vital lesson about the contemporary rise of dictatorships, the inadequacies of liberalism to combat them, and the dangerous enthusiasm of the masses for autocratic rule.

Welles's *Caesar* constituted the inaugural production of the Mercury Theater in New York, a new radical company, partly funded by left-wing organizations, which consciously targeted a working-class and African-American clientele, charged low ticket prices, and held to a radical manifesto of both entertaining and informing its audience through a repertoire of plays that had a special bearing on contemporary life. To that end, the text of Shakespeare's *Julius Caesar* was profoundly cut and simplified; scenes were reorganized, the identity of speakers changed, and the last two acts of the play almost completely eliminated. The tragedy's second half (the vengeance of Caesar accomplished through the machinations of Antony, the appearance of the ghost and the initiation of civil war) was especially condensed not, as in the late eighteenth and nineteenth centuries, to buttress the otherwise fragile heroism of Brutus, but in order to sharpen the focus on three protagonists in the tragedy generated by dictatorship: Caesar, Brutus, and the mob.

Under the direction of Welles, this populist *Julius Caesar* also subordinated Shakespeare's text to experimental and bruising performance strategies better to bind Roman (and Tudor) past to Europe's Fascist present. Rejecting the vastly elaborate scenography and stately choreography expected of productions of Shakespeare in the nineteenth century, the set was bare and urban in design, comprising a series of stacked platforms reaching back to the blood-red brick wall of the theatre itself, its pipes, hoses and radiators fully on view. Contemporary dress-code and the choreography of Fascism (with its salutes, processions and massed ranks of spectators all familiar from magazine illustrations or newsreel footage of 1930s Italy and Germany) presented Caesar as a ranting military dictator surrounded by uniformed henchmen and rowdy workers, and Antony as his rabble-rousing replacement (Figure 8.2). The conspirators hid behind overcoats, up-turned collars and large fedoras. Brutus was set apart as a troubled liberal politician in a double-breasted pin-stripe suit. The original score for trumpet, horn, percussion and organ (including bugle calls and drum beats) was composed to evoke Fascism's military parades, while the remarkably complex and piercing columns of light which, pouring down from overhead or

Fig. 8.2 Antony in Orson Welles's *Julius Caesar: The Death of a Dictator* (1937).

streaming up from below, singled out and shadowed members of the cast were suggestive of the spectacular staging of the night-time Nuremberg rallies.

Shakespeare's Caesar was now contrived as a vilification of the Italian dictator Mussolini since, in the legitimating political discourse of Fascism, the *duce* had constructed and was continuing to disseminate both at home and abroad a close identification between himself and the Roman general (see Chapters 4 and 7). So successful was the reproduction of Mussolini's attire and gesture (the dark, tightly belted military uniform, the head thrown back, the Fascist salute) that reviewers frequently noted a remarkable physical resemblance between this 'sawdust' Caesar and the Italian dictator (the large brow, the staring eyes, the jutting chin). The identification was brought most vividly to the attention of audiences at the very beginning of the performance. Shakespeare's opening scene, in which the Roman tribunes berate the commoners for celebrating Caesar's triumph and forgetting Pompey's, was both shortened and postponed. Instead, the utter darkness and the ominous tones of the overture were abruptly interrupted by a shaft of light, a voice crying 'Caesar', and the sudden presence on the New York stage of the Roman dictator dressed in contemporary Fascist uniform, saluting a responsive crowd.

In the context of this insistently anti-Fascist production of *Julius Caesar*, Welles was adamant that there was no place for Shakespeare's equivocations about the dictator:

Caesar is almost a cartoon dictator; he doesn't have to be played that way, but he can never be played sympathetically. He can either be full of pompous boast or ice-cold genius, but there's no love between him and Brutus. There's nothing that makes it a story of betrayal at all.

(Orson Welles in *This is Orson Welles*, 1998: 301)

This is an emblematic tyrant of few frailties, little indecision and no human warmth, whose accelerating accumulation of powers is fast destroying the traditional freedoms of the state.

Nonetheless, the scene of the assassination was carefully choreographed to portray some of the difficulty of eradicating dictatorship. The conspirators are disposed in a diagonal line leading from the back of the stage. Rolling forward from one to the other, Caesar is stabbed by each in turn. At the footlights, the chief conspirator is left, leaning against a wall. Caesar falls to his knees and turns to Brutus as if to his last hope of safety. Without a word, Brutus takes his dagger out of his pocket as Caesar clutches at his collar. Only the dying cry of Caesar breaks the silence. Had Welles contrived identification between this Caesar and Hitler, the scene might then have better matched eighteenth- and nineteenth-century performances of Virtue victorious over Tyranny, but in the 1930s the evocation of Mussolini might still provide some small correspondence with Shakespeare's distinctions between the public image and the less daunting person.

Prior to the assassination scene, moreover, Welles had already begun to characterize Brutus as a tragic liberal who would become an heroic failure. In one of the weekly bulletins issued by the Mercury Theater company, the director provocatively described the chief conspirator as 'the eternal, impotent, ineffectual, fumbling liberal; the reformer who wants to do something about things but doesn't know how and gets it in the neck in the end. He's dead right all the time, and dead at the final curtain.' On stage, he substantiated the description by himself playing the noble Roman – against the dominant tradition of preceding American theatre (including that of the Booth brothers) – as no high-minded moralist and man of action, but a dreamer, tentative, self-conscious and bewildered.

The criticisms reviewers made of this rendition of Shakespeare's Brutus missed the radicalism of *Julius Caesar: The Death of a Dictator*, which took as its overriding theme not the necessity of eradicating European dictatorship, but the ineffectiveness of liberalism in a world where the masses desire dictatorship and, therefore, are capable of generating and regenerating Fascism – a world of which the United States is a part. Hence the highlight of the New York production was a much adapted and extended version of the death of Cinna the poet. His murder is recounted in Plutarch's biographies. On his way to the forum to mourn at Julius Caesar's funeral pyre, this friend of the dictator is ironically mistaken for Cinna the conspirator and orator, who had publicly denounced the dictator moments after the assassination. As a result, the poet is torn to pieces by the savage crowd (*Caesar* 68.2–4 and *Brutus* 20.5–6). In Shakespeare's tragedy, the scene of Cinna the Poet's death occurs immediately after Mark Antony has whipped the plebeians into a frenzy; as an echo or repetition in miniature of the conspirators' assassination of Julius Caesar it uncomfortably connects the supposedly noble republican rationale of Brutus with the base passions of the mob (who are seeking instance revenge for the murder of their beloved leader), the ritual sacrifice of a tyrant with the bestial onslaught on a man of letters. Consequently, until this moment, Act 3.3 was invariably omitted from American productions of Shakespeare's play.

In the memorably brutal version staged by Welles, a gang surround the poet, who disappears altogether in their midst save for one raised hand and one last scream. The mob rushes him away down the ramp at the back of the stage, as if he were being devoured by an animal. The mob which appeared on stage in *The Death of a Dictator* was identified by the director with 'the hoodlum element you find in any big city after a war, a mob that is without the stuff that makes them intelligently alive, a lynching mob, the kind of mob that gives you a Hitler or a Mussolini'. For Orson Welles, then, what permanently removes dictatorship is not the act of assassination, but the education of the masses. And what might best make them become 'intelligently alive' is clearly political drama such as this radical production of Shakespeare's *Julius Caesar.*

The 1937 modern-dress production of *Julius Caesar: The Death of a Dictator* was a huge success and came to be much admired for its unconventional staging and its extraordinary topicality; the *New York Post* for 12 November 1937, for example, commented that 'if the play ceases to be Shakespeare's tragedy, it does manage to become ours'. And throughout its long run and its subsequent road tour, Orson Welles attempted robustly to fulfil his company's manifesto promise to educate as well as entertain. Lectures on Shakespeare's play and its contemporary relevance were offered to schools, and huge blocks of seats were made available for school and college bookings. Educative brochures were composed especially for these young audiences, and single-sheet mock-ups of tabloid newspapers carried banner headlines such as 'Dictator Slain, Rome Revolts' to demonstrate graphically the play's engagement with contemporary political concerns about Fascism. Although it was not the first American production to dress Shakespeare's *Julius Caesar* in modern trappings, *Death of a Dictator* was hugely influential on the modernizing style of many subsequent performances of the play and on the strategies developed to teach it at American schools.

Julius Caesar is still read in many high schools, and a vast pedagogic literature exists for teachers on how best to demonstrate the vital currency of both Roman republican history and Elizabethan drama. For example, in *Ready-to-Use Activities for Teaching Julius Caesar* (1993), one of a whole series of works each dedicated to a single Shakespeare play, the author argues that although American teenagers are no longer particularly familiar with the historical Julius Caesar in the absence of Latin classes on his *Gallic Wars*, they can – with the right encouragement – identify nonetheless with the

Elizabethan play's themes. As one 'focusing activity', the book suggests students be asked to improvise the scenario of a conversation, in a public park in Washington, DC, between two young, idealistic United States senators:

> Clark has recently been discussed as a possible vice-presidential candidate for the next election. Brook was elected recently because she believes strongly in the principles of representative democracy as stated in the U.S. Constitution. Clark has learned of a movement to abolish the United States House of Representatives and the Senate in favor of allowing the President to remain in office for life. Clark tells Brook that a group of other Senators and Representatives fear the President's increasing power and plan to assassinate the President. For the plan to succeed, Clark needs Brook's help. Improvise the dialogue between them.
>
> (J. W. Swope 1993: 23)

Whereas Shakespeare's Brutus and Cassius had been taken to heart by John Wilkes Booth as exemplary agents for an American assassination, here assassination becomes one possible outcome of an imaginary scenario peopled by the fictitious American senators Brook and Clark. Now *Julius Caesar* is not a stirring guide to real action in American political life, but improvising American political action is a guide to understanding, and passing examinations in, the Elizabethan play.

At the start of the twenty-first century, however, American audiences of Shakespeare's *Julius Caesar* have again been asked to take its staging of both political assassination and its tragic consequences as a challenging exploration of an acute and pressing political crisis of international dimensions. The play was revived, for example, at the Chicago Shakespeare Theater in December 2002, closing only a month before the invasion of Iraq. In local press interviews, the director Barbara Gaines gave an account of her preparations for the production which stood to attract intrigued readers to attend a performance. In the months leading up to the opening – when international dispute was escalating over the necessity and the legitimacy of overthrowing the Iraqi regime, and when Congress was investing in the President of the United States the power to declare war and initiate an invasion – the director would read the *Chicago Tribune* and the *New York Times* before arriving for rehearsal and, as it seemed, entering seamlessly into the world of ancient Rome. There the names may have been Brutus, Julius Caesar and Antony, not Colin Powell, Saddam Hussein and George Bush, but to Gaines the ancient power struggles now took on an intense familiarity.

As a text assigned for study at school, the director recalled, Shakespeare's *Julius Caesar* had been flat and predictable:

> But now I understand – thanks to the horrible situation in the world today – what it's about. The conspirators all end up dead, end up hurting their country. The questions asked are, 'Is the assassination of a world leader really the answer to complex questions? If this person is assassinated, how does it change the assassinated leader and the people around the assassinated leader? Does violence itself do good? Does it heal? How has history changed?' Shakespeare just asks the questions. He doesn't moralize. He just asks. The time couldn't be more right [to stage *Julius Caesar*].
>
> (Barbara Gaines, quoted in the *Chicago Tribune*,
> 15 December 2002)

Gaines represents her production to its potential audience variously as a mode of political interrogation, a challenge to the existing order or a patriotic stimulus to national debate. Her goal, she concludes, is for people to leave the theatre needing to ask questions of their government and of themselves.

As in the New York production of 1937, the use of contemporary dress and props in the performances at the Chicago theatre provided a strong visual invitation to see the Elizabethan drama of Roman tyrannicide and its failures as a warning for the American present, while the disposition of vocal actors among the audience at all three levels of the theatre was designed to heighten engagement with the play's crowd scenes. When Julius Caesar arrives in Act 1.2, the stage swarms with police officers wearing flak-jackets, helmets and assault rifles, while most of his entourage are formally dressed in tuxedoes, business suits or evening gowns. Brutus is played as a brooding, divided politician and agonized intellectual (identified here by his sweater and wire-rimmed glasses), Antony as a playboy. Cinna is beaten to death and stripped of his jacket and shoes in 3.3, while in 5.5 Brutus impales himself on his knife to the sound of heavy gunfire offstage.

Both near the opening and the close of the performance, reporters, photographers and television crews mill round the Roman characters further to alert audiences that this representation of the assassination of Julius Caesar anticipates (in, perhaps, only modestly more extravagant terms) the news which might soon appear in American and international media. Although the director took care to express her political neutrality (stating explicitly that she did not blame the Republican Party for the current desire in the United States to overthrow the government of Saddam Hussein), her production graphically displayed a sense that on such tyrannicide there would inevitably follow catastrophic war. Grim, swirling clouds and dark storms were projected over the performance space, and the face of Caesar lit up red skies. Hostile reviewers were quick to spot the despised liberal credentials this seemed to bring to Shakespeare's *Julius Caesar*: 'to the extent that the production has a political message . . . it's that of the holier-than-the-Democrats Left, insisting that because even the heroes are flawed there's no difference between them and villains' (www.aislesay.com).

Another notable modern-dress production of the play was staged in New York at the Belasco Theater in spring 2005, coinciding roughly with the Ides of March and with the second anniversary of the invasion of Iraq, and it too was criticized in right-wing quarters as another example of Shakespeare distorted into knee-jerk liberalism. Notably the first major revival of *Julius Caesar* on Broadway since that of Orson Welles almost seventy years earlier, again *mise en scène* and the presentation of Brutus supported most of the weight of the production's political conception. The director Daniel Sullivan set the play in a ravaged state, a city of crumbling grandeur strewn with scaffolding and rubble. One of the banners which flew over it bore the face of Caesar – a face which, for some reviewers, seemed to recall that of Saddam Hussein. In the first half, Roman politicians wore business suits; commoners carried security passes around their necks. The assassination took place in a boardroom inside the Senate (Figure 8.3), access to which required passage through metal detectors. In the second half, among the headless statues and the ruined facades, Brutus and Cassius, Octavius and Antony wore camouflage fatigues and berets, and carried assault rifles. The conflict and the suicides were bloody and noisy, accompanied by the sounds of explosive gunfire and overhead helicopters.

Most of the press coverage of the production was devoted to evaluation of the acting style of the Hollywood film star Denzel Washington, who had been cast as Brutus. For some critics, his self-questioning timbre and tired, doubting look marked the anxieties of an actor insufficiently experienced for such complex Shakespearean roles. For others, it belonged wholly appropriately to a Brutus who should indeed exude an unsettled air of 'someone who hears the world as a symphony of mixed signals'. In at least

Fig. 8.3 The assassination scene in a New York production of Shakespeare's *Julius Caesar* (2005).

one of his many publicity interviews, however, the star of this *Julius Caesar* attempted to fix an even more provocative analogy for its potential audiences than concern with the morality of killing a dictator and its aftermath. According to the *New York Times* for 3 April 2005, when interviewed in his Belasco dressing room, Washington pulled out a magazine photograph of President George W. Bush surrounded by his inner circle and then asked who would lead the rebellion 'if he decided he wanted to make himself King, like Julius Caesar'. Asked by the journalist, in turn, who would be Brutus, 'the conflicted honorable man', he replied: 'You know, the obvious one is Colin Powell. But I don't know. Condoleezza might be Brutus. You just don't know.' The comparison here of George W. Bush with Julius Caesar is, as we have seen in the preceding

chapter, no passing fancy. Its use interlocks the New York production with the widespread left-liberal critiques of the Bush
administration which had begun to escalate in the years after the
invasion of Iraq, a critique couched in terms of its aggressive imperialism and increasingly Caesarian mode of government. Readers of
the interview are thus invited by the star of the production to see
its decayed marble city differently – no longer now a reflection of
Iraq in the post-invasion present but, even more disturbingly, of the
neo-classical capital of the United States in the near future – riddled
with decay and corruption, in need of radical purification and
renewal.

While the analogies advertised and employed in these recent
revivals of Shakespeare's *Julius Caesar* may seem to some theatre critics merely superficial gimmicks of setting, costume and casting
undertaken in order to generate publicity and good box office,
they constitute nonetheless a fresh phase in the rich tradition of
staging Shakespeare's Roman tragedy as an American play and are
tightly bound up with widespread political polemic concerning
American imperialism and a Caesarian presidency. Such techniques
of analogy are thus indicative of the continuing and profound
attraction of Julius Caesar and his assassination (especially, but not
exclusively, in the form of Shakespeare's reconstruction of its instigation and its consequences) as mechanisms for interrogating
American political policy and its global repercussions in the twenty-
first century.

9

DIVINITY

Whether planned or thrust upon him, Julius Caesar had already accrued an aura of divinity and even some rituals of worship before he died. Divinity was an integral feature of absolute and hereditary rule in antiquity; as queen of Egypt, for example, Cleopatra VII was also venerated as a mother goddess. The touch of divinity would enable a Roman ruler to share in the continuous and permanent authority of the gods, rather than the merely temporary authority of magistrates.

Signs of the construction of a divine Caesar had existed from early on: his youthful claims to descent from the goddess Venus; the sacred powers he won when appointed as Rome's most senior priest in 63 BC; the catalogue of portents and miracles which appeared to accompany his life. But in 46 BC, although the dictator had already been revered for a few years in the province of Asia as a god made manifest and saviour of all mankind, in Rome his divinity still required further development. Cicero summarizes dismissively the divine honours Julius Caesar accumulated from 46 to 44 BC as a couch, an image, a pediment and a priest (*Philippics* 2.110). As we have seen in Chapter 8, the senate, having granted Caesar the right to clothe his body ceremonially in triumphal dress, decreed that his image (an ivory statue similarly attired) was to be carried in festal procession from its location in the temple of Jupiter to the Circus, and there placed alongside other images of the Roman gods on a cushioned couch. His house was to be adorned with a pediment; temples were to be built – one specifically for the worship of the new god, another for his Clemency – and Mark Antony appointed as their priest. Many other measures also helped elevate Caesar to a god of state in his own lifetime: his statue in every temple at Rome and in the municipalities, the month of his birth renamed Iulius, public sacrifices on his birthday, offerings for his welfare on other anniversaries, the honorific title *Iuppiter Iulius*, and all such decrees of deification inscribed in letters of gold on silver tablets for display at the feet of Capitoline Jupiter.

The list of portents and prodigies which immediately preceded the assassination begins with a brief observation by Cicero, and then undergoes embellishment and amplification in subsequent retellings. The horses which Caesar had promised and then dedicated to the river Rubicon in exchange for a safe crossing now refused to eat and wept copious tears. A bull he sacrificed was found to have no heart. He was warned of the impending danger by a soothsayer and, the very night before the Ides, his wife Calpurnia dreamt that the pediment which newly adorned their house collapsed and that her husband was stabbed in her arms, whereas Caesar dreamt he flew above the clouds and clasped the hand of Jupiter.

After the assassination, some of Caesar's followers were quick to position him as martyr, saviour and god. During the somewhat unorthodox funeral rites, Antony was said to have displayed to the crowd the dictator's bloodstained robe and a wax figure of his wounded body, eulogizing Caesar the while as a heavenly being. The consuls, however, did not yet endorse any popular move to recognize Caesar officially as a god, and ordered the demolition of an altar which had been erected unofficially in the forum, during

April 44 BC, on the spot where the corpse had been cremated. Nevertheless, by July deification was secured. For, when holding games in that month (the month in which his adoptive father had been born), Augustus himself recalls that

> on the very days of my games, a comet was visible over the course of seven days, in the northern region of the heavens. It rose at about the eleventh hour of the day and was bright and plainly seen from all lands. The common people believed that this star signified that the soul of Caesar had been received among the spirits of the immortal gods. On this account, it was added as an adornment to the head of the statue of Caesar that I not long afterwards dedicated in the Forum.
>
> (Pliny the Elder, *Natural History* 2.94 trans. Ramsey and Licht 1997:159)

The account given by Augustus of the sighting of a comet is distant from the actual event, a recollection of some twenty years later (preserved subsequently within Pliny the Elder's description), and the comet itself constitutes only one of many unusual disturbances of nature said to have occurred in the year after the assassination. In addition to the general pallor and weakness of the sun, these included an eclipse, crop failure, earthquakes, thunderbolts, storms and inundations. Augustus appears at first not to have given official sanction to the popular understanding of the comet's appearance as sign of Caesar's elevation to heaven (apotheosis) and transformation into a star (catasterism), since the appearance of a comet was conventionally understood to be a sinister omen and, unlike a star, it had no permanency. Nonetheless, the meteorological phenomenon came to be fictionalized and bestowed with supernatural importance in Ovid's ambitious and hugely influential poem *The Metamorphoses* (*c.*AD 8).

The epic narrative of change culminates, in its fifteenth book, with the deification of human beings, the last, most recent and

most spectacular of which is Julius Caesar's metamorphosis into a
god. Now it is on the authority of Jupiter himself that Venus
descends from Olympus to free her descendant's soul before his
body is burned:

> 'Meanwhile transform the soul, which shall be reft
> from this doomed body, to a starry light,
> that always god-like Julius may look down
> in future from his heavenly residence
> upon our Forum and our Capitol.'
> Jupiter hardly had pronounced these words,
> when kindly Venus, although seen by none,
> stood in the middle of the Senate-house,
> and caught from the dying limbs and trunk
> of her own Caesar his departing soul.
> She did not give it time so that it could
> dissolve in air, but bore it quickly up,
> toward all the stars of heaven; and on the way,
> she saw it gleam and blaze and set it free.
> Above the moon it mounted into heaven,
> leaving behind a long and fiery trail,
> and as a star it glittered in the sky.
>
> (*Metamorphoses* 15.840–50,
> trans. B. More, 1922)

Translated backward in time, even more dramatically, to the very
moment when Julius Caesar's muscular and majestic body receives
its fatal wounds, the transformation of his soul into a heavenly
entity was graphically captured in the cycles of illustrations to
Ovid's work which circulated widely throughout Europe in the
Renaissance (see Figure 9.1 for an Italian example).

Although the comet of 44 BC appears not to have had a part in

150. *Iulius Cæfar Veneris beneficio in Cometam mutatur.*

Fig. 9.1 Caesar is transformed into a comet, by A. Tempesta (1606).

subsequent senate discussion concerning Caesar's precise religious status, his divinity was formally recognized by act of the senate and people two years later. Caesar was now officially *Divus Iulius* (the divine Julius), and his veneration from East to West provided a model for the creation of the ruler cult of the Roman emperors that was to last for centuries to come.

We might think the apotheosis and catasterism of Julius Caesar, the elevation of a Roman statesman to heaven and godhood, too specific to the needs of the Roman emperors and too constrained by the idiosyncratic religious practices of pagan antiquity to have a significant place in post-Christian theological discourse. Moreover, ever since Jesus commanded the disciples of the Pharisees in

Matthew's Gospel 'Render therefore unto Caesar the things which are Caesar's; and unto God the things that are God's' (Matthew 22.21), the title 'Caesar' has been a keyword in definitions of the difference, even the outright opposition, between Church and State. Yet on an interior wing of a vast altarpiece designed by the painter Konrad Witz around 1435 for a church in Basel, we observe the encounter of a subject with a prince of the Church where the two characters are identified as Antipater and Julius Caesar. Antipater kneels on the left in supplication, displaying from under his plain cloak an array of bleeding wounds. Caesar, looking down at him from the right, is depicted wholly against historical conventions more as pope than Roman general. Majestic and richly costumed in an imperial robe, he wears a pontifical tiara and sits installed on a papal throne, one hand open in a gesture of leniency, the other clutching the sceptre of his authority. Unattractive and overweight, Julius Caesar wears the recognizable physiognomy of Eugène IV (pope from 1431 to 1447), while at the same time calling to mind God the Father here embodied in his representative on earth.

In tempera and gold leaf on oak, the panel refers to an anecdote narrated by the first-century historian Josephus in his widely diffused work *The Jewish Wars* (1.195–200). Antipater, the curator of Judaea (and father of Herod the Great), finds his loyalty on trial before Julius Caesar at a meeting held in Syria in 47 BC. The soldier strips off his clothes in order to expose the numerous scars he has recently won fighting for the Roman general in Egypt. Impressed by this corporeal demonstration of Antipater's devotion, Caesar promotes him to the procuratorship of all Judaea and orders that this honour be inscribed and displayed back in Rome as a memorial to both his own justice and his soldier's valour. Through an understanding of this historical event as a symbolic prefiguration of Christianity, the internal panel of the fifteenth-century altarpiece at Basel displays the idea of continuity between Roman and Christian justice.

For medieval Christianity, every earthly event is capable of bearing a spiritual meaning. Past events have prophetic value as prefigurations of Christ's incarnation and passion, because God directs the course of events thus. History becomes a mirror in which humanity can see its redemption. Created by medieval theologians, this theory of historical symbolism was popularized in sermons and plays, stained-glass cycles and encyclopaedic books, the most successful of which – and the one from which the altarpiece draws its meaning – was the *Speculum humanae salvationis* (*The Mirror of Human Salvation*).

Compiled at the very beginning of the fourteenth century most probably by a monk, the prologue to the *Speculum* argues that man may know his maker from the scriptures if he is learned, but if unlearned he must be taught by pictures. Christ is the pivot in the didacticism which follows: each chapter contains four images: three refer to events before Christ and constitute the 'prototype' or sign, one refers to the life of Christ and is the 'antitype', or fulfilment. Under or surrounding the images extensive text written in Latin verse explains their relationship to each other for the benefit of those who are to teach the book's uneducated audience. Part of the text in chapter 39 declares:

> Antipater, a vigorous soldier, was accused before emperor Julius,
> That he had been a disloyal and hurtful soldier to the Roman empire;
> On that account he, undressing, stood naked before the emperor.
> And before all displayed to him the scars of his wounds,
> And said there was no need to clear himself with words,
> Because the scars would be seen to acclaim his loyalty;
> Seeing this, Caesar approved his explanation

And confirmed that he was a loyal and vigorous soldier.
Christ was excellently prefigured by this Antipater,
Because he himself always stands on our behalf before his
    Father,
And with his own scars displays that he has been a
    vigorous soldier
And that he has fulfilled his Father's command just like a
    loyal soldier;
On that account God does not cease to honour so loyal a
    soldier,
And is ready to grant whatever he has asked.

(trans. from the Latin text cited in
Lutz and Perdrizet 1907: 80)

Accompanying a translation of the text, in a manuscript of the *Speculum* dated to 1325–30 from a monastic library in southern Germany, we are shown on the left a representation of Christ at the Last Judgement. He displays his wounds (and the instruments of his torture) to his Father as he intercedes for mankind and receives his Father's forgiveness. On the right, Antipater similarly exposes his wounds to Julius Caesar (Figure 9.2). Although crowned, robed, sceptred and seated at a lower level than God, the youthful Julius Caesar here possesses strikingly similar features and delivers an identical gesture of forgiveness. As a visual exegesis of the text, the characters of the prototype are removed from their initial historical environment and their composition is designed to mirror the antitype. The spectator's gaze is drawn from left to right, from Christian to Roman event, from fulfilment to foreshadow. Composition and juxtaposition together create symbolic meaning. For the medieval viewer, Julius Caesar becomes a witness to filial obedience and the truth of the gospels. In typological history, Caesar is the preparation and the shadow of God, who is the fulfilment and the Light.

Fig. 9.2 Christ displays his wounds to his Father; Antipater displays his to Caesar.
Speculum humanae salvationis (*c*.1325–30).

As many as four hundred manuscripts of the *Speculum* from the fourteenth and fifteenth centuries have survived in Latin and in various translations. Although highly influential on the religious iconography of northern Europe (as the Basel altarpiece testifies), its historical symbolism had much less impact in Italy. There, at the start of the fourteenth century, at the same time as manuscripts of the *Speculum* began their circulation, the poet Dante presented Julius Caesar not as the pagan shadow of God but as his earthly counterpart. In his view, Caesar politically, as well as theologically, paved the way for Christ.

Journeying through Hell, Purgatory and Paradise in his vernacular poem *La Divina Commedia* (*The Divine Comedy*), Dante famously comes upon the Roman senators Brutus and Cassius alongside Judas Iscariot in the last section of the lowest circle of Hell, in its nethermost pit (*Inferno*, Canto 34.61–7). There all three sinners are punished for betraying their respective masters: the absolute betrayer Lucifer devours them in his three mouths. An illustration of Dante's text from a manuscript of 1478 now in the

Vatican shows the bat-winged 'emperor of the woeful realm' locked in ice at the centre of the earth (Figure 9.3). At this, the greatest distance from God, he is cut off from all warmth, light and love. Possessed of three heads (coloured pale yellow, red and black), and in a travesty of the Trinity, Lucifer dangles the three figures from his mouths. As Dante clambers down the dreadful creature in order to reach Purgatory on the other side of the world, his guide Virgil (on whose back he clings) observes that the greatest punishment is reserved for Judas:

Fig. 9.3 Cassius, Judas, and Brutus in the mouths of Lucifer.
Illustration of Dante's *Inferno* (c.1478).

With head inside, he plies his legs without.
   Of the two others, who head downward are,
The one who hangs from the black jowl is Brutus;
See how he writhes himself, and speaks no word.
   And the other, who so stalwart seems, is Cassius.

           (*Inferno* 34.63–7. Trans. H. W. Longfellow, 1895)

Lucifer devours Judas for eternity as betrayer of God, the supreme spiritual authority. He devours Brutus and Cassius as betrayers of the first Roman emperor, the supreme civil authority.

Underlying Dante's conception of the depths of Hell are the twin authorities of the Holy Roman Empire and the pope (at a time of profound schism between them). According to *Monarchia* (*On Monarchy*, c.1316), Dante's political treatise written in Latin, empire overseen by a single world-ruler is essential for peace, and for the moral liberty and well-being of its citizens. It is the ideal mode of universal government. The emperor (or, as Dante generally terms him, the monarch) is chosen by God Himself to lead men to live good and virtuous lives and thus attain temporal happiness, an earthly paradise. The ancient Roman empire (and its rule by a single individual) was ordained by God to have universal jurisdiction and thus provide a state of world peace and well-being within which to receive Christ. As in heaven, so on earth. The monarchical mode of government of Caesar and his successors closely corresponds to the spiritual rule of the one divine Lord.

In 1302, Boniface VIII had issued a papal bull that reasserted the Church's ultimate authority, both spiritual and temporal, over mankind. To the ambassadors at his court, he declared, 'I am Caesar, I am the Emperor.' Dante (who had himself been one such ambassador on behalf of the city of Florence) became a strong opponent of such claims. With the empire currently weakened and its emperor absent, with the Church currently excessively focused on material gain and secular politics, Dante presented a desire for the rebirth of a strong Roman empire and a new Roman emperor to be its earthly guide. The pope must be exclusively a spiritual guide, chosen by God to lead men to salvation and to the happiness of eternal life in heaven.

When Dante as protagonist of *La Divina Commedia* reaches Paradise, he hears a brief hymn to universal empire uttered by the spirit of Justinian (the celebrated lawgiver and a Christian Caesar). In his narrative of Rome's history from Aeneas to the present inglorious struggle in Italy between political factions, Justinian recalls Julius Caesar as the founder of empire. He is presented as the first figure to have participated directly in God's imperial design. He is the divine emperor who seized the Roman eagle – sacrosanct banner and bird of God – in order to make war across Europe (*Paradiso*, Canto 6.55–72).

However, Julius Caesar himself resides neither in Dante's Paradise nor in his Hell. It is in Purgatory, on a green meadow, before a noble castle, that the poet sees paraded the great heroes of antiquity who were born before the coming of Christ and (because they did not worship him) cannot attain a fully blessed state. They include Julius Caesar, armed and hawk-eyed (*Inferno*, Canto 4.123). Cato, perhaps surprisingly, is not located here but nearer to Paradise, as sentinel posted at the base of the mountain of Purgatory. Having committed suicide to escape the tyranny of Caesar, his soul stands as an example of the love of liberty, and liberty being the goal of monarchy, supersedes it. In Dante's medieval vision, however, Brutus and Cassius cannot be defenders of liberty like Cato because they murdered Caesar and thus betrayed the empire of which Caesar was the first sovereign. Their infernal punishment as a trio with Judas equates the two acts of betrayal – of Caesar and of Christ. It places Caesar on a par with Christ and thus transfers to him some of Christ's divinity. Caesar is sacralized.

Divinity has not always become the dictator so well. Traces of

Christ do emerge, for example, in Shakespeare's play *Julius Caesar* (1599), where Rome's 'colossus' suffers the same number of stab wounds as Christ – 'three-and-thirty' (5.1.53) – not the twenty-three of the ancient sources. Earlier on in the play, however, comparison with Christ is presented as a rhetorical device with which to tempt him: in Act 2, the conspirator Decius is determined to persuade a superstitious Caesar to attend the senate on the Ides of March, so he plays up to the dictator's godly aspirations. He suggests a sacral interpretation of Calpurnia's terrifying dream:

> It was a vision fair and fortunate:
> Your statue spouting blood in many pipes,
> In which so many smiling Romans bathed,
> Signifies that from you great Rome shall suck
> Reviving blood and that great men shall press
> For tinctures, stains, relics, and cognizance.
> This by Calpurnia's dream is signified.
>
> (2.2.84–90)

'Tinctures', 'stains' and 'relics' all evoke the corporeality of the Catholic veneration of the saints, while the theme of blood is suggestive of medieval cult, which featured not only the propagation of Christ's blood in holy phials but also miraculous tales of statues and paintings of him that bled. To this Christological image of the dictator as a redeemer who, in an heroic act of self-sacrifice, sheds (or even, in Decius' metaphor, lactates) blood for his people, Shakespeare's protagonist responds positively and, in doing so, is condemned to die. Here 'immortal' Caesar, who in Cassius's sardonic view has 'now become a god', is marked as a holy saviour only in a grotesque parody he is too arrogant to recognize. From the perspective of English Protestantism, the play at this point reads as a satire on papal Rome with Julius Caesar standing in for the pope as Antichrist.

By the late nineteenth century, outrage or at the very least embarrassment greeted the publication of a biography of Caesar by the celebrated historian of England and Ireland, James Antony Froude, which concluded climatically with an explicit and sustained comparison between Caesar and Christ:

> [Caesar] fought his battles to establish some tolerable degree of justice in the government of this world; and he succeeded, though he was murdered for doing it.
>
> Strange and startling resemblance between the fate of the founder of the kingdom of this world and of the Founder of the Kingdom not of this world, for which the first was a preparation. Each was denounced for making himself a king. Each was maligned as the friend of publicans and sinners; each was betrayed by those whom he had loved and cared for; each was put to death; and Caesar also was believed to have risen again and ascended into heaven and become a divine being.
>
> (*Caesar: A Sketch* 1879: 494)

For Froude, as for Dante, there were political as well as theological grounds for casting Julius Caesar as precursor of and parallel to Jesus Christ. As a determined admirer of and campaigner for empire, Froude visited many of the British colonies. His essays and histories – idolizing the past, revelling in force, afraid of decadence, racially deterministic – helped significantly to delay the dissolution of the British empire. In the collapse of the Roman republic, Froude found an essential history lesson for the English: free nations cannot govern subject provinces. So, in his biography of Caesar, the patrician party is denounced as corrupt, the democratic as anarchic, and Caesar is forced by necessity rather than ambition to overthrow the constitution and create a military monarchy better fitted for imperial government. In his last chapter, in further echoes of

Dante, Froude argues that the Roman general came into the world at a special time and for a special purpose. His work on earth was to establish order and good government in order to make possible the introduction of Christianity. The Victorian historian then concludes by giving Caesar, the Roman empire and (by extension) the British a touch of holiness, the authority of God.

This recourse to the medieval tenets of military absolutism, aggressive imperialism, and a providential dictatorship that paved the way for Christianity proved too shocking for Froude's Victorian contemporaries, even though praise of Caesar had by now become popular currency in histories of the later Roman republic published in Britain and elsewhere. Whilst the historian's other books sold in hundreds of thousands and were enthusiastically consumed all over the English-speaking world, reviewers of *Caesar: A Sketch* commented critically that it is always the worshippers of heroic force who grovel before Caesar, the militarists who recognize in him an instrument of Heaven. The benefits of empire for Christianity, they protested, should not reflect unreal glory on the process by which despotism was first established. It would be easier to draw an absolute contrast between Caesar and Christ than the strange and startling resemblances which Froude had proposed. 'Neither the heavenly nor the earthly king is honoured by rendering to Caesar that which is not Caesar's.' Froude was forced consequently to suppress his controversial hyperbole, and in later editions of his biography the final paragraph was omitted.

A century later, an altogether different purpose appears to be served by an extensive and hugely elaborate comparison between Julius Caesar and Jesus Christ that has circulated from the late 1980s in newspaper articles, a monograph (itself published in a number of different languages), radio and television broadcasts and on the Internet. In *Jesus was Caesar: On the Julian Origin of Christianity. An Investigative Report* (2005), on his own website and on other web discussion boards, Francesco Carotta (an 'independent philosopher and linguist') presents the hypothesis that the story of the life of Christ is based on preceding biographies of Julius Caesar. Carotta is persuaded four times over: by the resemblance of Caesar's iconography to that of Jesus (the oak wreath worn by one Roman bust corresponding to the crown of thorns); by the congruence of Jesus' life with that of Caesar (down to the narrative function of people and the phonetic similarity of place names); by the re-emergence of Caesar's words and actions in the gospels (miraculous victories become victorious miracles); and by the patterning of the Easter liturgy not on the gospels but on the burial rituals of the Roman statesman.

A highly abridged version of Carotta's so-called *Vitae Parallelae* (or *Parallel Lives*, in the manner of Caesar's ancient biographer Plutarch) indicates the flavour of his arguments and the kind of criticism it would attract:

Both Caesar and Jesus start their rising careers in neighboring states in the north.

Both have to cross a fateful river. Once across the rivers, they both come across a patron/rival.

Both are continually on the move, finally arriving at the capital, where they at first triumph, yet subsequently undergo their passion.

Both have good relationships with women and have a special relationship with one particular woman.

Both have encounters at night.

Both of them are great orators and of the highest nobility, yet nevertheless both are self-made men. Both struggle hard and ultimately triumph, hence each has a 'triumphal entry'.

Both have an affinity to ordinary people – and both run afoul of the highest authorities.

Both are contentious characters, but show praiseworthy clemency as well.

Both have a traitor. And an assassin who at first gets away. And one who washes his hands of it.

Both are accused of making themselves kings. Both are dressed in red royal robes and wear a crown on their heads.

Both get killed.

Both die on the same respective dates of the year.

Both are deified posthumously.

Both leave behind priests. Both have a posthumous heir.

From such sweeping and often superficial parallels, however detailed and justified at book length, Carotta concludes that the Gospel of Mark constitutes a corrupted retelling of the Roman civil war from Julius Caesar's crossing of the Rubicon to his assassination, funeral and apotheosis. Jesus has therefore been constructed in divine Caesar's image, his cult a transposition of that of Caesar. This metamorphosis of *Divus Iulius* into the Messiah occurred, according to Carotta, during the reign of Vespasian. Its purpose? Better to integrate the Jews into the empire.

Carotta is not the only person to have put forward such eccentric views, and their contrast with medieval theology could not be sharper. Where once comparison was undertaken in order to glorify Christ and give witness to the truth of the gospels, or to give divine authority to monarchy and empire, now it is undertaken to undermine both the divinity and the historicity of Jesus, and the empire of modern Christianity. To this end, the divinity and the primacy of Caesar is proclaimed. Caesar is no longer the shadow of Christ, but Christ the shadow of Caesar.

BIBLIOGRAPHY

Ancient sources

The context of production and respective historical value of the following literary sources are discussed in many of the general works on Julius Caesar listed below. The monographs on Caesar also include frequent discussion of additional sources such as inscriptions, monuments, coins and other material remains.

Main sources cited and translations used (if not my own):

(a) contemporary

Julius Caesar (100–44 BC): *Commentaries on the Gallic War (de bello Gallico)* and additional book on the final campaigns by Aulus Hirtius, translations from the Loeb Classical Library by H. J. Edwards (Cambridge, Mass., 1917). *Commentaries on the Civil War (Bellum civile)*, translations from the Loeb Classical Library by A. G. Peskett (Cambridge, Mass., 1914) or The World's Classics by J. Carter (Oxford, 1997). *Commentaries on the Alexandrian, African and Spanish Wars* by anonymous continuators of Caesar's account.

Cicero (106–43 BC): Letters, speeches, philosophical and rhetorical works. Translations from Penguin Classics: *Cicero: Selected Works* by M. Grant (Harmondsworth, 1960) and *Cicero: Selected Political Speeches* by M. Grant (Harmondsworth, 1969).

Sallust (86–35 BC): *The War of Catiline.*

(b) later

Nicolaus of Damascus (b. 64 BC): *Bios Kaisaros*, a biography of Augustus.

Ovid (43 BC – AD 18): *Metamorphoses*, an epic poem. Translation from B. More (ed.), *Ovid. Metamorphoses* (Boston, 1922).

Velleius Paterculus (*c.* 19 BC – after 31 AD): *Roman Histories.*

Valerius Maximus (reign of Tiberius): *Memorable Words and Deeds.*

Lucan (AD 39–65): *Civil War* (*Bellum civile or Pharsalia*), an epic poem. Translations from The World's Classics by S. H. Braund (Oxford, 1999).

Plutarch (*c.*AD 45–125): *Parallel Lives*, including *Caesar* and *Brutus*. Translations from Loeb Classical Library by B. Perrin (Cambridge, Mass., 1919) or Penguin Classics, *Plutarch. Makers of Rome* by I. Scott-Kilvert (Harmondsworth, 1965).

Suetonius (*c.*AD 70–140): Biographies of *The Twelve Caesars*, including the *Life of the Deified Julius* (*Divus Julius*). Translations from the Loeb Classical Library by J. C. Rolfe (Cambridge, Mass., 1913).

Appian (AD 90–160): *Roman History: The Civil Wars.*

Cassius Dio (AD 155–235): *Roman History.* Translations from Loeb Classical Library by E. Cary (Cambridge, Mass., 1916).

General works & reception

Baehr, P. (1998) *Caesar and the Fading of the Roman World: A Study in Republicanism and Caesarism.* New Brunswick, NJ.

Cairns, F., and Fantham, E. (eds.) (2003) *Caesar against Liberty? Perspectives on his Autocracy.* Cambridge.

Canfora, L. (1999) *Giulio Cesare. Il dittatore democratico.* Rome. In English available as (2007) *Julius Caesar: The People's Dictator.* Trans. M. Hill and K. Windle. Edinburgh.

Chevallier, R. (ed.) (1985) *Présence de César: Hommage au Doyen M. Rambaud.* Paris.

Christ, K. (1994) *Caesar: Annäherungen an einen Diktator.* Munich.

Garland, R. (2003) *Julius Caesar.* Bristol.

Gelzer, M. (1968) *Caesar: Politician and Statesman.* Cambridge, Mass. Trans. P. Needham. First edition published in German, 1921.

Grant, M. (1969) *Julius Caesar.* London.

Gundolf, F. (1924) *Caesar. Geschichte seines Ruhms.* Berlin. Trans. J. W. Hartmann as *The Mantle of Caesar.* London, 1929.

Kamm, A. (2006) *Julius Caesar: A Life.* Abingdon.

Meier, C. (1995) *Caesar.* London. Trans. by D. McLintock. First edition published in German, 1982.

Southern, P. (2001) *Julius Caesar.* Stroud, Glos.

Weinstock, S. (1971) *Divus Julius.* Oxford.

Welch, K. and Powell, A. (eds.) (1998) *Julius Caesar as Artful Reporter: The War Commentaries as Political Instruments*. London.

Woolf, G. (2006) *Et Tu, Brute? The Murder of Caesar and Political Assassination*. London.

Wyke, M. (ed.) (2006) *Julius Caesar in Western Culture*. Oxford.

Yavetz, Y. (1983) *Julius Caesar and his Public Image*. London. First published in German, 1979.

Bibliographic Notes

Chapter 1 Caesar's Celebrity

Caesar's portraits: Toynbee, J. M. C. (1957) 'Portraits of Julius Caesar', *Greece and Rome* 4.1: 2–9; *The Times* (20 September 2003); http://www.bestofsicily.com/mag/art108.htm (accessed 5 February 2007); http://festaseattle.com/archaeology.htm (accessed 6 February 2007).

On ancient sources about Caesar (in addition to pervasive discussion within general works on Caesar): Ahl, F. M. (1976) *Lucan: An Introduction*. Ithaca: esp. 190–230; Johnson, W. R. (1987) *Momentary Monsters: Lucan and His Heroes*. Ithaca: esp. 101–34; Masters, J. (1992) *Poetry and Civil War in Lucan's* Bellum Civile. Cambridge; Morford, M. P. O. (1996²) *The Poet Lucan: Studies in Rhetorical Epic*. Bristol. First edition 1967; Wardle, D. (1997) '"The sainted Julius": Valerius Maximus and the dictator', *Classical Philology* 92: 323–45; Narducci, E. (2002) *Lucano: Un'epica contro l'impero*. Rome; Pelling, C. (2002) *Plutarch and History: Eighteen Studies*. London: 253–65; Gleicher, J. (2002) 'On Plutarch's *Life of Caesar*', *Interpretation* 29.3: 265–79.

Caesar's fame: Weinstock, S. (1971) *Divus Julius*. Oxford; Braudy, L. (1986) *The Frenzy of Renown: Fame and its History*. Oxford: 55–111; Baehr, P. (1998) *Caesar and the Fading of the Roman World: A Study in Republicanism and Caesarism*. New Brunswick, NJ: 1–88; Garland, R. (2003) *Julius Caesar*. Bristol: 95–113; Pelling, C. (2006) 'Judging Julius Caesar', in Wyke, M. (ed.) *Julius Caesar in Western Culture*. Oxford: 3–26.

Caesar in Middle Ages: Beer, J. M. A. (1976) *A Medieval Caesar*. Geneva; Spiegel, G. M. (1993) *Romancing the Past: The Rise of Vernacular Prose*

Historiography in Thirteenth-Century France. Berkeley; Croizy-Naquet, C. (1999) *Écrire l'histoire romaine au début du XIIIe siècle:* L'Histoire ancienne jusqu'à César *et les* Faits des Romains. Paris.

Reception of ancient Rome: Graf, A. (1882) *Roma nella memoria e nelle immaginazioni del medio evo*. Turin: 248–303; Reinhold M. (1984) *Classica Americana: The Greek and Roman Heritage in the United States*. Detroit; Bondanella, P. (1987) *The Eternal City: Roman Images in the Modern World*. Chapel Hill; Cavallo, G., Fedeli, P. and Giardina, A. (eds.) (1999²) *Lo spazio letterario di Roma Antica*. Rome, four volumes. First edition 1989; Edwards, C. (ed.) (1999) *Roman Presences: Receptions of Rome in European Culture, (1789–1945)*. Cambridge; Wyke, M. and Biddiss, M. (eds.) (1999) *Uses and Abuses of Antiquity*. Berne; Giardina, A. and Varchez, A. (2000) *Il mito di Roma da Carlo Magno a Mussolini*. Rome; (2001) *Roma antica nel medioevo: Mito, rappresentazioni, sopravvivenze nella 'Respublica Christiana' dei secoli IX–XIII*. Milan; Joshel, S. R., Malamud, M. and McGuire, D. (2001) *Imperial Projections: Ancient Rome in Modern Popular Culture*. Baltimore; Waquet, F. (2001) *Latin or the Empire of the Sign: From the Sixteenth to the Twentieth Centuries*. London. Trans. J. Howe. First published in French 1998; Goldhill, S. (2004) *Love, Sex & Tragedy: How the Ancient World Shapes Our Lives*. London; Hopkins, A. and Wyke, M. (eds.) (2005) *Roman Bodies: From Antiquity to the Eighteenth Century*. Rome.

Metabiography: Montserrat, D. (2000) *Akhenaten: History, Fantasy and Ancient Egypt*. London; Warner, M. (1981) *Joan of Arc: The Image of Female Heroism*. New York.

Classical reception studies: Hardwick, L. (2003) *Reception Studies*. Greece & Rome New Surveys in the Classics no. 33. Oxford; Settis, S. (2006) *The Future of the 'Classical'*. Cambridge. Trans. A. Cameron; Martindale, C. and Thomas, R. F. (2006) (eds.) *Classics and the Uses of Reception*. Oxford.

Chapter 2 Audacity and Adventurism

Ancient sources on Caesar's kidnap by pirates: Vell. Pat. *Roman Histories* 2.41.3–42.3; Val. Max. 6.9.15; Plutarch, *Caesar* 1.8–2.7; Suet. *Deified Julius* 4.1–2 and 74.1; Polyaenus 8.23.1.

Plutarch & childhood anecdotes: Pelling, C. (1990) 'Childhood and personality in Greek biography', in Pelling, C. (ed.) *Characterization and Individuality in Greek Literature*. Oxford: 213–44; Duff, T. (2003) 'Plutarch on the childhood of Alkibiades (*Alk.* 2–3)', *Proceedings of the Cambridge Philological Society* 49: 89–117.

Valerius Maximus: Bloomer, W. M. (1992) *Valerius Maximus and the Rhetoric of the New Nobility*. London; Skidmore, C. (1996) *Practical Ethics for Roman Gentlemen: The Work of Valerius Maximus*. Exeter; Wardle, D. (1997) '"The sainted Julius": Valerius Maximus and the dictator', *Classical Philology* 92: 323–45.

Pinelli: Pinelli, B. (1818–19) *Istoria Romana, inventata, disegnata ed incisa da Bartolomeo Pinelli Romano*. Rome; Fagiolo, M. and Marini, M. (1983) *Bartolomeo Pinelli 1781–1835 e il suo tempo*. Rome; Olson, R. J. M. (2001) 'An album of drawings by Bartolomeo Pinelli', *Master Drawings* 39: 12–44.

'Little Caesar and the pirates': Saylor, S. (1999) 'Little Caesar and the pirates', in *The House of the Vestals*. London: 137–86; Saylor in preface to Ashley, M. (ed.) (1996) *Classical Whodunnits: Murder and Mystery from Ancient Greece and Rome*. London; Homepage of Saylor www.stevensaylor.com includes interviews, newspaper reviews of his books, biography (visited 19 October 2006); review by Allan Massie of *The House of the Vestals* in the *Times Literary Supplement* n.5045 10 December 1999, reviews by classicists inc. Mary Beard in *TLS* n.4962 8 May 1998, Barbara Levick in *TLS* n.5100 29 December 2000. On JFK and the PT-109 incident, see Hamilton, N. (1992) *JFK: Life and Death of an American President. Volume 1: Reckless Youth*. New York: esp. 652–4; Renehan, E. J. (2002) *The Kennedys at War 1937–1945*. New York: 1–2 and 256–73.

Detective fiction, history, and the historical novel: Todorov, T. (1977) *The Poetics of Prose*. Oxford: 42–52; White, H. (1978) *Tropics of Discourse: Essays in Cultural Criticism*. Baltimore; Cowart, D. (1989) *History and the Contemporary Novel*. Carbondale: 1–30; Ruprecht, L. A. (1997) 'Clio and Melpomene: In defense of the historical novel', *Historical Reflections* 23.3: 389–418; O'Gorman, E. (1999) 'Detective fiction and historical narrative', *Greece & Rome* 46.1: 19–26; Chernaik, W., Swales, M. and Vilain, R. (eds.) (2000) *The Art of Detective Fiction*. Basingstoke.

Cutter's Island: Panella, V. (2000) *Cutter's Island: Caesar in Captivity*. Chicago; reviews at http://ancienthistory.about.com/library/weekly/aa120500a.htm (downloaded 19 October 2006);

http://www.worldandi.com/specialreport/2001/March/Sa21425.
htm (downloaded 19 October 2006).

Xena and fantasy television: *Xena: Warrior Princess* (1995–2001), production company Pacific Renaissance, distributors MCA Universal
Studios (Los Angeles), Episode 36 Series 2.12 'Destiny', first broadcast 27 January 1997, teleplay R. J. Stewart and S. L. Sears, director
(also producer and series creator) R. Tapert. Websites which are
still running and contain a message board, episode guides, articles
and interviews include www.whoosh.org and www.xenaville.com
(visited 20 December 2006); Morreale, J. (1998) '*Xena: Warrior
Princess* as feminist camp', *Journal of Popular Culture* 32.2: 79–86;
Inness, S. A. (1999) *Tough Girls: Women Warriors and Wonder Women
in Popular Culture*. Philadelphia; Helford, E. R. (2000) 'Feminism,
queer studies, and the sexual politics of *Xena: Warrior Princess*' in
Helford (ed.) *Fantasy Girls: Gender in the New Universe of Science
Fiction and Fantasy Television*. Maryland: 135–62; Early, F. and
Kennedy, K. (eds.) (2003) *Athena's Daughters: Television's New
Women Warriors*. Syracuse: 11–52.

Rise of Rome and computer games: *Rise of Rome* designed by Ensemble
Studios and published by Microsoft in October 1998 as an extension
to their original *Age of Empires*; gamers' review of *The Rise of Rome* by
Pete Hines at http://www.avault.com/reviews published 22 October
1998 (visited 23 March 2006); Nicastro, N. (1999) 'Simulated
Caesars', *Archaeology* 52.1: 79–81; Friedman, T. (1999) '*Civilization*
and its discontents: Simulation, subjectivity and space' in G. M.
Smith (ed.) *On a Silver Platter: CD-Roms and the Promises of a New
Technology*. New York: 132–50; Darley, A. (2000) *Visual Digital
Culture: Surface Play and Spectacle in New Media Genres*. London; Ryan,
M.-L. (2001) 'Beyond myth and metaphor: The case of narrative in
digital media', *Game Studies* 1.1. Available at www.gamestudies.org;
Atkins, B. (2006) 'What are we really looking at? The future-
orientation of video game play', *Games and Culture* 1.2: 127–40.

Chapter 3 Courage, Cruelty and Military Acumen

Ancient sources on Caesar's campaigns in Gaul: Caesar *Gallic War* bks.
1–7 and Hirtius *Gallic War* bk. 8; Sallust *Cat.* 54.4; Cicero *de
provinciis consularibus oratio ad senatum*; Vell. Pat. *Roman Histories*

2.46–7; Plut., *Caesar* 15–27, *Cato* 51; Suet. *Deified Julius* 24–5; Dio *Roman History* 38.31–40.44; Pliny *Natural History* 7.92; Appian *Civil Wars* 2.17.

Cicero's support in 56 B.C.: Butler, H. E. and Cary, M. (eds.) (1924) *M. Tulli Ciceronis. De provinciis consularibus oratio ad senatum.* Oxford.

The Gallic war and Caesar's commentaries: Hammond, C. (trans.) (1996) *Caesar: The Gallic War.* Oxford: xi–xlix; Welch, K. and Powell, A. (eds.) (1998) *Julius Caesar as Artful Reporter: The War Commentaries as Political Instruments.* London; Seager, R. (2003) 'Caesar and Gaul: Some perspectives on the *Bellum Gallicum*', in Cairns, F. and Fantham, E. (eds.) *Caesar against Liberty? Perspectives on his Autocracy.* Cambridge: 19–34. For the military historian's perspective: Fuller, J. F. C. (1965) *Julius Caesar: Man, Soldier, and Tyrant.* London: 97–165; Dupuy, T. N. (1969) *The Military Life of Julius Caesar: Imperator.* New York: 25–100; Goldsworthy, A. (2006) *Caesar: The Life of a Colossus.* London: 184–356.

Medieval adaptations of Caesar's *Gallic War*: Flutre, L-F. and Sneyders de Vogel, K. (eds.) (1937) *Li Fet des Romains. Compilé ensemble de Saluste et de Suetoine et de Lucan. Texte du XIIIe siècle.* Paris; Parodi, E. G. (1889) 'Le storie di Cesare nella letteratura italiana dei primi secoli', in Monaci, E. (ed.) *Studi di filologia Romanza.* Volume 4. Rome: 237–501; Beer, J. M. A. (1976) *A Medieval Caesar.* Geneva; Spiegel, G. M. (1993) *Romancing the Past: The Rise of Vernacular Prose Historiography in Thirteenth-Century France.* Berkeley: 99–151; Croizy-Naquet, C. (1999) *Écrire l'histoire romaine au début du XIIIe siècle:* L'Histoire ancienne jusqu'à César *et les* Faits des Romains. Paris.

Renaissance responses to Caesar's war in Gaul: Sharrat, P. (1972) 'Peter Ramus and imitation: Image, sign and sacrament', *Yale French Studies* 47: 19–32; Dubois, M. C.-G., (1985) 'César et Ramus' in Chevallier, R. (ed.) *Présence de César: Hommage au Doyen M. Rambaud.* Paris: 109–18; Baillet, M. R. (1985), 'César chez Machiavel', in Chevallier: 67–76; Hale, J. R. (1990) *Artists and Warfare in the Renaissance.* New Haven: esp. 196–7; Mackenzie, L. (2006) 'Imitation gone wrong: The "pestilentially ambitious" figure of Julius Caesar in Michel de Montaigne's *Essais*', in Wyke, M. (ed.) *Julius Caesar in Western Culture.* Oxford: 131–47; Wintjes, J. (2006) 'From "Capitano" to "Great Commander": The military

reception of Caesar from the sixteenth to the twentieth centuries',
in Wyke: 269–84.

Ancient sources on surrender of Vercingetorix: Caesar *Gallic War*
7.89.3–4; Florus 1.45.26; Plutarch 27.5; Dio *Roman History*
40.41.1–3.

Archaeological evidence for Vercingetorix and his campaigns against
Caesar: MacKendrick, P. (1971) *Roman France*. London: 33–58;
Exhibition Catalogue (1994) *Vercingétorix et Alésia*. Catalogue de
l'exposition au Musée des Antiquités Nationales de Saint-
Germain-en-Laye. Paris; Special Edition of *L'Archéologue* (1998)
Hors-Série 1; Goudineau C. (1995) *César et la Gaule*. Paris;
Goudineau (2001) *le dossier vercingétorix*. Arles.

Vercingetorix and French nationalism: Deforges, R. (ed.) (1977) *Eugène
Sue. Les Mystères du peuple: ou Histoire d'une Famille de Prolétaires à
travers les âges. De la Gaule à la Révolution de 1848*. Two volumes. Paris;
Harmand, M. J. (1985) 'Un refus du témoignage Césarien:
L'iconographie de la reddition de Vercingétorix depuis cent ans', in
Chevallier: 423–39; Simon, A. (1989) *Vercingétorix et l'idéologie française*.
Paris; (1994) *Vercingétorix et Alésia*; Cabanel, P. (2001) 'Nations anti-
quaires et antiquités nationales', *L'antiquité*: 49–58; Goudineau (2001);
Pucci, G. (2006) 'Caesar the foe: Roman conquest and national
resistance in French popular cuture', in Wyke: 190–201.

Asterix: official website http://www.asterix.com and blog
http://www.doubleclix-blog.com (both visited 2 November 2006);
Stoll, A. (1978) *Astérix: l'épopée burlesque de la France*. Brussels. First
edition 1974; Nye, R. B. (1980) 'Death of a Gaulois: René
Goscinny and Astérix', *Journal of Popular Culture* 14.2: 181–95;
Martin, M. P.-M. (1985) 'L'image de César dans "Asterix" ou
comment deux Français sur trois aujourd'hui voient César', in
Chevallier: 459–81; Beaulieu, J.-P. (1991) 'Astérix et les Romains:
de la psychanalyse à la sociologie', *Romance Notes* 32.2: 169–77.

Chapter 4 Revolution and Risk-Taking

Ancient sources on crossing the Rubicon: Vell. Pat. *Roman Histories*
2.49.4; Lucan *Civil War* 1.183–232; Plutarch *Caesar* 32 and *Pompey*
60; Suet. *Deified Julius* 31–2; Appian *Civil Wars* 2.35; Dio *Roman
History* 41.4.1.

Suetonius' Rubicon: Butler, H. E. and Cary, M. (eds.) (1982²) *Suetonius. Divus Julius.* Bristol: 84–5. First edition 1927; Canfora, L. (1999) *Giulio Cesare: Il dittatore democratico.* Rome: 158–65.

Plutarch's Rubicon: Edwards, M. J. (ed.) (1991) *Plutarch: The Lives of Pompey, Caesar and Cicero.* Bristol: ad loc.; Duff, T. (1999) *Plutarch's Lives: Exploring Virtue and Vice.* Oxford: 79–80; Pelling, C. (2004) 'Plutarch on the outbreak of the Roman civil war' in Heftner, H. and Tomaschitz, K. (eds.) *Ad Fontes! Festschrift für Gerhard Dobesch.* Wien: 317–27.

Lucan's Rubicon: Ahl, F. M. (1976) *Lucan: An Introduction.* Ithaca: 210–11; Johnson, W. R. (1987) *Momentary Monsters: Lucan and His Heroes.* Ithaca; Morford, M. P. O. (1996) *The Poet Lucan: Studies in Rhetorical Epic.* Bristol: esp. 77–8. First edition 1967; Masters, J. (1992) *Poetry and Civil War in Lucan's Bellum Civile.* Cambridge: 1–10; Braund, S. H. (ed. and trans.) (1999) *Lucan: Civil War.* Oxford. First published 1992; Narducci, E. (2002) *Lucano: Un'epica contro l'impero.* Rome: 194–5; Walde, C. (2006) 'Caesar, Lucan's *Bellum Civile,* and their Reception', in Wyke, M. (ed.) *Julius Caesar in Western Culture.* Oxford: 45–61.

Medieval and early Renaissance versions of Caesar's Rubicon: Flutre, L.-F. and Sneyders de Vogel, K. (eds.) (1937) *Li Fet des Romains. Compilé ensemble de Saluste et de Suetoine et de Lucan. Texte du XIIIᵉ siècle.* Paris; Wyss, R. L. (1957) *Die Caesarteppiche: Und ihr ikonographisches Verhältnis zur Illustration der "Faits des Romains" im 14. und 15. Jahrhundert.* Bern: 61–83; Heuzé, M. Ph. (1985) 'Comment peindre le passage du Rubicon?', in Chevallier, R. (ed.) *Présence de César: Hommage au Doyen M. Rambaud.* Paris: 57–65; Spiegel, G. M. (1993) *Romancing the Past: The Rise of Vernacular Prose Historiography in Thirteenth-Century France.* Berkeley: esp. 167–71.

Cesare Borgia's Rubicon: Yriate, C. (1886) 'Le graveur d'épées de César Borgia', *Les lettres et les arts* 1 February: 163–86 and March: 339–61; Yriate (1889) *César Borgia.* 2 volumes. Paris; Bradford, S. (1976) *Cesare Borgia: His Life and Times.* London: esp. 69–84; Exhibition catalogue, Fondazione Memmo, Rome (2002) *I Borgia.* Milan: 178–237.

Napoleonic Rubicons: Napoléon (1866) *Histoire de Jules César. Tome Deuxième: Guerre des Gaules.* Paris: esp. 515–7; Poignault, M. R. (1985) 'Napoleon Iᵉʳ et Napoleon III Lecteurs de Jules Cesar', in

Chevallier: 329–45; Thody, P. (1989) *French Caesarism from Napoleon 1 to Charles de Gaulle.* Basingstoke; Giardina, A. and Varchez, A. (2000) *Il mito di Roma da Carlo Magno a Mussolini.* Rome: 123–59; Baguley, D. (2000) *Napoleon III and His Regime: An Extravaganza.* Baton Rouge; Cowling, M. and Martin, J. (2002) *Marx's Eighteenth Brumaire: (Post)modern Interpretations.* London; Carver, T. (2004) 'Marx's *Eighteenth Brumaire of Louis Bonaparte*: Democracy, dictatorship, and the politics of class struggle', in Baehr, P. and Richter, M. (eds.) (2004) *Dictatorship in History and Theory: Bonapartism, Caesarism, and Totalitarianism.* Cambridge: 103–27; Hemmerle, O. B. (2006) 'Crossing the Rubicon into Paris', in Wyke: 285–302.

Mussolini's Rubicon: Susmel, E. and D. (eds.) (1958), *Opera Omnia di Benito Mussolini.* Florence: (vol. 25) 287 and (vol. 26) 21–2; Lyttelton, A. (1987) *The Seizure of Power: Fascism in Italy 1919–29.* London. First edition 1973; Berezin, M. (1997) *Making the Fascist Self: The Political Culture of Interwar Italy.* Ithaca: esp. 70–140; Laurence, R. (1999) 'Tourism, townplanning and *romanitas*: Rimini's Roman heritage' in Wyke, M. and Biddiss, M. (eds.) *Uses and Abuses of Antiquity.* Basle: 187–205: Wyke, M. (1999) 'Sawdust Caesar: Mussolini, Julius Caesar, and the drama of dictatorship', in Wyke: 167–86; Dunnett, J. (2006) 'The rhetoric of *romanità*: representations of Caesar in Fascist theatre', in Wyke (2006): 244–65.

Metaphoric Rubicons (some samples): 'Bush across the Rubicon' by Robert Fisk, posted 14/15 September 2002 and 'Bush crosses the Rubicon', posted 11 November 2002, http://www.counterpunch.org/fisk0914.html and http://www.counterpunch.org/fisk1111.html (both downloaded 21 November 2006); 'Have we crossed the Rubicon?' by Brian D. Chapin, posted 14 February 2003 http://realpolitik.us/archives/000610.php (also on Bush and Iraq; downloaded 21 November 2006); 'The hanging of Saro-Wiwa: Abacha crosses the Rubicon' by Mobolaji Aluko, posted 10 November 1995 http://www.nigerdeltacongress.com/tarticles/The%20hanging.htm (Rubicon as boundary of moral and political decency, irreversible consequences at level of state; downloaded 21 November 2006); Rubicon Insurance and Risk Management http://www.rubiconinsurance.com (visited 21 November 2006);

'The Rubicon 4WD Trail, California' by Glenn Wakefield, http://www.4x4now.com/trcar.htm (a dangerous, four-wheel drive trail in the Sierra Nevada through which the American river Rubicon flows, labelled 'a rubithon of rockcrawling'; visited 21 November 2006); the New Zealand band 'Rubicon' signed to Wildside Records http://www.wildesiderecords.com/artist.cfm?i=35 (band name to indicate a decision to change artistically and to pursue that change relentlessly, visited 21 November 2006); Maidment, J. and Logan, W. H. (1874) *The Dramatic Works of John Crowne. With Prefatory Memoir and Notes. Volume 4.* Edinburgh: 101.

Chapter 5 Lust, Luxury and Love

Suetonius on Caesar's extravagant expenditure and sexual promiscuity: Suet. *Deified Julius* 22.2, 46–7, 49–52.

Ancient sources on Caesar and Cleopatra in Egypt: Caesar *Civil War* 3.107; *The Alexandrian War* 33; Lucan *Civil War* 10.53–171; Plut. *Caesar* 48–9; Suet. *Deified Julius* 52.1; Appian *Civil Wars* 2.90; Dio *Roman History* 42.9, 42.34–5, 42.44; Florus 2.13.56.

Lucan's Cleopatra and Caesar: Ahl, F. M. (1976) *Lucan: An Introduction.* Ithaca: esp. 222–30; Johnson, W. R. (1987) *Momentary Monsters: Lucan and his Heroes.* Ithaca: esp. 101–34; Berti, E. (ed.) (2000) *M. Annaei Lucani. Bellum Ciuile Liber X.* Florence; Narducci, E. (2002) *Lucano: Un'epica contro l'impero.* Rome–Bari: esp. 245–7; Walde, C. (2006) 'Caesar, Lucan's *Bellum Civile* and their reception', in Wyke, M. (ed) *Julius Caesar in Western Culture.* Oxford: 45–61.

The medieval adulterers: Flutre, L.-F. and Sneyders de Vogel, K. (eds.) (1937) *Li Fet des Romains. Compilé ensemble de Saluste et de Suetoine et de Lucan. Texte du XIIIᵉ siècle.* Paris; Beer, J. M. A. (1976) *A Medieval Caesar.* Geneva: 155–68; Spiegel, G. M. (1993) *Romancing the Past: The Rise of Vernacular Prose Historiography in Thirteenth-Century France.* Berkeley: 153–82; Croizy-Naquet, C. (1999) *Écrire l'histoire romaine au début du XIIIᵉ siècle:* L'Histoire ancienne jusqu'à César *et les* Faits des Romains. Paris: esp. 240–3, 248–9 and 252–7.

Petrarch's Triumph of Love: Wilkins, E. H. (trans.) (1962) *The Triumphs of Petrarch.* Chicago; Carnicelli, D. D. (ed.) (1971) *Lord*

Morley's Tryumphes of Fraunces Petrarcke. Cambridge, Mass.; Eisenbichler, K. and Iannucci, A. A. (eds.) (1990) *Petrarch's Triumphs: Allegory and Spectacle*. Ottawa; Berra C. (ed.) (1999) I Triumphi *di Francesco Petrarca*. Bologna; Ludovici S. S. (1978) *Francesco Petrarca* I Trionfi: *Illustrati nella miniatura da codici precedenti del sec. XIII ad sec. XVI*. Rome: Vol. I: 177–9 and Vol. II: plate 88.

The medieval courtly lovers: Settegast, F. (ed.) (1881) *Li Hystore de Julius Cesar: Eine altfranzösische Erzählung in Prosa von Jehan de Tuim*: Halle; Spiegel: 182–213; Collet, O. (ed.) (1993) *Le Roman de Jules César*. Geneva; Collet (1993) *Étude Philologique et Littéraire sur Le Roman de Jules César*. Geneva; Collet (2001) '"Translatio imperii": la route des Flandres', in *Roma antica nel medioevo: Mito, rappresentazioni, sopravvivenze nella 'Respublica Christiana' dei secoli IX–XIII*. Milan: 309–25.

Handel's *Giulio Cesare in Egitto*: Trans. into English by D. McAdoo (1967) from libretto published with recording of the opera in the RCA Victor opera series, Handel, *Julius Caesar*. New York City Opera Chorus and Orchestra. Conductor J. Rudel; Winton, D. (1970) *Handel and the Opera Seria*. London; Monson, C. (1985) '"Giulio Cesare in Egitto": From Sartorio (1677) to Handel (1724)', *Music & Letters* 66.4: 313–43; Néraudau, J.-P. (1985) 'Le "Giulio Cesare" de Haendel, ou l'héroïsme à l'opéra', in Chevallier, R. (ed.) *Présence de César: Hommage au Doyen M. Rambaud*. Paris: 263–74; Strohm, R. (1985) *Essays on Handel and Italian Opera*. Cambridge; Winton, D. & Knapp, J. M. (1987) *Handel's Operas 1704–1726*. Oxford: esp. 483–526; Questa, C. (1999) 'Roma nell'immaginario operistico' in Cavallo, G., Fedeli, P. and Giardina, A. (eds.) *Lo spazio letterario di Roma Antica*. Volume 4: *L'attualizzazione del testo*. Rome: esp. 315–25. First edition 1991; Burrows, D. (1994) *Handel*. Oxford; review by D. L. Groover of Houston Grand Opera's 2003/4 version of *Giulio Cesare* archived at www.houstonpress.com (downloaded 29 July 2006). Cf. C. Ward, *Houston Chronicle*, 31 October 2003 and S. Cantrell, *Dallas Morning News*, 4 November 2003.

Shaw's *Caesar and Cleopatra*: Shaw, G. B. (1901) *Three Plays for Puritans*. London; Reinert, O. (1960) 'Old history and new: Anachronism in *Caesar and Cleopatra*', *Modern Drama* 3.1: 37–41; Weintraub, S.

(1962) 'Shaw's Mommsenite Caesar', in Shelley, P. A. and Lewis, A. O. (eds.) *Anglo-German and American-German Crosscurrents*. Volume 2. Chapel Hill, N. Carolina: 257–72; Crompton, L. (1969) *Shaw the Dramatist*. Lincoln, Nebraska: esp. 59–73; Couchman, G. W. (1973) *This Our Caesar: A Study of Bernard Shaw's* Caesar and Cleopatra. The Hague; Bertolini, J. A. (1981) 'Shaw's ironic view of Caesar', *Twentieth Century Literature* 27.4: 331–42; Wisenthal, J. L. (1988) *Shaw's Sense of History*. Oxford; Saunders, M. S. (2001) 'From metropolis to "impossible edges": Shaw's imperial abjects', *Annual Review of Bernard Shaw Studies* 22.1: 99–115; Slater, N. W. (2006) 'Shaw's Caesars', in Wyke: 228–43.

Caesar and Cleopatra in cinema: Deans, M. (1946) *Meeting at the Sphinx: Gabriel Pascal's Production of Bernard Shaw's* Caesar and Cleopatra. London; Costello, D. P. (1965) *The Serpent's Eye: Shaw and the Cinema*. Notre Dame, Indiana: esp. 127–9 and 142; Hughes-Hallett, L. (1990) *Cleopatra: Histories, Dreams and Distortions*. London: 329–64; Hamer, M. (1993) *Signs of Cleopatra: Histories, Politics, Representation*. London: 104–34; Wyke, M. (2002) *The Roman Mistress: Ancient and Modern Representations*. Oxford: 244–320; Cyrino, M. (2005) *Big Screen Rome*. Malden, MA: 121–58.

Caesars Palace: Since 2005, the website www.caesars.com has been integrated into that of the new parent company Harrah's Entertainment, www.harrahs.com (visited 21 November 2006); Martin, M. R. (1985) 'César à Las Vegas, ou les clefs d'un royaume', in Chevallier: 509–16; Spanier D. (1992) *Welcome to the Pleasuredome: Inside Las Vegas*. Reno, Nevada; Hess, A. (1993) *Viva Las Vegas: After-Hours Architecture*. San Francisco: esp. 84–99; Malamud, M. (1998) 'As the Romans Did? Theming ancient Rome in contemporary Las Vegas', *Arion* 6.2: 11–38; Malamud, M. and McGuire, D. (2001) 'Living like Romans in Las Vegas: The Roman world at Caesars Palace', in Joshel, S., Malamud, M. and McGuire, D. (eds.) *Imperial Projections: Ancient Rome in Modern Popular Culture*. Baltimore: 249–69; Schwartz, D. G. (2003) *Suburban Xanadu: The Casino Resort on the Las Vegas Strip and Beyond*. New York.

Advertising: Williamson, J. (1978) *Decoding Advertisements: Ideology and Meaning in Advertising*. London; Hartigan, K. V. (2002) *Muse on*

Madison Avenue: Classical Mythology in Contemporary Advertising.
Frankfurt; Schroeder, J. E. (2002) *Visual Consumption.* London:
esp. 92–114.

Chapter 6 Triumphalism

Ancient sources on Caesar's triumphs: Vell. Pat. *Roman Histories*
2.56.1–2; Plut. *Caesar* 55.1–2 and 56.4; Suet. *Deified Julius* 37 and
38.2; Appian *Civil Wars* 2.101; Dio *Roman History* 43.19–24 and
43.42.

Ancient sources on other especially relevant triumphs: Plut. *Life of
Aemilius Paullus* 32–5; Appian *The Punic Wars* 8.66 (on triumph of
Scipio Africanus); Josephus *Jewish War* 7.121–57 (on triumph of
Vespasian and Titus).

Caesar, the Roman triumph, and its reception: Payne, R. (1962) *The
Roman Triumph.* London: esp. 120–40; Versnel, H. S. (1970)
*Triumphus: An Inquiry into the Origin, Development and Meaning of
the Roman Triumph.* Leiden; Weinstock, S. (1971) *Divus Julius.*
Oxford: 60–79; McCormick, M. (1986) *Eternal Victory: Triumphal
Rulership in Late Antiquity, Byzantium, and the Early Medieval West.*
Cambridge: 11–34; Miller, A. (2001) *Roman Triumphs and early
Modern English Culture.* Basingstoke. On Frederick II: Abulafia, D.
(2002²) *Frederick II: A Medieval Emperor.* London: esp. 302–5. First
edition 1988.

Petrarch's *Trionfi*: Wilkins, E. H. (trans.) (1962) *The Triumphs of Petrarch.*
Chicago; Carnicelli, D. D. (ed.) (1971) *Lord Morley's Tryumphes of
Fraunces Petrarcke.* Cambridge, Mass.; Eisenbichler, K. and Iannucci,
A. A. (eds.) (1990) *Petrarch's* Triumphs*: Allegory and Spectacle.*
Ottawa; Berra C. (ed.) (1999) I Triumphi *di Francesco Petrarca.*
Bologna.

Mantegna's *The Triumphs of Caesar*: Blunt, A. (1975) *The Triumph of
Caesar by Andrea Mantegna.* London; Martindale, A. (1979) *The
Triumphs of Caesar by Andrea Mantegna.* London; *Caesar Triumphans:
Rotoli disegnati e xilografie cinquecentesche da una collezione privata
parigina* (1984). Florence; Lightbown, R. (1986) *Mantegna.* Oxford:
esp. 140–53, 424–33, and pls. 101–118; Massing, J. M. (1990) 'The
triumphs of Caesar by Benedetto Bordon and Jacobus
Argentoratensis: Its iconography and influence', *Print Quarterly*

7.1: 2–21; Martineau, J. (ed.) (1992) *Andrea Mantegna*. Milan: esp. 350–6; Halliday, A. S. (1994) 'The literary sources of Mantegna's *Triumphs of Caesar*', *Annali della Scuola Normale Superiore di Pisa* 24.1: 337–96.

Renaissance triumphal entries: Chartrou, J. (1928) *Les entrées solennelles et triomphales à la Renaissance (1484–1551)*. Paris; Carandente, G. (1963) *I trionfi nel primo rinascimento*. Naples; Bonner, M. (1979) *Italian Civic Pageantry in the High Renaissance*. Florence; Jacquiot, J. (1985) 'César dans les entrées royales et dans les medailles à la renaissance', in Chevallier, R. (ed.) *Présence de César: Hommage au Doyen M. Rambaud*. Paris: 137–45; Strong, R. (1984) *Art and Power: Renaissance Festivals 1450–1650*. Suffolk: esp. 7–11 and 44–50; Bonner, M. (1986) *The Majesty of the State: Triumphal Progresses of Foreign Sovereigns in Renaissance Italy (1494–1600)*. Florence; Graham, V. E. (1990) 'The entry of Henry II into Rouen in 1550: A Petrarchan triumph', in Eisenbichler and Iannucci: 403–13; Wisch, B. and Munshower, S. S. (eds.) (1990) *'All the World's a Stage' . . .: Art and Pageantry in the Renaissance and Baroque. Part 1: Triumphal Celebrations and the Rituals of Statescraft*. Pennsylvania; Wintroub, W. (1998) 'Civilizing the savage and making a king: The Royal Entry Festival of Henri II (Rouen, 1550)', *Sixteenth Century Journal* 29.2: 465–94; Temple, N. (2006) 'Julius II as second Caesar', in Wyke, M. (ed.) *Julius Caesar in Western Culture*. Oxford: 110–27.

Napoleonic military spectacles: Truesdell, M. (1997), *Spectacular Politics: Louis-Napoleon Bonaparte and the Fête Impériale, 1849–1870*. Oxford: esp. 136–55.

Chapter 7 Liberty and Tyranny

For Caesar's government and the ancient sources, see the monographs on Julius Caesar listed above.

Caesarism in political theory and historiography generally: Momigliano, A. (1956) 'Per un riesame della storia dell'idea di Cesarismo', *Rivista Storica Italiana* 68: 220–9; Yavetz, Y. (1971) 'Caesar, Caesarism, and the Historians', *Journal of Contemporary History* 6.2: 184–201; Mangoni, L. (1976) 'Cesarismo, Bonapartismo, Fascismo', *Rivista trimestrale dell'istituto Gramsci* 17.3:

41–61; Yavetz, Y. (1983) *Julius Caesar and his Public Image*. London: 10–57; de Giorgi, F. (1984) 'Scienze umane e concetto storico: il cesarismo', *Nuova rivista storica* 68.3/4: 323–54; Christ, K. (1994) *Caesar: Annäherungenan einen Diktator*; Munich; Chevallier, R. (ed.) (1995) *Présence de César: Hommage au Doyen M. Rambaud*. Paris; Baehr, P. (1998) *Caesar and the Fading of the Roman World: A Study in Republicanism and Caesarism*. New Brunswick; Baehr, P. and Richter, M. (eds.) (2004) *Dictatorship in History and Theory: Bonapartism, Caesarism, and Totalitarianism*. Cambridge; Wyke, M. (ed.) (2006) *Julius Caesar in Western Culture*. Oxford.

Caesar in Renaissance political discourse: Blanc, M. P. (1985) 'De la transgression comme scandale à la transgression comme idéal: La double image de César dans l'oeuvre et la pensée de Petrarque', in Chevallier: 35–55; Baillet, M. R. (1985), 'César chez Machiavel', in Chevallier: 67–76; Mackenzie, L. (2006) 'Imitation gone wrong: The "pestilentially ambitious" figure of Julius Caesar in Michel de Montaigne's *Essais*', in Wyke: 131–47.

French and German Caesarism: Bonaparte, L. (1800) *Parallèle entre César, Cromwell, Monck et Bonaparte*. Paris; Marchand, M. (1836) *Précis des guerres de César*. Paris. Written under dictation from Emperor Napoleon Bonaparte; Romieu, A. (1850) *L'ère des Césars*. Paris; Napoléon (1865–6) *Histoire de Jules César*. Paris; Hegel, G. W. F. (1975) *Lectures on the Philosophy of World History. Introduction: Reason in History*. Cambridge. Trans. H. B. Nisbet from J. Hoffmeister's edition of *Berliner Vorlesungen* (1822–31); Mommsen, T. (1913) *The History of Rome*. London, five volumes. Trans. by W. P. Dickson from *Römische Geschichte* (1854–6, Berlin); Gundolf, F. (1924) *Caesar. Geschichte seines Ruhms*. Berlin. Trans. J. W. Hartmann as *The Mantle of Caesar*. London 1929; Sturmer, M. (1977) 'Caesar's laurel crown – the case for a comparative concept', *The Journal of Modern History* 49.2: 203–7; Poignault, M. R. (1985) 'Napoleon Ier et Napoleon III Lecteurs de Jules César', in Chevallier: 329–45; Pöschl, V. (1985) 'César en Allemagne de Mommsen à Christian Meier', in Chevallier: 407–12; Gollwitzer, H. (1987) 'The Caesarism of Napoleon III as seen by public opinion in Germany', *Economy and Society* 16.3: 357–404; Baehr, P. (1987) 'Accounting for Caesarism: Introduction to Gollwitzer', *Economy and Society* 16.3: 341–56; Mosse, G. L. (1987) *Masses and Man: Nationalist and Fascist*

Perceptions of Reality. Detroit: esp. 104–118; Thody, P. (1989) *French Caesarism from Napoleon 1 to Charles de Gaulle*. Basingstoke; Baehr (1998): 89–254; Giardina, A. and Varchez, A. (2000) *Il mito di Roma da Carlo Magno a Mussolini*. Rome: 123–59; Vance, N. (1997) *The Victorians and Ancient Rome*. Oxford: esp. 75–9; Baguley, D. (2000) *Napoleon III and His Regime: An Extravaganza*. Baton Rouge; Eliaeson, S. (2000) 'Constitutional Caesarism: Weber's politics in their German context', in Turner, S. (ed.) *The Cambridge Companion to Weber*. Cambridge: 131–48; Feuchtwanger, E. (2002) *Bismarck*. London; Baehr and Richter (2004).

Italian Fascism and Caesar: Ferrero, G. (1933) *The Life of Caesar*. Trans. A. E. Zimmern. London. (Abridged edition of first two volumes of *Grandezza e Decadenza di Roma*. 1902–4.); Treves, P. (1934) 'Interpretazioni di Giulio Cesare', *La Cultura* 13.9: 129–32; Seldes, G. (1935) *Sawdust Caesar: The Untold History of Mussolini and Fascism*. New York; Lombardo, N. (1941) *Cesare e Mussolini*. Brescia; Gianeri, E. (1945) *Il cesare di cartapesta: Mussolini nella caricatura*. Turin; Forzano, G. (1954) *Mussolini, autore drammatico: Campo di maggio, Villafranca, Cesare*. Florence; Diggins, J. P. (1972) *Mussolini and Fascism: The View from America*. Princeton; Boulay, M. Ch. (1985) 'L'image de César sous le fascisme d'après « L'enciclopedia Italiana » Treccani', in Chevallier: 373–90; Ceplair, L. (1987) *Under the Shadow of War: Fascism, Anti-Fascism, and Marxists, 1918–1939*. New York: 181–241; Bondanella, P. (1987) *The Eternal City: Roman Images in the Modern World*. Chapel Hill: 172–206; Visser, R. (1992) 'Fascist doctrine and the cult of *romanità*', *Journal of Contemporary History* 27: 5–22; Lepre, A. (1995) *Mussolini l'italiano: Il duce nel mito e nella realtà*. Milan: esp. 172–3; Quartermaine, L. (1995) '"Slouching towards Rome": Mussolini's imperial vision', in Cornell, T. J. and Lomas, L. (eds.) *Urban Society in Roman Italy*. London: 203–15; Falasca-Zamponi, S. (1997) *Fascist Spectacle: The Aesthetics of Power in Mussolini's Italy*. Berkeley: esp. 89–118; Bosworth, R. J. B. (1998) *The Italian Dictatorship: Problems and Perspectives in the Interpretation of Mussolini and Fascism*. London: esp. 58–81; Stone, M. (1999) 'A flexible Rome: Fascism and the cult of romanità', in Edwards, C. (ed.) *Presences*: 205–20; Wyke, M. (1999) 'Sawdust Caesar: Mussolini, Julius Caesar, and the drama of dictatorship', in Wyke and Biddiss, M. (eds.) *The Uses and Abuses of Antiquity*. Basle: 167–86; Griffiths, C. E. J. (2000) *The Theatrical Works of Giovacchino Forzano: Drama for Mussolini's Italy*. Lewiston, NY: 159–75; Fontana, B. (2004) 'The concept of Caesarism in Gramsci', in Baehr and Richter: 175–95; Dunnett, J. (2006) 'The rhetoric of *romanità*: representations of Caesar in Fascist theatre', in Wyke (2006): 244–65.

The American presidency and Caesar: Riencourt, A. de (1957) *The Coming Caesars*. New York; Meyer, F. S. (1957) 'Principles and heresies. America: No Imperial Rome', *National Review* 4.10: 233; Molnar, T. (1966) 'Imperial America', *National Review* 18.18: 409–11; Dirksen, E. (21 February 1966) 'The commander in chief', a 'Radio TV weekly report' archived at http://www.dirksencenter.org/Vietnam/February211966.htm (downloaded 12 January 2007); Liska, G. (1978) *Career of Empire: America and Imperial Expansion over Land and Sea*. Baltimore; Miller, A. S. (1981) *Democratic Dictatorship: The Emergent Constitution of Control*. Westport, CT; Grantham, D. W. (1988) *Recent America: The United States Since 1945*. Wheeling, Il.; Stromberg, J. R. (13 March 2001) 'Empire and reaction', www.antiwar.com/stromberg/pf/p-s031301.html (downloaded 12 January, 2007); Greenstein, F. I. (2001) *The Presidential Difference: Leadership Style from FDR to Clinton*. Princeton; Fisk, R. (13 September 2002) 'Bush across the Rubicon: The mantra that means this time it's serious' and 'George Bush crosses Rubicon – But what lies beyond?' (11 November 2002), both in the *Independent* (both articles are still archived on many websites of the American political left such as www.counterpunch.org, www.dissident.voice.org, and www.commondreams.org, all accessed on 15 January 2007); Foster, J. B. (2002) 'The rediscovery of imperialism', *Monthly Review* 54.6:1–16; Lapham, L. H. (2002) 'Hail Caesar!', *Harper's Magazine* 305.1831: 9–11; Chafe, W. H. (2003) *The Unfinished Journey: America Since World War II*. New York; Cox, M. (2003) 'The empire's back in town: or America's imperial temptation – again', *Millennium: Journal of International Studies* 32.1: 1–27; Johnson, C. (2004) *The Sorrows of Empire: Militarism, Secrecy, and the End of the Republic*. New York. Cf. Johnson, C. (12 September 2003) 'The scourge of militarism', www.motherjones.com/commentary/columns/2003/09/we_546_01.html; Byrd, R. C. (2004) *Losing America: Confronting a Reckless*

and Arrogant Presidency. New York; (22 October 2005) 'Et tu,
Brute?: The waning of the imperial presidency', *The Economist*;
Malamud, M. (2006) 'Manifest Destiny and the eclipse of Julius
Caesar', in Wyke: 148–69; Jones, T. (5 November 2006) 'Julius
Caesar had Gaul; Bush just has gall', *Observer*; Wyke, M. (2006) 'A
twenty-first-century Caesar', in Wyke: 305–23; Golub, P. S. (15
September 2006) 'Is democracy dying in the west?',
http://www.middle-east-online.com/english/Default.pl?id=17475
(downloaded 14 January 2007) and see its incorporation into a
weblog by 'Jo Swift' (19 September 2006) 'Bush: American Caesar'
archived at www.radicalleft.net/blog (accessed 14 January 2007).

Chapter 8 Assassination

Ancient sources on the excessive honours of 46–44 BC and the gestures
of kingship: Cic. *Phillipics* 2.85–7 and 2.110; Nic. Dam. *Aug.* 69–75;
Plut. *Caesar* 60–1; Suet. *Deified Julius* 76.1, 78–80.1; Appian *Civil
Wars* 2.106–9; Dio *Roman History* 43.14.6–7, 43.44–5, 44.3–11.

Some ancient sources on the assassination: Nic. Dam. *Aug.* 83–90;
Lucan *Civil War* 10.341–4; Plut. *Caesar* 63–6 and *Brutus* 14–17;
Suet. *Deified Julius* 80–2; Appian *Civil Wars* 2.111–18; Dio *Roman
History* 44.16–20.

On the ancient sources and the reception of the assassination generally:
Clarke, M. L. (1981) *The Noblest Roman: Marcus Brutus and His
Reputation*. London; Pelling, C. (2006) 'Judging Julius Caesar', in
Wyke, M. (ed.) *Julius Caesar in Western Culture*. Oxford: 3–26;
Toher, M. (2006) 'The earliest depiction of Caesar and the later tra-
dition', in Wyke: 29–44; Woolf, G. (2006) *Et Tu, Brute? The Murder
of Caesar and Political Assassination*. London.

The politics of Shakespeare's *Julius Caesar*. Miola, R. S. (1985) '*Julius
Caesar* and the tyrannicide debate', *Renaissance Quarterly* 38.2:
271–89; Wilson, R. (1987) '"Is this a holiday?": Shakespeare's
Roman carnival', *English Literary History* 54: 31–44; Spevack, M.
(ed.) (1988) *Julius Caesar*. Cambridge; Bushnell, R. W. (1990)
*Tragedies of Tyrants: Political Thought and Theater in the English
Renaissance*. Ithaca: esp. 143–53; Sinfield, A. (1992) *Faultlines: Cultural
Materialism and the Politics of Dissident Reading*. Oxford: 1–28; Blits, J.
H. (1993) *The End of the Ancient Republic: Shakespeare's* Julius Caesar.

Lanham, MD: 39–91; Daniell, D. (ed.) (1998) *The Arden Shakespeare: Julius Caesar.* Walton-on-Thames, Surrey: esp. 1–38; Hutchins, C. E. (2001) '"Who is here so rude that would not be a Roman?" England as anti-type of Rome in Elizabethan print and *Julius Caesar*', *The Ben Jonson Journal* 8: 207–27; Wells, R. H. (2002) '*Julius Caesar, Machiavelli, and the uses of history*', *Shakespeare Survey* 55: 209–18; Kewes, P. (2002) 'Julius Caesar in Jacobean England', *The Seventeenth Century* 17.2: 155–86; Bushnell, R. W. (2003) '*Julius Caesar*', in Dutton, R. and Howard, J. E. (eds.) *A Companion to Shakespeare's Works*. Volume 1: The Tragedies. Oxford: 339–56; Zander, H. (ed.) (2005) *Julius Caesar: New Critical Essays*. New York; Royle, N. (2006) 'Julius Caesar and the democracy to come', in Wyke: 205–27.

Romanitas in the United States: Reinhold, M. (1984) *Classica Americana: The Greek and Roman Heritage in the United States*. Detroit: 94–115; Bondanella, P. (1987) *The Eternal City: Roman Images in the Modern World*. Chapel Hill; Richard, C. J. (1994) *The Founders and the Classics: Greece, Rome, and the American Enlightenment*. Cambridge, MA; Malamud, M. (2000) 'The imperial metropolis: ancient Rome in turn-of-the-century New York', *Arion* 7.3: 64–108; Malamud, M. (2001) 'The greatest show on earth: Roman entertainments in turn-of-the-century New York City', *Journal of Popular Culture* 35.3: 43–58; Winterer, C. (2002) *The Culture of Classicism: Ancient Greece and Rome in American Intellectual Life, 1780–1910*. Baltimore; Malamud, M. (2006) 'Manifest destiny and the eclipse of Julius Caesar', in Wyke: 148–69; Wyke, M. (2006) 'A twenty-first-century Caesar', in Wyke: 305–23.

Shakespeare's *Julius Caesar* in the United States: Dunn, E. C. (1939) *Shakespeare in America*. New York; Ripley J. (1980) *Julius Caesar on Stage in England and America, 1599–1973*. Cambridge; Derrick, T. J. (1998) *Understanding Shakespeare's* Julius Caesar: *A Student Casebook to Issues, Sources, and Historical Documents*. Westport, Conn.; Greenwald, M. L. (2005) 'Multicultural and regendered Romans: *Julius Caesar* in North America, 1969–2000', in Zander: 319–32.

The Booths, Shakespeare's *Julius Caesar*, and Abraham Lincoln: Marker, L.-L. and Marker, F. J. (1976) 'Edwin Booth's *Julius Caesar*: A Promptbook study', *Nineteenth Century Theatre Research* 4.1: 1–21; Rogin, M. P. (1987) *Ronald Reagan, The Movie*. Berkeley: 84–90; Ripley (1980), 115–39; Furtwangler, A. (1991) *Assassin on the Stage:*

Brutus, Hamlet, and the Death of Lincoln. Urbana; Erdman, H. (1992) 'Two Booths and a bard: *Julius Caesar* and nineteenth-century theatrical ideals', *The Centennial Review* 36.3: 517–29; Derrick: 107–31.
Welles's *Julius Caesar*: Houseman, J. (1972) *Run-Through: A Memoir.* New York; France, R. (1977) *The Theatre of Orson Welles.* Lewisburg: 106–23; Ripley: 222–32; Leaming, B. (1985) *Orson Welles: A Biography.* London: 138–42; Brady, F. (1990) *Citizen Welles: A Biography of Orson Welles.* London: 120–8; France, R. (ed.) (1990) *Orson Welles on Shakespeare: The W.P.A. and Mercury Theatre Playscripts.* New York: 1–21 and 103–7; Callow, S. (1996) *Orson Welles: The Road to Xanadu.* London: 322–43; Welles, O., Bogdanovich, P. and Rosenbaum, J. (1998) *This is Orson Welles.* New York; Wyke, M. (1999) 'Sawdust Caesar: Mussolini, Julius Caesar, and the drama of dictatorship', in Wyke, M. and Biddiss. M. (eds.) *The Uses and Abuses of Antiquity.* Bern: 167–86; Axline, K. (2001) 'A "new deal" and a new direction: Welles' and Houseman's depression-era productions of *Macbeth, Doctor Faustus,* and *Julius Caesar*', *Theatre Studies* 45: 16–47; Casale, G. (2001) *L'incantesimo è compiuto: Shakespeare secondo Orson Welles.* Turin: 124–37; Anderegg, M. (2005) 'Orson Welles and after: *Julius Caesar* and twentieth century totalitarianism', in Zander: 295–305.
For George Bush, Iraq, and analogies from Roman history, see chapter 8 above.
Julius Caesar in Chicago, 2003: *Chicago Tribune* (15 December 2002); Shaltz, J. (2003) 'Julius Caesar', *Shakespeare Bulletin* 21.2: 37–8; www.oakparkjournal.com/TheaterReviews/Chicago-Shakespeare-Theater-Julius-Caesar-2002.html (downloaded 31 March 2004); www.aislesay.com/CHI-JULIUS.html (downloaded 31 March 2004).
Julius Caesar in New York, 2005: *New York Times* (3 and 4 April 2005); *Hollywood Reporter* (2 April 2005); *Variety* (4 April 2005); *Observer* (10 April 2005); Newsweek (18 April 2005); *New York Magazine* (18 April 2005); *United Press International* (8 May 2005); http://www.caesaronbroadway.com (downloaded 17 May 2005).

Chapter 9 Divinity

See chapter 1 (Celebrity) for Caesar's self-construction as unique, and chapter 8 (Assassination) for the honours of 46–44 BC.

Ancient sources on the comet, and the disturbances of nature just before and after Caesar's death: Cicero *On divination* 1.119; Virgil *Georgics* 1.466–8 and 487–8; Tibullus 2.5.71 and 75–6; Ovid *Metamorphoses* 15.783–802 and 843–50; Vell. Pat. 2.57.2 and 59.6; Val. Max. 1.6.13 and 8.11.2; Seneca *Natural Questions* 1.2.1; Pliny *Natural History* 2.93–4 and 98; Plut. *Caesar* 63 and 69.3–4; Suet. *Deified Julius* 81.1–3 and 88, *Augustus* 95; Appian *Civil Wars* 2.116 and 152–3; Dio *Roman History* 44.17, 45.7.1 and 17.

On the ancient sources and Caesar's divinity: Taylor, L. R. (1931) *The Divinity of the Roman Emperor*. Middletown, CT: esp. 58–99; Weinstock, S. (1971) *Divus Julius*. Oxford; Feeney, D. C. (1991) *The Gods in Epic: Poets and Critics of the Classical Tradition*. Oxford: 210–14; Ramsey, J. T. and Licht, A. L. (1997) *The Comet of 44 B.C. and Caesar's Funeral Games*. Atlanta; Wardle, D. (1997) '"The sainted Julius": Valerius Maximus and the dictator', *Classical Philology* 92: 323–45.

Speculum humanae salvationis: Lutz, M. M. J. and Perdrizet, P. (1907) *Speculum humanae salvationis, texte critique, traduction inédite de Jean Mielot (1448)*. Mulhouse; James, M. R. (1926) *Speculum humanae salvationis (being a reproduction of an Italian ms of the fourteenth century)*. Oxford; Barrucand, M. (1972) *Le retable du miroir du salut dans l'oeuvre de Konrad Witz*. Geneva; Hano, M. M. (1985) 'L'image de César dans la peinture du XVe au XIXe siècle', in Chevallier, R. (ed.) *Présence de César: Hommage au Doyen M. Rambaud*. Paris: 309–11; Niesner, M. (1995) *Das Speculum Humanae Salvationis: Der Stiftsbibliothek Kremsmünster*. Köln; Cardon, B. (1996) *Manuscripts of the* Speculum Humanae Salvationis *in the Southern Netherlands (c1410-c1470)*. Leuven.

Dante and empire: Kantorowicz, E. H. (1957) *The King's Two Bodies: A Study in Mediaeval Political Theology*. Princeton; Maillat, M. G. (1985) 'Dante et César', in Chevallier: 25–34; Mancusi-Ungaro, D. (1987) *Dante and the Empire*. Bern; Vallone, A. and Scorrano, L. (eds.) (1987) *La Divina Commedia: Paradiso*. Naples; Nassar, E. P. (1994) *Illustrations to Dante's Inferno*. London; Jacoff, R. (ed.) (1993) *The Cambridge Companion to Dante*. Cambridge; Shaw, P. (trans. and ed.) (1995) *Dante, Monarchia*. Cambridge; Woodhouse, J. (ed.) (1997) *Dante and Governance*. Oxford; 'Digital Dante', http://dante.ilt.columbia.edu.

Shakespeare's Christological Caesar: Kaula, D. (1981) '"Let us be sac-rificers": Religious motifs in *Julius Caesar*', *Shakespeare Studies* 14:197–214; Paster, G. K. (1989) '"In the spirit of men there is no blood": Blood as trope of gender in *Julius Caesar*', *Shakespeare Quarterly* 40.3: 284–98; Parker, B. L. (1995) 'The whore of Babylon and Shakespeare's *Julius Caesar*', *Studies in English Literature, 1500–1900* 35.2: 251–69; Royle, N. (2006) '*Julius Caesar* and the democracy to come', in Wyke, M. (ed.) *Julius Caesar in Western Culture*. Oxford: esp. 213 and 219.

James Antony Froude's biography: Reviews of Froude's *Caesar: A Sketch* in (1879) *The Edinburgh Review* 150: 498–523 and (1879) *The Quarterly Review* 148: 453–89; Dunn, W. H. (1961) *James Antony Froude: A Biography (1818–1856)* and (1963) *James Antony Froude: A Biography (1857–1894)*. Oxford; Turner, F. M. (1986) 'British politics and the demise of the Roman republic: 1700–1939', *Historical Journal* 29.3: 577–99; Rowse, A. L. (1987) *Froude. The Historian: Victorian Man of Letters*. Gloucester; Thompson, T. W. (1987) *James Antony Froude on Nation and Empire: A Study in Victorian Racialism*. New York; Vance, N. (1997) *The Victorians and Ancient Rome*. Oxford: esp. 228.

Caesar / Christ on the Internet: 'Divus Julius' Homepage of Francesco Carotta http://www.carotta.de (visited 4 October 2006); 'Christ a Myth?' Homepage of Gary Courtney http://www.users.big-pond.com/pontificate (visited 4 October 2006); supportive discussion in 'Jesus Christ = Julius Caesar?' by E. J. de Meester, http://home-3.tiscali.nl/~meester7/engjesus.html (visited 4 October 2006); various critical reviews by Michael Turton at http://michaelturton2.blogspot.com/2005/04/was-j-caesar-really-j-christ.html (dated 1 April 2005, retrieved 5 October 2006) and http://michaelturton2.blogspot.com/2005/04/carotta-part-ii-jesuswas-not-julius.html (dated 2 April 2005, retrieved 5 October 2006); posts about Carotta's theory from the Internet Infidels Discussion Board (December 2004 to August 2006) at http://www.iidb.org/vbb/showthread.php?t=109654&pp=25 (visited 23 July 2007).

ILLUSTRATION CREDITS

Map   Map © copyright 2007, Ancient World Mapping Center (www.unc.edu/awmc). Used by permission.

Fig. 1.1   © Copyright The Trustees of The British Museum.

Fig. 1.2   Reproduced by permission of the Syndics of the Fitzwilliam Museum, Cambridge.

Fig. 1.3   © Bibliothèque Nationale, Paris/The Bridgeman Art Library, London.

Fig. 1.4   © The Metropolitan Museum of Art, New York.

Fig. 1.5   Reproduced by permission of the Syndics of the Fitzwilliam Museum, Cambridge.

Fig. 2.1   © The British Library Board. All Rights Reserved (N.TAB.2019/9).

Fig. 2.2   Reproduced by kind permission of NBCU Photo Bank.

Fig. 2.3   Microsoft product screen shot reprinted with permission from Microsoft Corporation.

Fig. 3.1   Reproduced by permission of Bayerische Staatsgemäldes-ammlungen, Alte Pinakothek, Munich.

Fig. 3.2   © Musée Crozatier, Le Puy-en-Velay, France/Giraudon/ The Bridgeman Art Library, London.

Fig. 3.3   www.asterix.com © 2007 Les Editions Albert Rene/ Goscinny-Uderzo.

Fig. 3.4   www.asterix.com © 2007 Les Editions Albert Rene/ Goscinny-Uderzo.

Fig. 4.1   © Musée du Louvre, Paris, France/The Bridgeman Art Library, London.

Fig. 4.2   From C. Yriate, *César Borgia* (1889:1).

Fig. 4.3   From the private collection of Robert Gurval.

Fig. 5.1   Reproduced by permission of Bibliothèque Nationale de France.

Fig. 5.2a   Courtesy of Senate House Library, University of London.

279

Fig. 5.2b   Courtesy of Senate House Library, University of London.

Fig. 5.3   Photograph courtesy of BFI Stills.

Fig. 5.4   Reproduced by kind permission of Greenline Interiors.

Fig. 6.1   The Royal Collection © 2007 Her Majesty Queen Elizabeth II.

Fig. 6.2a   Courtesy of The Warburg Institute, London.

Fig. 6.2b   Courtesy of The Warburg Institute, London.

Fig. 7.1   © Punch Ltd www.punch.co.uk.

Fig. 7.2   Reproduced by permission of the University of Heidelberg.

Fig. 7.3   A 1966 Herblock Cartoon, copyright by *The Herb Block Foundation.*

Fig. 8.1   Library of Congress, Prints and Photographs Division (repro. no. USZ62-6862).

Fig. 8.2   Reproduced by permission from the Special Collections of The New York Public Library.

Fig. 8.3   Sara Krulwich/The New York Times/Redux.

Fig. 9.1   Photographic Archive, The Warburg Institute (*The Illustrated Bartsch* B.17.151.638-787).

Fig. 9.2   Reproduced by permission of the Kremsmünster Stiftsbibliothek.

Fig. 9.3   © Biblioteca Apostolica Vaticana (Vatican).

INDEX